The Diffused Story of the Footwashing in John 13

Contrapuntal Readings of the Bible in World Christianity

Series Editors: K. K. Yeo, Melanie Baffes

Just as God knows no boundaries and incarnation happens in shared space, truth does not respect borders and its expression in various contexts is kaleidoscopic. As God's church is birthed forth from local cultures, it is called into a catholic community—namely world Christianity. This series values the twofold identity of biblical interpretations that seek to engage in contextual theology and, at the same time, become part of a global and "many-voiced" conversation for the sake of mutual understanding. By promoting contrapuntal readings that hold contextual and global biblical hermeneutics in tension, this series celebrates interpretations in three movements: (1) those based on the biblical text that honor multiple and interacting worldviews (reading the world biblically/theologically); (2) those that work at the translatability of the biblical text to uphold various dynamic vernaculars and faithful hermeneutics for the world (reading the Bible/theology contextually); and (3) those that respect the cross-cultural and shifting contexts in which faithful communities are embedded, and embody, real-life issues.

International Advisory Board

Walter Brueggemann, William Marcellus McPheeters Professor Emeritus of Old Testament, Columbia Theological Seminary (USA)

Adela Yarbro Collins, Buckingham Professor of New Testament Criticism and Interpretation, Yale Divinity School (USA)

Kathy Ehrensperger, Research Professor of New Testament in Jewish Perspective, University of Potsdam (Germany)

Justo L. González, Emeritus Professor of Historical Theology, Candler School of Theology, Emory University (USA)

Richard A. Horsley, Distinguished Professor of Liberal Arts and the Study of Religion Emeritus, University of Massachusetts—Boston (USA)

Robert Jewett (1933–2020), Emeritus Professor of New Testament, Heidelberg University (Germany)

Brigitte Kahl, Professor of New Testament, Union Theological Seminary (USA)

Peter Lampe, Professor of New Testament Theology, Heidelberg University (Germany)

Tremper Longman III, Robert H. Gundry Professor Emeritus of Biblical Studies, Westmont College (USA)

Daniel Patte, Professor Emeritus of Religious Studies, New Testament, and Christianity, Vanderbilt University (USA)

Volumes in the Series (2018–2021)

Volume 1: *Text and Context: Vernacular Approaches to the Bible in Global Christianity*, edited by Melanie Baffes

Volume 2: *What Has Jerusalem to Do with Beijing? Biblical Interpretation from a Chinese Perspective* (Twentieth Anniversary Edition), K. K. Yeo

Volume 3: *Chinese Biblical Anthropology: Persons and Ideas in the Old Testament and in Modern Chinese Literature*, Cao Jian

Volume 4: *Cross-textual Reading of Ecclesiastes with Analects: In Search of Political Wisdom in a Disordered World*, Elaine Wei-Fun Goh

Volume 5: *The Cambridge Dictionary of Christianity*, 2 vols., edited by Daniel Patte

Volume 6: *An Ethic of Hospitality: The Pilgrim Motif in Hebrews and the Refugee Problem in Kenya*, Emily Jeptepkeny Choge

Volume 7: The *Diffused Story of the Footwashing in John 13: A Textual Study of Bible Reception in Late Imperial China*, Yanrong Chen

"This book provides an interdisciplinary perspective on how the biblical text of footwashing in John 13 was perceived by the Chinese Christian textual communities in the seventeenth century. The diffused story, as investigated by Yanrong, not only contributes a groundbreaking scholarly work for readers but also offers a constructive lens for those who are challenged in the pursuit of theological contextualization."

—**Fuk Tsang Ying**, Divinity School of Chung Chi College, The Chinese University of Hong Kong

"Chen Yanrong's exquisite study of a single moment in the Gospel narrative—Jesus' washing of his disciples' feet—in twenty-six texts from the Ming and Qing dispels the myth of the missing Roman Catholic Bible. Chen's meticulous analysis shows how Bible stories were transmitted in paraphrase, in catechisms and pedagogical texts, though poetry, commentary and art—and how these interpretations of Christ recalibrate our understanding of the contextualization of Christianity in China."

—**Chloë Starr**, Professor of Asian Theology and Christianity, Yale Divinity School

"Scholars have long been puzzled on how the Chinese Catholic community was able to transmit biblical stories, especially the ones related to Jesus, in the absence of a Bible in the Chinese language. This excellent study by Dr. Chen Yanrong gives us an important answer. She methodically reconstructs how the washing of the feet in the Gospel of John was transmitted over and over through Chinese texts in the seventeenth and eighteenth centuries, progressively building a textual community which identifies itself in various ways with the figures of Peter and the other disciples."

—**Thierry Meynard**, SJ, Professor of Philosophy, Sun Yat-sen University, Guangzhou, China

"The author is highlighting how the biblical narrative of the foot-washing was received by readers in late Ming and Qing dynasties through various genres which ranged from traditional (Western) books to follow the readings given at Mass to catechetical literature to spiritual exercises, and which addressed both Chinese Catholics and outsiders. The author develops the innovative insight that the biblical narratives were already available to Chinese readers centuries before a complete (Catholic) Bible translation appeared."

—**Wim François**, Professor of Early Modern Church and Theology, KU Leuven, Belgium

"With her meticulous analysis of the many ways missionaries and their local converts in China translated the biblical story of Jesus washing the feet of his apostles, Yanrong Chen excavates the history of Christianity in East Asia from a new, and enlightening, angle. By showing how much a translation is influenced by the audience it is translated for, she also enhances our understanding of translations as cross-cultural interactions everywhere they occur."

—**Donald Leslie Baker**, Professor of Asian Studies, University of British Columbia

The Diffused Story of the Footwashing in John 13

A Textual Study of Bible Reception
in Late Imperial China

Yanrong Chen

FOREWORD BY
Nicolas Standaert

◥PICKWICK *Publications* • Eugene, Oregon

THE DIFFUSED STORY OF THE FOOTWASHING IN JOHN 13
A Textual Study of Bible Reception in Late Imperial China

Contrapuntal Readings of the Bible in World Christianity 7

Copyright © 2021 Yanrong Chen. All rights reserved. Except for brief quotations in critical publications or reviews, no part of this book may be reproduced in any manner without prior written permission from the publisher. Write: Permissions, Wipf and Stock Publishers, 199 W. 8th Ave., Suite 3, Eugene, OR 97401.

Pickwick Publications
An Imprint of Wipf and Stock Publishers
199 W. 8th Ave., Suite 3
Eugene, OR 97401

www.wipfandstock.com

PAPERBACK ISBN: 978-1-5326-5311-7
HARDCOVER ISBN: 978-1-5326-5312-4
EBOOK ISBN: 978-1-5326-5313-1

Cataloguing-in-Publication data:

Names: Chen, Yanrong, author. | Standaert, Nicolas, foreword.

Title: The diffused story of the footwashing in John 13 : a textual study of Bible reception in late imperial China / by Yanrong Chen ; foreword by Nicolas Standaert.

Description: Eugene, OR : Pickwick Publications, 2021. | Contrapuntal Readings of the Bible in World Christianity 7. | Includes bibliographical references and indexes.

Identifiers: ISBN 978-1-5326-5311-7 (paperback). | ISBN 978-1-5326-5312-4 (hardcover). | ISBN 978-1-5326-5313-1 (ebook).

Subjects: LCSH: Bible. Gospel of John. | Bible. John XIII, 1–20—Criticism, interpretation, etc. | Footwashing (Rite). | Bible—Hermeneutics—China.

Classification: BS2615.2 C54 2021 (print). | BS2615.2 (ebook).

Scripture texts in this work are taken from the New American Bible, revised edition © 2010, 1991, 1986, 1970 Confraternity of Christian Doctrine, Washington, D.C. and are used by permission of the copyright owner. All Rights Reserved. No part of the New American Bible may be reproduced in any form without permission in writing from the copyright owner.

02/05/21

This book is dedicated to my grandmother GUO Yufeng 郭玉凤

who is a living example of illiterate Chinese readers of Gospel stories.

Contents

List of Illustrations | ix
Foreword by Nicolas Standaert | xiii
Abbreviations | xv
Notes on Multilingual Primary Sources Quoted in the Text | xvii
Acknowledgments | xix
Introduction | xxi

1. Textual Substances in Place of a Chinese Bible | 1
2. The Footwashing Pericope and the Three-Layer Framework | 8

Part I: Equivalent Narratives in Scriptural Books

3. Corresponding Chinese Versions Varying in Words | 21
4. *Shengjing zhijie*: Straight Explanation of Sacred Scriptures | 36
5. *Misa jingdian*: Classic and Canon on the Mass | 49
6. *Guxin shengjing*: Old and New Holy Scriptures | 64

Part II: Varied Narratives Composed by Missionaries and Chinese Converts

7. Diverged Versions Made for Chinese Readers | 77
8. Biography and Illustrations Integrated | 98
9. Works Prepared by Missionaries | 115
10. Works of Chinese Clergies and Laity | 129

Part III: Divergent Narratives in Versatile Texts

11. Reinvented Versions in Differing Compositions | 149
12. Writings and Images for Outsiders to Learn of Christianity | 179

13. Texts to Foster Chinese Christian Religiosity among Insiders | 193
14. Disparate Chinese Compositions | 206

15. Conclusion: The Footwashing Case and the Bible in China | 218

Bibliography | 225
Index of Authors | 231
Index of Subjects | 233
Scripture Index | 237

Illustrations

1. *Shengjing zhijie*, the first page of its index, BnF Chinois 6722, vol. mulu, f. 8a | 39

2. *Shengjing zhijie*, the page explaining the feast day of Jesus Establishing the Eucharist, BnF Chinois 6723, vol. 9, f. 49a | 41

3. *Shengjing zhijie*, the first page of the footwashing text in the jing section of scripture, BnF Chinois 6723, vol. 9, f. 49b | 42

4. *Shengjing zhijie*, the first page of the footwashing text in the zhen section of commentary, BnF Chinois 6723, vol. 9, f. 51a | 43

5. *Misa jingdian*, cover page in Chinese, *CCT ZKW XB* vol. 15, p. 3 (photo by author) | 50

6. *Misa jingdian*, cover page in Latin, *CCT ZKW XB* vol. 15, p. 5 (photo by author) | 51

7. *Misa jingdian*, the first page in which the Mass on the feast day of Establishing the Eucharist starts, *CCT ZKW XB* vol. 15, p. 286 (photo by author) | 52

8. *Misa jingdian*, the first half of conducting the footwashing ceremony, *CCT ZKW XB* vol. 15, p. 292 (photo by author) | 54

9. *Misa jingdian*, the second half of conducting the footwashing ceremony, *CCT ZKW XB* vol. 15, p. 293 (photo by author) | 55

10. *Missale Romanum* (1570), the first page of general rubrics, a Plantin print of the Antwerp edition (Antverpiae, 1589) preserved at KU Leuven Libraries, Maurits Sabbe Library (photo by author) | 58

11. *Misa jingdian*, the first page of general rubrics, *CCT ZKW XB* vol. 15, p. 49 (photo by author) | 59

12. *Guxin shengjing*, the beginning of the footwashing text in John verses, *CCT ZKW XB* vol. 33, p. 624 (photo by author) | 66

13. *Guxin shengjing*, the beginning of the commentary on the John verses, *CCT ZKW XB* vol. 33, p. 627 (photo by author) | 68
14. *Yanxing jilüe*, a random page showing print features, *CCT ARSI* vol. 4, p. 276 (photo by author) | 102
15. *Chuxiang jingjie*, the footwashing page, BnF Chinois 6750 | 106
16. *Evangelicae Historiae Imagines*, the footwashing plate, a modern reprint based on the engravings by Antonius III Wierix (1596–1624), in Natalis, *Imagenes de la historia evangelica* (Barcelona, 1975; photo by author) | 107
17. *Chuxiang jingjie*, the page of Coronation, BnF Chinois 6750 | 111
18. *Evangelicae Historiae Imagines*, the Coronation plate, in Natalis, *Imagenes de la historia evangelica* (Barcelona, 1975; photo by author) | 112
19. *Shengti yaoli*, a random page containing a note to further reading, *CCT BnF* vol. 18, p. 270 (photo by author) | 119
20. *Moxiang shengong*, the footwashing page full of handwritten notes, *VZX CK* vol. 38, p. 653 (photo by author) | 123
21. *Tianzhu shengjiao kouduo*, the footwashing text corrected, *CCT ZKW XB* vol. 20, p. 39 (photo by author) | 133
22. *Tianjiao mingbian*, the page of the footwashing text, *CCT ZKW XB* vol. 10, p. 495 (photo by author) | 140
23. *Shengti yaoli*, the page of the footwashing text, *CCT BnF* vol. 18, p. 274 (photo by author) | 141
24. *Jincheng shuxiang*, an image of the four Evangelists, in Standaert, *An Illustrated Life of Christ Presented to the Chinese Emperor*, p. 112 (photo by author) | 180
25. *Jincheng shuxiang*, the page of footwashing illustration and text, BnF Chinois 6757 II | 181
26. An image of The Last Supper: The Washing of Feet by Theodore / Philippe Galle, in Standaert, *An Illustrated Life of Christ Presented to the Chinese Emperor*, p. 243 (photo by author) | 182
27. *Tizheng bian*, a random page with handwritten phonetic writing, *CCT ZKW XB*, vol. 27, p. 525 (photo by author) | 191
28. *Yesu shengti daowen*, the page containing the footwashing prayer, *CCT BnF* vol. 18, p. 295 (photo by author) | 199

29. *Fasciculus sacrarum litaniarum*, the page containing the footwashing prayer, *Fasciculus sacrarum litaniarum* (Augustae Vindelicorum, 1614), p. 295 | 200

30. *Tianxue mengyin*, the page of the footwashing text in verse, BnF Chinois 7065, f. 8b | 210

31. *Tianxue mengyin*, the page of the footwashing text in prose, BnF Chinois 7065, f. 11b | 211

Foreword

ONE OF THE FASCINATING characteristics of the Gospels is that they are not written in Aramaic, which was the common language of Judea spoken by Jesus and his disciples, but in Greek. Because the Gospels translated Jesus' words into a language other than his own, they carry, so to speak, within themselves the dynamic of translation: they not only can but need to be translated into other languages. Moreover, there is not merely one Gospel, but there are four different Gospels, each with its own characteristics in length, literary style, form, and intended audience. Because the Gospels were retranslated in this way, they carry within themselves a second dynamic, namely that they can and need to be retranslated into various styles and forms for different audiences from different cultures.

What about the translation of the Bible into Chinese? Here, we face a striking feature: although the Catholic mission started in China at the end of the sixteenth century, it was not until the 1960s that a full Chinese Catholic Bible was published. This is much later than the multiple Protestant translations, which were already published from the early nineteenth century onward. Thus, strictly speaking, the history of a Catholic Bible translation is very short and would not require a long analysis. Yet, there are two ways to complement this story by investigating what happened with Catholic biblical texts in the Chinese context before this first publication of a full translation. On one hand, it is possible to look at partial translations of biblical texts, clearly meant as translations; on the other hand, we can take into account various texts that are not translations in the narrow sense of the word, but rather reinterpretations of biblical stories into a wide variety of styles and forms.

This double approach is precisely what Dr. Yanrong Chen has done for the seventeenth and early eighteenth century. She approaches the topic in a very original way, being the first to discuss it from this perspective. First, she has selected one biblical passage—the story of the footwashing in John 13—as a unique story line for her investigation and as a guide through the texts. Next, she has applied a strict method of narrative analysis to the prototype in the Latin Vulgate translation, which was commonly used at that time, and to three direct Chinese translations of the prototype. By looking at three dimensions (text, story, and fabula), this method allowed her to discover changes that took place in the translation of the narratives. Finally, she extended the analysis to a wide variety of retranslations, included in twenty-six different texts, most of which have not yet been the object of academic study. They represent a broad diversity of forms and linguistic and literary styles: catechisms, guides for meditation, sermons, study notes, reading digests, illustrated lives of Christ, etc. Each of them targeted a different audience: the ingroup and outgroup of Christians, elites and commoners, newcomers and already-practicing Christians. Chen's overview gives an extremely rich picture of how the Gospel passage not only was translated but also retranslated in line with the original dynamic of the Gospels sketched above. As such, the study not only sheds a new and comprehensive light on the spread of biblical stories in early Christian communities—despite the absence of a full Bible translation—but also connects different texts that are often categorized as specific genres.

The research presented in this book also has a wider significance for understanding Chinese Christian communities in the seventeenth century. A unique characteristic of the cultural contacts between China and Europe at that time is that a widespread print culture was available in China. As a result, European books that travelled to China were translated and published into Chinese or became the origin of other Chinese printed texts. The consequence was the creation of a textual community in which these texts circulated and were transformed into rituals, including a ceremony of washing feet. One can even state that the community partially drew its identity from these shared texts, to such an extent that the community itself is represented in the texts. The fact that biblical narratives also circulated among many different texts indicates that they were an integral part of this shared heritage and that the community identified itself with these narratives. Given this significance, one may wish that the work of Yanrong Chen will be the source of inspiration for further studies on this rich collection of Chinese Christian texts.

Nicolas Standaert
October 2019
Leuven, Belgium

Abbreviations

BnF	Bibliothèque nationale de France (National Library of France), Paris
CCT-Database	Ad Dudink and Nicolas Standaert, Chinese Christian Texts Database http://heron-net.be/pa_cct/index.php/About/Index
CCT ARSI	*Yesuhui Luoma dang'anguan MingQing tianzhujiao wenxian* 耶穌會馬檔案館明清天主教文獻 (Chinese Christian Texts from the Roman Archives of the Society of Jesus), 12 vols. Edited by Nicolas Standaert 鐘鳴旦 and Ad Dudink 杜鼎克. Taipei: Ricci Institute, 2002
CCT BnF	*Faguo guojia tushuguan MingQing tianzhujiao wenxian* 法國國家圖書館明清天主教文獻 (Chinese Christian Texts from the National Library of France), 26 vols. Edited by Nicolas Standaert, Ad Dudink and Nathalie Monnet 蒙曦. Taipei: Ricci Institute, 2009
CCT ZKW XB	*Xujiahui cangshulou MingQing tianzhujiao wenxian* 徐家匯藏書樓明清天主教文獻續編 (Sequel to Chinese Christian Texts from the Zikawei Library), 34 vols. Edited by Nicolas Standaert, Ad Dudink and Wang Renfang 王仁芳. Taipei: Ricci Institute, 2013
VZX CK	*Fandigang tushuguancang MingQing zhongxi wenhua jiaoliushi wenxian congkan* 梵蒂岡圖書館藏明清中西文化交流史文獻叢刊 (第一輯), 44 vols. Edited by Ren Dayuan 任大援, Zhang Xiping 張西平, and Federico Masini 馬西尼. Zhengzhou: Daxiang chubanshe, 2014
WX	*Tianzhujiao dongchuan wenxian* 天主教東傳文獻. Edited by Wu Xiangxiang 吳相湘. Taipei: Xuesheng shuju, 1965
WXXB	*Tianzhujiao chuhan* 天主教東傳文獻續編, 3 vols. Edited by Wu Xiangxiang. Taipei: Xuesheng shuju, 1966

List of the Twenty-Six Chinese Christian Books

Chinese Title	Romanization of the Title	Copies Consulted	Chapter
聖經直解	Shengjing zhijie	BnF Chinois 6722–6723	3, 4
彌撒經典	Misa jingdian	CCT ZKW XB vol. 15	3, 5
古新聖經	Guxin shengjing	CCT ZKW XB vol. 28–34	3, 6
言行紀略	Yanxing jilüe	CCT ARSI vol. 4	7, 8
出像經解	Chuxiang jingjie	BnF Chinois 6750	7, 8
聖體要理	Shengti yaoli	CCT BnF vol. 18	7, 9
默想神功	Moxiang shengong	VZX CK vol. 38	7, 9
照永神鏡	Zhaoyong shenjing	CCT ZKW XB vol. 19	7, 9
口鐸日抄	Kouduo richao	CCT ARSI vol. 7	7, 10
天主聖教口鐸	Tianzhu shengjiao kouduo	CCT ZKW XB vol. 20	7, 10
週年瞻禮口鐸	Zhounian zhanli kouduo	CCT BnF vol. 9	7, 10
天教明辨	Tianjiao mingbian	CCT ZKW XB vol. 6–12	7, 10
進呈書像	Jincheng shuxiang	BnF Chinois 6757 II	11, 12
龐子遺詮	Pangzi yiquan	CCT ARSI vol. 2	11, 12
提正編	Tizheng bian	BnF Chinois 6942 and CCT ZKW XB vol. 27	11, 12
萬物始元	Wanwu shiyuan	CCT BnF vol. 13	11, 13
聖教源流	Shengjiao yuanliu	CCT BnF vol. 23 and CCT ARSI vol. 3	11, 13
耶穌聖體禱文	Yesu shengti daowen	CCT BnF vol. 18	11, 13
默想工夫	Moxiang gongfu	CCT BnF vol. 22	11, 13
進善錄	Jinshan lu	CCT BnF vol. 25	11, 13
四字經文	Sizi jingwen	CCT ARSI vol. 2	11, 14
天學蒙引	Tianxue mengyin	BnF Chinois 7065	11, 14
誦吾主耶穌念珠默想規條	Song wuzhu yesu nianzhu moxiang guitiao	BnF Chinois 7349	11, 14
思正恩言	Sizheng enyan	CCT BnF vol. 22	11, 14
超性俚吟	Chaoxing liyin	CCT ZKW XB vol. 17	11, 14
七克真訓	Qike zhenxun	A copy at Hong Kong Baptist University	11, 14

Notes on Multilingual Primary Sources Quoted in the Text

- Words in non-English languages do not appear in italics unless they are book titles in Chinese or Bible verses in Latin.

- Latin verses from the Bible are from *Sixto-Clementine Vulgate* (1592). English translations of the Bible are from the *New American Bible, revised edition* © 2010, 1991, 1986, 1970 Confraternity of Christian Doctrine, Washington, DC and are used by permission of the copyright owner. All Rights Reserved. No part of the New American Bible may be reproduced in any form without permission in writing from the copyright owner.

- The romanization of Chinese words and phrases follows the modern Mandarin *pinyin* system (but not in italics), so, for example, 北京 is Beijing, instead of Peking. The original historical materials remain the same, so "Peking" remains Peking.

- Chinese names follow the convention of the family name first. If a European missionary's Chinese name is referred to in a primary source, his name is noted in parentheses.

- Chinese book titles and names are written in both *pinyin* and Chinese characters when appearing for the first time in this book. Both traditional and simplified Chinese characters may be adopted according to original references.

- Primary Chinese texts are punctuated. Transcriptions of the primary sources adopt traditional Chinese characters in order to keep them as close to the original as possible. For rarely used variants, their conventional forms are used. In some cases, if a character is not readable, it is replaced with a question mark in square brackets. Empty square brackets show spaces intentionally left blank in the primary sources.

xvii

- The first principle for translating primary Chinese sources (book titles, expressions, and sentences) into modern English is to convey their meanings in the context of history. A literal approach is adopted at the cost of the elegance of English sentences to retain the authentic sense of materials.

Acknowledgments

THIS BOOK IS PART of my doctoral dissertation. During my time at the University of Leuven, my advisor Nicolas Standaert provided me with guidance and freedom to cultivate my exploration of interdisciplinary subjects, methods, and multi-linguistic skills as much as I could. Scholars from Leuven—among whom are Ad Dudink, Noël Golvers, Carine Defoort, Wim François, and Pieter Vermeulen—and scholars outside of Leuven—including Chloë Starr (Yale Divinity School), Thierry Meynard (Sun Yat-Sen University), Jean-Paul Wiest (Seattle), R. G. Tiedemann (London), Eugenio Menegon (University of Boston), XIAO Qinghe (Shanghai University), Paul Mariani (Santa Clara University)—all gave me comments in different stages of my study and writing. I express my sincere thanks to these dear colleagues, working across many continents and across many fields, for their input as I undertook this research.

My sincere thanks extend to my colleagues in the Department of Sinology, other colleagues in the Faculty of Arts, the Faculty of Theology and Leuven Language Institute who offered warm support to me along the way. The libraries (the East Asian Library, the Manuscript Department, Interlibrary Loan Department, and Maurits Sabbe Library) not only effectively assisted my research but also allowed particular pages to be reproduced in this book. It is the people in the libraries who enabled me to complete this task. I give special thanks to them for their great work.

In a later period of revising the book manuscript, I gained insights from colleagues at the Ricci Institute at the University of San Francisco, which include but are not limited to M. Antoni J. Ucerler, WU Xiaoxin, Mark Mir, Stephen Ford, Steven Pieragastini, Jeanhyoung Soh, thanks to the Luce Foundation. I also received kind suggestions from Timothy Matovina and John Fitzgerald from the University of Notre Dame. Mario Cams (University of Macau) and WU Huiyi (Needham Research Institute at Cambridge University) read earlier versions more than once and always encouraged me. LI Ji (the University of Hong Kong), Michael Puett (Harvard University), Christian Meyer (Free University of Berlin), and Lauren

Pfister (Hong Kong Baptist University) helped me in this stage too. To all of them, I am very thankful.

Eventually, this book could not have materialized without K. K. Yeo and Melanie Baffes, the editors of this series. It is the editors' contributions that shaped the manuscript into a form acceptable to larger audiences beyond academics such as college students. I am indebted for their careful work and tremendous support for taking this book to its final stage with Wipf and Stock Publishers.

I have been lucky to have these colleagues, including those I failed to mention. Many of them have become my friends, and some very close friends along this journey. I would like to express thanks to them for their friendship and to my family for their love.

Yanrong Chen
San Jose, March 2020

Introduction

A Known History of the Bible in China

EUROPEAN MISSIONARIES MICHELE RUGGIERI, SJ (1543–1607), and Matteo Ricci, SJ (1552–1610), landed on the mainland of Ming China as early as 1583, officially initiating the history of Christianity in China. Except for a few Siberian Orthodox missionaries in Beijing, only Catholic orders and congregations were involved in the China mission before the nineteenth century, and that was through the late Ming and the Qing dynasties. The missionaries in China comprised Jesuits, Franciscans, Dominicans, Augustinians, Lazarists, Missions Étrangères, and individuals directly sent by Propaganda Fide.[1]

The next three hundred years witnessed the flourishing development of Christian conversion, setbacks, and difficulties. The peak success of the mission—if we mark it by the number of registered converts—reached the reported conversion of two hundred thousand souls (ca. 1700).[2] That was approximately 0.13 percent of some one hundred fifty million people at that time.[3] The geographical span of the mission covered major provinces from cities to rural areas over the country, wherein Chinese Christian communities were kept alive due to irregular visits by European missionaries and Chinese priests. The downfalls included a series of persecutions and the Chinese Rites Controversy, which eventually led to the Yongzheng emperor (1678–1735; reign 1723–1735) forbidding Christianity in China in 1723.

The aftermath of the European missionaries' encounters with natives in late imperial China was that localized Chinese Christian communities emerged through cross-cultural conversations and inter-cultural collaborations. One unique aspect of the Christian community in China is that

---

1. Unless specified with other denominations, all Christianity-related activities, people, and works in China this book explores fall under the category of the Roman Catholic Church.

2. Standaert, *Handbook of Christianity in China*, 380–86.

3. Deng, "China's Population Expansion and Its Causes during the Qing Period, 1644–1911," 2.

a large number of Chinese texts—approximately 1,050—were produced, circulated, and preserved in the forms of published books, manuscripts, handwritten copies, pamphlets, and sheets.[4] Issues of Christianity, including the religion and themes on morals and philosophy, took up a significant portion of these texts. More striking is that the impressive collection of Chinese Christian texts did not contain a single book that had been authorized as a Chinese version of the Bible.

Translating the Bible was indeed a huge project, especially in the historical background of sixteenth-and-seventeenth-century Europe after the Council of Trent (1545–1563). As for the mission in China, the verdict is simple: there did not exist a Chinese Bible in the Catholic Church until the mid-twentieth century. Between 1964 and 1968, the first complete Catholic Bible was published in Hong Kong. The work is *Sigao shengjing* 思高聖經, named in honor of Duns Scotus, due to teamwork led by Gabriele Allegra OFM (1907–1976) and translated based on Hebrew, Aramaic, and Greek texts.[5]

Rethinking the History from a Reception Perspective

Beyond this mainstream narrative, our understanding can be deepened and broadened. The history of the Bible in China should not be told on the basis of only several masterpieces. Studying several translations of the Bible, the book, or parts of the Bible is off-limits. Fixing an original edition against which the correspondence of the translation can be compared is not enough.

The fact that the Bible has been translated into a range of languages suggests translatability and universality of everything contained within it. The translatable "everything" entails biblical accounts, messages, stories, and words. In this regard, the China mission represents a fabulous case; it needs only inspection through a perspective of reception. Chinese Bible reception occurred in reality prior to a full publication of the Bible translation, and it can be discovered from the experiences of Chinese readers in the seventeenth and eighteenth centuries.

To start with, Chinese Christians claimed access to the Bible, their knowledge, and learning of the Bible in conversations and writings. In a large number of fragments, they referred to "shengjing" (聖經), a collocation in modern Mandarin Chinese that primarily refers to the Christian Bible. The first character, "sheng," means "holy, sacred, sage," and the second

---

4. See CCT Database.

5. Camps, "Father Gabriele M. Allegra, OFM (1907–1976) and the Studium Biblicum Franciscanum."

one, "jing," inclusively refers to canons, classics, Scriptures, and sacred texts.[6] Missionaries also employed the same Chinese expression, "shengjing," to quotes incorporated in their writings. In addition, there are miscellaneous allusions to the Bible at different levels found in Chinese Christian texts as well. Teachings of Jesus and theological matters from the Bible were rendered into the Chinese language. Verses in the New Testament and Old Testament were paraphrased and explained in a manner appropriate to Chinese audiences. Pieces of evidence substantiated a phenomenon diverging from the mainstream narrative: biblical content was made accessible in Chinese and conveyed to Chinese audiences.

It is just a preliminary conclusion to know that Chinese readers did receive the Bible. The question is how to understand this Chinese reception of the Bible without a Chinese Bible translation. In this work, I propose rethinking the history with new perspectives and nuances that can be inserted into existing scholarship on the Bible in China. I hope to open a new window to more Chinese Christian texts because previous studies have not mentioned the copious biblical and parabiblical texts that facilitated actual communication of the Bible.

In Search of Chinese Biblical and Parabiblical Texts

In recent decades, more and more Chinese-language Christian books have been uncovered from libraries and hidden collections all over the world. Among them are texts containing biblical content in various textual forms, lengths, literary styles, images, or other types of medium. Not limited to written words and images, the numerous Chinese Christian texts that went beyond translations of the Bible expressed and delivered biblical content to audiences in late Ming and early Qing China.[7] What has yet to be explained is the dissemination of copies, commentaries, and interpretations of those texts.

Departing from the abundant textual sources, I look for biblical traces. In this book, I choose one biblical account, namely the footwashing story from the Gospel of John, to look for its traces through Chinese Christian works. The footwashing story as a central theme guides my search for biblical and parabiblical texts. Following the footwashing prototype, I have located a great variety of Christian texts in which many Chinese renditions of the footwashing story were delivered to different audiences. I invite two methods of study for these textual materials: one is a narrative analysis that focuses

6. Chen, "Christian Biblical Tradition in the *Jing* Chinese Culture."
7. Chen, "Jesuit Order (China)," 1135–37.

on the footwashing prototype and its various Chinese renditions; the other is an overview of composite characteristics of Chinese Christian books in which the footwashing texts are found. More specifics of both methods are explained later when I employ them to examine those texts.

The interdisciplinary nature of this study places this book at the crossroads of several fields. Its topic locates it in the history of Christianity in China in the context of world Christianity. Its methodology and orientation make use of tools from literary analysis, textual studies, biblical studies, and translation studies. I am indebted to two particular works for the courage to propose this new approach to the history of the Bible in China and to continue the exploration of a large amount of Chinese Christian texts. Nicolas Standaert's article, "The Bible in Early Seventeenth-Century China," provides an overview and informative sources on many biblical and parabiblical texts beyond a few translations.[8] This article considers for the first time that devotional and spiritual books relate to the Chinese Bible in the seventeenth century. Chloë Starr, in her article "Reading Christian Scriptures: The Nineteenth-Century Context," adopts a similar view by adding parabiblical texts to the array of Chinese translations of the Protestant Bible in the nineteenth century.[9] Her stress on Chinese readers' role enriches the conventionally outlined history of the Bible in China; moreover, this study inspires more scholarly attention to literary styles and forms of Chinese Christian writings, one example of which is Starr's book, *Chinese Theology*.[10]

Building upon constructive scholarship and, meanwhile, challenging the current outlook on the history of the Bible in China, this book intends to retrace routes through which biblical topics were conveyed to different kinds of Chinese audiences. The absence of a Chinese Bible translation from the late sixteenth century through the eighteenth century is certain, given that this book strives to add more strokes to the picture in which Chinese people of the time encountered the Bible. The focus on the footwashing account and its appearances in the Chinese language and contexts can help demonstrate a single biblical account's Chinese renditions and their trajectories to arrive at Chinese audiences. Two methods—narrative analysis and uncut textual examination—are integrated to facilitate a possible way to understand the mechanism of rendering biblical contents into texts in a manner accessible and appropriate to Chinese audiences. With the proper methodology, the collection of Chinese Christian texts uncovered in this book serves as a case to stand for the alternative approach for

---

8. Standaert, "The Bible in Early Seventeenth-Century China."
9. Starr, "Reading Scripture in Nineteenth-Century China."
10. Starr, *Chinese Theology*.

understanding the history of Bible in late imperial China — not a history of translation projects but a process of integrating biblical contents into Chinese texts of the time.

Plan of the Book

In order to unlock windows for exploring the complexity and richness of communicating biblical contents through Chinese text culture, this study involves multiple dimensions for analyzing the collection of Chinese Christian texts that incorporate the footwashing story. It is centered on a spectrum built upon almost disparate versions of the single biblical account, from renditions precisely the same as the prototype in the Bible to the ones that represent the biblical account with only one sentence or phrase in Chinese. At the same time, these versions appealing to Chinese audiences of all sorts of types and different purposes are worked out in Christian books of shared or distinguished genres and readerships that form a textual network.

Accordingly, I structure this book with steps and leaps. Taking steps in how the prototype was conveyed in the Chinese language with diversified alterations, I trace the mutations that the footwashing account undergoes as it travels from one Chinese version to another. The leaps bridge individual Chinese biblical and parabiblical texts, through which I present the ways that several different versions of the footwashing story are incorporated in books of similar styles and forms which share certain textuality and intertextuality.

Chapter 1 adds more details to what is introduced here with specific textual sources. That includes the works relevant to the history of Bible in China, the bits and pieces referring to biblical contents scattered throughout Chinese Christian texts, and finally, the generic appearances of the footwashing story in the Chinese context and its prototype *in situ* in the Bible pericope. Chapter 2 elaborates on a specific three-layer framework of the narrative analysis and applies it to the original footwashing pericope in the Latin Vulgate. Chapters 1 and 2 lay the foundation for this book, which unfolds a wide range of Chinese footwashing narratives and Christian books of various genres and readerships.

The remaining chapters, from Chapter 3 to Chapter 14, comprise three parts. Each part is organized in the same way. Chapter 3, Chapter 7, and Chapter 10 are lined up to demonstrate the itineraries of the original footwashing story to diversified Chinese versions. They focus on the three-layer narrative analysis of the twenty-six Chinese footwashing fragments. Other chapters in the three parts report on investigations of the twenty-six

Chinese Christian books wherein the footwashing fragments are found. The focus is the genres of these books and the experience of their audiences. Still, each part has its own high point as each takes a unique approach to understanding these books' genres.

In Part I, three books are gathered, including two commentary works and one handbook for mass. Their footwashing texts are literally corresponding to the original biblical pericope but still are divergent from one another. They contain Bible verses translated into Chinese for different contexts to use. Chapter 3 showcases the three Chinese versions with narrative components being identical to the prototype, although the three Chinese texts vary from one another. Chapter 4, Chapter 5, and Chapter 6, respectively, examine each of the three books and their roles in the history of Christianity in China.

Part II presents nine books that incorporate Chinese footwashing narratives of a great variety. Chapter 7 brings in the nine versions that are by and large close to the prototype, but a great diversity of obvious changes can be observed in these books. From catechism to guides for meditation, from sermons to the faithful's study notes and reading digests, these nine books are of different writing forms and styles, not only accessible to audiences inside the Christian communities but also open to outsiders. They are organized, however, according to their indicated authorships—missionaries or Chinese Christians. Chapter 8 explores the life of Jesus Christ and illustrations in the same series of the same author. Chapter 9 introduces a catechetical book, a work to teach and to assist meditation, and another anthology of devotional lectures, all of whose production was supervised by missionaries. Chinese Christians' personal writings to defend their conversion, their journals recording daily conversations within a local Christian community, and sermons prepared by Chinese clergies are covered in Chapter 10.

Part III collects fourteen books. The footwashing stories found therein are rewritten; sometimes only the core narrative unit is left. Chapter 11 encompasses the fourteen dissimilar versions diverging further from the prototype with simplified narrations but creative writing. They are grouped according to shared compositions, readerships, functions, and similar contexts. Chapter 12 presents the books of literary and scholarly composition that let them circulate beyond Christian circles to non-Christian readers, even opponents who could familiarize themselves with Christianity. The books in Chapter 13 are primarily for practicing insiders, some to improve their doctrinal training and some to assist them in their spiritual exercises with prayers and meditative texts. Chapter 14 clusters books that cannot be described under a category of the church textual tradition but are Christian works using Chinese literary writing models of the time.

There might be discrepancies in the ways the twenty-six books are placed in the three parts, especially if assessing these Chinese Christian books from a Western point of view. For instance, two books of commentary and a liturgy book are in Part I. It is also possible to sort out individual books differently. For example, the books in Part II can be arranged according to their readerships, just as those in Part III could be labeled according to whether missionaries or Chinese authors took the leading role in producing them. Nevertheless, the organization of the three parts is an attempt to provide a holistic view from different perspectives. The intention for using different approaches in each part is to show the complexity. It is another gain if one can process the dynamics of these books with multi-dimensioned views beyond the point of merely categorizing them in bibliographies. It is hardly plausible to label all the Chinese Christian texts with the conventional classification, after all. Only by breaking boundaries and endeavoring to bring in a constructive view may we discover a better understanding of the building of the Christian literary tradition in the Chinese context. This book is a step toward that goal.

1

Textual Substances in Place of a Chinese Bible

Individual Efforts to Prepare Chinese Translations

SINCE THE BEGINNING OF the China mission from the early modern times through the twentieth century, although a Chinese Bible was absent, missionaries in China did make impressive efforts. Even when not every priest could possess a Bible in Europe, Jesuits in China had already requested the Bible from Europe and permission to translate the Bible into Chinese. A beautifully embellished polyglot edition of the Bible published in Antwerp with parallel translations in Septuagint, Vulgate, and Syriac arrived in Beijing in 1604.[1] Continuously, in 1615, Pope Paul V (papacy: 1605–1621) granted permission for the Jesuits to translate the Bible into the erudite language proper to the Chinese literati.[2] This privilege was asked in regard to training native Chinese clergies. Another permission came along for priests, allowing them to wear a headpiece while celebrating mass and to celebrate the mass and recite the canonical hours in literary Chinese.[3] This permission to translate the Bible into Chinese did not lead to immediate execution, but it was reflected in translating Gospel verses (see chapter 4) and in making a Chinese version of the Roman Missal (see chapter 5).

Incidentally, there have been some individual attempts in the Catholic Church to make a Chinese Bible, though not in the sense of making use of the permission granted in 1615.[4] Antonio Laghi, FM, translated Genesis and part of Exodus, a task that was continued by Francesco Jovino, FM (1677–1737), who then translated the Old Testament up to the book of Judges. Their manuscripts were lost. François d'Entrecolles, SJ (1663–1741), translated the book of Tobit only, and the work was published. Jean

---

1. Standaert, "The Bible in Early Seventeenth-Century China," 35.
2. Bontinck, *La lutte autour de la liturgie chinoise*, 36–44.
3. Standaert, *Handbook of Christianity in China*, 621.
4. Zetzsche, *The Bible in China*, 26.

Basset, MEP (1662–1707), had a set of incomplete translations of the New Testament. Louis de Poirot, SJ (1735–1813), translated an almost complete version of the Bible, except for some prophetic books, but the translation was not approved for publication.

The end of the nineteenth century onward brought about more Catholic missionaries' efforts. Joseph Dejean, MEP (1834–1895), translated the Gospels in 1893, and they were printed in Hong Kong. Several Chinese Jesuits continued translations. In 1897, Laurence Li Di 李杕, SJ (1849–1911), published a translation of the New Testament. So did Joseph Xiao Jingshan 蕭靜山, SJ (1855–1924), in 1922. Ma Xiangbo 馬相伯, SJ (1840–1939), also completed a translation of the Gospels. Another Chinese layman, John Wu Jingxiong 吳經熊 (1899–1986), published the Psalter in 1946 and the New Testament in 1949. The nineteenth and twentieth centuries witnessed many Bible translations done by Protestant missionaries, who already had published two translations of the Bible before setting foot in mainland China. The earliest Protestant translations of the Bible by Robert Morrison (1782–1835) and Joshua Marshman (1768–1837) even used manuscripts of the New Testament done by Catholic pioneer Jean Basset as a base. These individual Catholic works, whether having survived or not, by no means brought about a Chinese Bible.

Allusions to the "Bible" in Chinese Sources

The lack of a Chinese Bible prompts me to turn to a large number of Chinese Christian books, manuscripts, and pamphlets that were published by private printing houses or remained as handwritten copies. If the Bible was not readable in Chinese, which texts did Chinese Christians rely upon while articulating their belief? I have searched any available Chinese Christian texts preserved in libraries or reproduced in facsimiles with a consistent agenda, looking for the means by which the Bible was communicated to and between Chinese of the time. The search has proved to be unique, as scattered biblical messages, words, and doctrines can be spotted throughout Chinese Christian texts. Hence, many biblical and parabiblical Chinese Christian texts converge. All sorts of matters of doctrine and devotion conveyed in the Bible were brought to life even in different styles of Chinese as well. The following shows a series of fragments as an example.

As early as the beginning of the China mission, Jesus' words and teachings, a series of statements of beliefs and norms, and accounts of the apostles and salvation history had been presented in Chinese Christian books. For instance, *Xinbian xizhuguo tianzhu shilu* 新編西竺國天主實錄 (1584) by

Michele Ruggieri rendered prayers in Chinese. Matteo Ricci at the same time prepared the Our Father, the Hail Mary, and the Ten Commandments for Chinese converts to recite, and these became another book, *Tianzhu jiaoyao* 天主教要 (1605), which was republished later and widely distributed under the title *Shengjing yüelu* 聖經約錄 (1610).[5]

In addition, there are a handful of Christian books containing sentences and passages to speak of biblical stories and pericopes. Original Bible verses and long passages can be seen in more than several texts. For instance, pericopes from the Book of Job in the Old Testament were translated word by word and commented on in *Shengjing zhijie* 聖經直解 (1636–1642) by Manuel Dias, SJ (Junior) (1574–1659). The verse of Job 1:21 in the Latin Vulgate (*Nudus egressus sum de utero matris meae, et nudus revertar illuc*) can find its exact equivalent in Chinese in a literary style (昨日赤身出私母之胎。翌日赤身入塚公母之胎。).[6]

In addition to knowledge of the Bible and fundamental Christian doctrines, worldviews and values as taught by the Bible were communicated among Chinese Christians, friends of missionaries, and even their opposing Buddhist and Islamic scholars. For example, a non-Christian mathematician in the Qing court learned of biblical chronology and thus became more interested in comparing Chinese and biblical chronologies in order to look for the origin of the world.[7]

Even if isolated and out of context, these and many more miscellaneous allusions to the Bible at different levels found in Chinese Christian texts suggest that biblical contents were accessible in Chinese. The absence of an official Chinese edition of the Bible did not prevent Chinese reception of the Bible. The teachings of Jesus were rendered into Chinese, verses in the sacred books were rewritten or paraphrased, and theological matters deriving from the Bible were explained to Chinese audiences. Including converts within the Christian community and the ones outside of their circle, Chinese readers encountered the Christian Bible at a certain level.

The Footwashing Story *in Situ*

In order to show a full picture of how specific biblical content was delivered to which kind of Chinese audiences, I choose one case to focus on: the footwashing story recording that Jesus washed the feet of the

---

5. *CCT ARSI*, vol. 1, 1–116.

6. BnF Chinois 6723, vol. 14, 11.

7. Dudink, "Biblical Chronology and the Transmission of the Theory of Six 'World Ages' to China," 90.

apostles at the Passover dinner before he was seized. This account as a theme has inspired different forms of expression ranging from paintings to sculptures through the Catholic tradition. The very biblical origin is solely documented in the Gospel of John, as the Synoptic Gospels contain no reference to the footwashing episode. The textual sources to retrieve the footwashing pericope is John 13:1–15 from the Vulgate Latin Bible, specifically, the *Sixto-Clementine Vulgate* (1592).

1. Ante diem festum Paschæ, sciens Jesus quia venit hora ejus ut transeat ex hoc mundo ad Patrem: cum dilexisset suos, qui erant in mundo, in finem dilexit eos.
2. Et cœna facta, cum diabolus jam misisset in cor ut traderet eum Judas Simonis Iscariotæ:
3. sciens quia omnia dedit ei Pater in manus, et quia a Deo exivit, et ad Deum vadit:
4. surgit a cœna, et ponit vestimenta sua, et cum accepisset linteum, præcinxit se.
5. Deinde mittit aquam in pelvim, et cœpit lavare pedes discipulorum, et extergere linteo, quo erat præcinctus.
6. Venit ergo ad Simonem Petrum. Et dicit ei Petrus: Domine, tu mihi lavas pedes?
7. Respondit Jesus, et dixit ei: Quod ego facio, tu nescis modo: scies autem postea.
8. Dicit ei Petrus: Non lavabis mihi pedes in æternum. Respondit ei Jesus: Si non lavero te, non habebis partem mecum.
9. Dicit ei Simon Petrus: Domine, non tantum pedes meos, sed et manus, et caput.
10. Dicit ei Jesus: Qui lotus est, non indiget nisi ut pedes lavet, sed est mundus totus. Et vos mundi estis, sed non omnes.
11. Sciebat enim quisnam esset qui traderet eum; propterea dixit: Non estis mundi omnes.
12. Postquam ergo lavit pedes eorum, et accepit vestimenta sua, cum recubuisset iterum, dixit eis: Scitis quid fecerim vobis?
13. Vos vocatis me Magister et Domine, et bene dicitis: sum etenim.
14. Si ergo ego lavi pedes vestros, Dominus et Magister, et vos debetis alter alterius lavare pedes.

15. Exemplum enim dedi vobis, ut quemadmodum ego feci vobis, ita et vos faciatis.[8]

To Chinese audiences in the late sixteenth century, the footwashing story of Jesus and his disciples was unique and intriguing. First of all, there would not be confusion because the footwashing story and the particular occasion associated with washing feet did not exist in any non-Christian Chinese tradition. Confucius and Buddha were not portrayed as washing their students' feet before they suffered or were captured. There were no other anecdotes of washing feet in Chinese literature overlapping with the role of Jesus in the biblical story. Chinese incorporation of the Christian biblical footwashing account should be bereft of intercultural hermeneutics and accommodation to non-Christian concepts. Meanwhile, Chinese audiences would face fewer obstacles in understanding this story than in understanding other theological subjects. Washing feet is a daily activity, after all, and the episode is purely human in its scope. Besides, its storyline in the Bible pericope is straightforward enough that no prior knowledge or sophisticated reasoning is required to comprehend it. Therefore, the clear narration of the footwashing event and its uniqueness make the story a good theme for tracking down Chinese expressions of the biblical story.

As a case study, the footwashing account's comprehensibility is balanced with its complexity. It is a notoriously complicated case to liturgists, exegetes, and academics. For instance, should the footwashing be practiced in liturgy and, if so, how should it be done? Could women receive this rite? The biblical reference is tightly bound up with ritual and liturgy insofar as it is performed on Holy Thursday in specific circumstances that have caused arguments by missionaries and theologians both in the Catholic and Protestant Church about the role of footwashing in pastoral practice.[9] Commentators and scholars in biblical studies also view the footwashing story from different perspectives and emphasize its significance in different domains. For instance, Dunn strictly considers it as an experience of spiritual cleansing.[10] Weiss argues that it was a ceremony in the historical context to symbolize the experience of martyrdom within the Johannine community.[11] John Thomas looks at it as a community rite.[12] In recent studies, some say that it is a preparatory ritual

---

8. *Vulgata Clementina*, John 13:1–15.

9. Chauncy, *A Discourse Concerning Unction and Washing of Feet*, 26; Brooks, *A Discourse Investigating the Doctrine of Washing the Saint's Feet*; Forney, *The Christian Ordinances*.

10. Dunn, "The Washing of the Disciples' Feet in John 13:1–20."

11. Weiss, "Foot Washing in the Johannine Community."

12. Thomas, *Footwashing in John 13 and the Johannine Community*.

for burial.[13] Some call it a welcoming and loving gesture, with which the host shows hospitality in God's house.[14] Alternatively, it is considered a servant's action, one that reverses social conventions of defining the relationship between Jesus and his disciples.[15] To sum up, the complexity of this account opens a floodgate of possibilities to render and to explain the footwashing story in many ways. The Chinese footwashing texts collected in this book also diverge from one another in different ways.

I scanned almost all the available Chinese Christian texts preserved in libraries or reproduced in facsimiles for the footwashing theme. The search has brought about dozens of Chinese renditions, and they carry out assorted versions of the footwashing story that lay out the premise of this work. Twenty-six examples are exhibited and analyzed in this book. They incorporate the prototype in many different ways and are found in the form of excerpts from Chinese Christian books of all sorts. These fragments meet two conditions: at first, they contain Chinese expressions of washing feet that in different Chinese language styles and characters could be "zhuozu" (濯足), "xizu" (洗足), "jianzu" (湔足), or "xijiao" (洗腳); in addition, they depict the very event of Jesus—not others—washing the disciples' feet. As a whole, these texts put together a picture of the footwashing story's diversified message prepared for Chinese audiences in the absence of a Chinese Bible.

Case Study Questions and Approach

These twenty-six texts incorporating the footwashing story forged a medium between the footwashing pericope in the Bible that was originally written in Latin and Chinese audiences who did not read Latin at all. Given the footwashing origin in the Latin Vulgate Bible, this book analyzes and compares Chinese texts with the Latin verses. In this book, I study these texts in the hope of solving the Chinese reception issue of the Bible that can be divided into two questions: How did one account in the Bible fall into transformed pieces in the Chinese language? How did the texts that represented the biblical content relate to their Chinese audiences? Both areas entail a series of inquiries that led to the research in this book.

The first question deals with the biblical story and its Chinese appearances. It asks what the different Chinese versions of the single footwashing account are. The answer is oriented toward Chinese renditions of the biblical prototype. It brings about such concerns as: Was there one version or more

13. Neyrey, "The Footwashing in John 13:6–11."
14. Coloe, "Welcome into the Household of God."
15. Matson, "To Serve as Slave."

of the footwashing account appearing in Chinese? How was the prototype reshaped in each version? To what extent did the Chinese renditions remain the same as the prototype in the Latin Bible? How were the Chinese versions similar to or different from one another?

For the second question, how did the Chinese texts of the biblical account raise and connect to their audiences? Specifics of the answer lie in the Chinese Christian books that represented the biblical account and contexts to read them. It entails such concerns as: In which kinds of books were the footwashing story incorporated? What was the nature and purpose of an individual one? How should it be read? Who were its target readers, and how did they encounter those books? To them, what did the embodiments of the biblical story mean? Were those books in circulation? Did they relate to each other? Were they completely distinct or independent from one another, or did they share certain textuality or readerships?

These strings of inquiries and interests converge to a primary methodology that is beside the established fields but opens an interdisciplinary channel for future research. Answering these questions requires a new approach. I employ narrative analysis, which serves as a lens for me to detect the existence of the biblical prototype's transformations in the Chinese language. Meanwhile, a balanced observation of all the involved Chinese Christian books guides me to obtain a reader's experience of the Chinese biblical and parabiblical texts. The integration of the methods and materials will be demonstrated in later chapters.

2

The Footwashing Pericope and the Three-Layer Framework

Reading the Footwashing Narrative through Three Layers

THE BIBLE ITSELF HAS a narrative character. Moreover, narrative is one of the most comprehensive and effective ways to convey what is documented in the Bible, simultaneously encompassing biblical figures, names, verses, and teachings. Regarding the footwashing account, an inherent narrative case, the verses of John 13:1–15 unfold a footwashing storyline in three phases. The opening verses 1–3 set a background; this event occurred at the Passover dinner. In verses 4–11, the pericope records actions and speeches. Verses 4–5 depict the movements and actions of Jesus, who first rose from supper and took off his outer garments. He took a towel and tied it around his waist, then he poured water into a basin and began to wash the apostles' feet and dry them with the towel around his waist. Verses 6–10 cover the dialogues between Jesus and Peter. Peter initially refused what Jesus was about to offer; he did not understand the action. Jesus explained his motive a bit but did not explicitly spell out the enigma. To be enlightened, Peter turned his attitude around and asked for washing of his whole body. Jesus again intervened and said to Peter, "Whoever has bathed has no need except to have his feet washed, for he is clean all over; so you are clean, but not all." Verse 11 is transitional, for it interpolates an interpretation of the previous verse. Verses 12–15 close the episode with a speech of Jesus. Jesus instructed the disciples about what he had done and what legacy the disciples should continue carrying on.

Roughly paraphrasing and describing what the Bible verses convey is not enough for scholarly examination. It is particularly far from answering how the footwashing account's appearances in scores of Chinese renditions communicated biblical messages to Chinese audiences.

Theological studies on the footwashing story and textual examination of its representation in the Bible often take a narrative perspective.[1] So does my approach. My close reading of the footwashing story starts with its narrativity; more important is that the analysis involves the travel of the story across languages and cultures. This study has a dual-focus on the footwashing story's origins in Latin in the Bible as well as twenty-six versions incorporated into Chinese Christian texts. While comparing the biblical origin with every version of Chinese writings, I consider narrative as an effective means of "translating" content between different linguistic and cultural contexts. The Latin prototype as a reference point can shed light on the narrative components in each Chinese version, thereby allowing us to compare them all.

The mission of this study is not to pair every Latin verse with Chinese sentences because of the varied Chinese renditions of the story. While the footwashing narrative crosses languages and contexts, the biblical pericope has to be parsed so that the essence of the footwashing account can be presented without involving linguistic words. To do so, I employ a structural method to uncover narrative features of the story. The specific tool I have adopted and tailored from narratology is called "three-layer framework." It helps to retrieve the prototype narrative from its textual embodiment in the Latin pericope, revealing its essential narrative components thoroughly. It also helps to construe a representation of each Chinese version of the footwashing story in a way so that each can be compared with the Latin prototype, respectively.

As a structural tool or device of narrative analysis, the three-layer framework interprets a text by making distinctions between different levels in a text and unveiling how each layer interweaves to make the narrative text, to give "a description of a narrative text to the extent that they are narrative."[2] The crucial operation is separating a narrative text in three dimensions, an idea that has been commonly developed and accepted among literary critics and narratologists. To keep consistency, I use the theory shaped by Mieke Bal. Bal has a series of terms to elucidate dividing a text into three dimensions (text, story, and fabula) and to recognize what constitutes each. In Bal's terms, the three layers of a narrative text can be explained as follows:

---

1. Richter, *Die Fusswaschung im Johannesevangelium*; Lohse, "Die Fusswaschung (Joh 13, 1–20)"; Dunn, "The Washing of the Disciples' Feet in John 13:1–20"; Thomas, *Footwashing in John 13 and the Johannine Community*; Matson, "To Serve as Slave"; Coloe, "Welcome into the Household of God"; Weiss, "Foot Washing in the Johannine Community."

2. Bal, *Narratology*, 10.

> A narrative text is a text in which an agent or subject conveys to an addressee ("tells" the reader) a story in a particular medium, such as language, imagery, sound, buildings, or a combination thereof. A story is the content of that text and produces a particular manifestation, inflection, and "coloring" of a fabula; the fabula is presented in a certain manner. A fabula is a series of logically and chronologically related events that are caused or experienced by actors.[3]

Bal's theory has gained classical status in narratology, but it has never been applied to the footwashing narrative nor to any Chinese Christian texts. In this book, I use it to analyze the current case in both Latin and Chinese texts.

The footwashing narrative texts crossing languages and contexts can be viewed through the three-layer framework. The biblical pericope of John 13:1–15 is a narrative *text*. The verses are part of the Gospel of John, serving audiences of the Bible. Text-layer words in the Vulgate Bible are in the Latin language, through which readers can read the footwashing account in Latin; comparatively, text-layer words in the twenty-six Chinese footwashing versions are all in Chinese but with different styles and forms, for different types of audiences. As in its everyday use of the word "story," the footwashing "story" that I have been referring to so far in this book corresponds to the *story* layer termed in this framework. This layer gives the storyline that shows Jesus washing his disciples' feet. The footwashing episode is accounted with a particular logic and sequences that are determined by story-layer aspects. The event happens at a specific place and time, and it involves specific actions and speeches. These elements constitute the nucleus story and collectively belong to the *fabula* layer of a narrative text. The fabula-layer elements in the Latin pericope shape the core unit of the footwashing prototype in the first place. Also, they are essential for rendering the biblical story in another language. The changes of each fabula-layer element can be uncovered from their Chinese embodiments.

The three-layer framework provides an accessible model for us to formulate an interpretative description of the original footwashing story and the role it serves in the Chinese context. Later in this chapter, I will analyze the pericope in the Latin Vulgate. The result of uncovering the prototype's narrative components at each layer will become a fixed reference point for examining each Chinese text in later chapters.

---

3. Bal, *Narratology*, 10.

Fabula-Layer Elements

The fabula layer forms the core of a story with elements. It contains substances for making a story by providing bases that include events, actors, time, and place. The essence of an event—an event with a time sequence in particular—lies in its plots that enable transitions from one state to another. The occurring of an event requires an agent to perform an action whereby at least one actor must get involved. In addition, a location and time should be specified for the event to take place. These are prerequisites to set up an event.

In the footwashing prototype, the fabula-layer elements comprise the event of Jesus washing his disciples' feet, its background, actors, and the plot. The background setting is the Passover dinner. The leading actor is Jesus, whose individual role designates him as a protagonist, whereas the disciples play supporting roles. The names of Peter and Judas are mentioned as part of the narrative; hence, the two stand out as main actors from the rest of the group. The plot of the event is made up of actions and speeches. An array of Jesus' actions indicates his movements before and after washing his disciples' feet. The conversations between Jesus and Peter and the instructions of Jesus in the end are the two sections of speech occurring during the event.

Verses 1–3 situate the footwashing event in a specific setting: the time and location for it to take place is the day of Passover (*diem festum Paschæ*) and when the supper was done (*cœna facta*) at the dining table. Jesus, the protagonist, appears at the very beginning. Jesus knowing (*sciens Jesus*) is the first action as part of the plot. Another action part is that the devil entered the heart of another actor, Judas, who would betray Jesus (*diabolus jam misisset in cor ut traderet eum Judas*).

Verses 4–5 document a series of actions that make up the main plot of the narrative. According to these verses, Jesus began to wash (*cœpit lavare*) beside the dining table. He first rose from the dining table and took off his outer garment. Continuing, he took a towel and had it girded around his waist; he then poured water into a basin, and afterward, he began to wash and to wipe the feet with the towel. With these actions taking place, Jesus is the only actor; yet, his disciples (*discipulorum*) are supposed to be present.

Verses 6–10 directly cite dialogues between Jesus and Peter. Three turns in total show that Peter's attitude changed, and Jesus revealed somehow what would come in the near future. During the conversations, the rest of the disciples are collectively referred to when Jesus said "you" in the plural form (*vos*).

Verse 11 interpolates an interpretation of the previous verse. It contains no fabula element but is of importance for analyzing story-layer aspects.

Verses 12–15 record another series of actions. Immediately after washing the feet of the disciples (*Postquam ergo lavit pedes eorum*), Jesus put on his garment and sat back at the dining table. Then he spoke to the disciples, lecturing them about what had been done and leaving them with the lessons of footwashing.

The fabula-layer elements expressed in the original Latin pericope appear different while being transformed into Chinese texts. The Chinese versions' fabula layers also vary from one another. Changes mainly fall into three types. In some cases, an original fabula element remains the same as it is in the prototype. Sometimes, an element from the prototype is entirely left out. More often, an original fabula-layer element is reframed so that it appears in different manners in Chinese narratives; for instance, certain elements are simplified, some are imposed with a connotation that differs from the prototype, occasionally extra elements are added upon existing elements. Every Chinese footwashing narrative's fabula layer is a collection of alternations. The various fabula layers recreated in Chinese Christian books will be demonstrated case by case in the ensuing chapters.

Story-Layer Aspects

The story layer makes each storyline unique, even those with the same fabula-layer elements. It organizes fabula-layer elements in different manners to build distinguishable versions of storytelling. Story-layer aspects are determined in the first place by a narrator whose presence is not always visible. The narrator is the person who personally "knows/witnesses/experiences" the event that is constituted by the collection of fabula-layer elements. Like a journalist reporting a live event in front of a camera, the narrator "tells/narrates" the event by manipulating how to present the fabula-layer elements. Strictly speaking, when a direct speech during the event occurs in a narrative text, it is the narrator who temporarily empowers the character to speak. The narrator transfers the function of "telling" to the character in the story as if the characters speak for themselves. While reading the story, we may feel that we can hear the characters without any medium, but in fact, it is the craft of the narrator who employs direct quotes.

It is not easy to track down the art of the narrator John in the footwashing prototype, as his voice is not always clearly raised. In John 13:1–3, the narrator introduces the footwashing event by depicting its settings. He directly presents what he sees with descriptions of the time, place, and other things that are not visible in a physical universe. Sometimes, the narrator's voice is implied through the protagonist Jesus. Verse 1 reads, "Jesus knew that his hour had come to pass from this world to the Father. He loved his own in the world and he loved them to the end." In this case, the narrator speaks for Jesus. When verse 2 states that "the devil had already induced Judas, son of Simon the Iscariot, to hand him over," the narrator's voice is explicit. He seems to see everything, including the devil entering the heart of Judas.

From verse 4 to verse 10, the narrator's presence is only logical because he directly presents the moves of Jesus and the conversations between Jesus and Peter. The narrator's involvement is more evident and subjective in verse 11. It reads, "For he knew who would betray him; for this reason, he said, 'Not all of you are clean.'" Herein, the narrator serves as an authoritative interpreter of the mind of Jesus. He points out what Jesus knew and what he implied in verse 10.[4] From verse 12 onward, the narrator steps back again to give the stage to Jesus by depicting his moves back to the dining table and quoting his final instructions.

There are many complexes playing a part as the story-layer aspects for creating a narrative in literary works. The footwashing prototype in the Bible is a case much simpler than *The Kite Runner*. Only two measures are relevant for consideration in this regard: the narrator's presentation manners, and focalization. Both presentational modes and focalization are story-layer aspects. Presentational modes decide how to organize the fabula-layer elements on the story level, so that in a way they manifest techniques to tell a story. Focalization is a control of all the techniques as it decides how to project the presentational modes.[5] These are crafts of the narrator to serve his intentions and points of view while telling a story.

Presentational modes in making a full novel involve a series of issues, such as frequencies, sequential ordering, and relations of characters. The presentational modes of the narrator, John, concern, for example, the way in which the narrator introduces actors, how he describes settings, and which actions he underscores. In the Latin prototype, the story-layer presentation deals with three fabula-layer elements, including the footwashing event's setting, actions, and speeches.

In verses 1–3, the main setting of the footwashing event is introduced in prolepsis because the narrator refers to what would occur ahead of this moment (such as Jesus returning to his Father). Verses 4–5 present actions

---

4. Culpepper, *Anatomy of the Fourth Gospel*, 35; Tenney, "The Footnotes of John's Gospel," 350.

5. Bal, *Narratology*, 142–61.

in typical progress with sequential movements, from Jesus rising from the supper to girding the towel around his waist, and then to pouring water into the basin. In comparison, verses 6–10 are presented in scenery duration. The conversations between Jesus and Peter involve neither moves nor pauses. What is important is the manner of presenting their conversations, which are recorded in a direct speech. Verse 11 inserts a pause in terms of unfolding the storytelling. This verse is an interpolation of the narrator, and the stream of the story freezes at this moment. Verses 12–15 echo verses 4–10 by first outlining sequential moves of Jesus and then presenting what Jesus said as the final instruction in a citation.

Focalization is another story-layer aspect, deciding how the presentational modes are executed. By definition, focalization controls the narrator's lens. It adjusts the relationship between the narrator who sees and what is seen by the narrator. Moreover, it filters what is to be presented and what is not, and then it directs from which vision the narrator proceeds with his experience of the event. The lens divides up the landscape where and when the event is taking place. Since the narrator with the lens often makes moves while observing an event, focalization also moves, in both spatial and temporal dimensions.

The application of focalization in the footwashing prototype is simpler than it is in a full-length novel. The protagonist role of Jesus always occupies the focus; meanwhile, the lens is generally set in a panoramic mode as the whole group of disciples is included during the event. Yet, focalization constantly changes, both in space and time.

In verses 1–3, which situate the footwashing event in scenery duration, the focus is simultaneously on Jesus and Judas. Verse 2 inserts that the devil had put into the heart of Judas Iscariot to betray Jesus. At this moment, the spotlight moves to Judas and his heart. The focalization returns to Jesus again as verse 3 continues with Jesus' inner thoughts. Here, the focalization also involves a time sequence. When alluding to the moments in the past and future (such as the return hour of Jesus to his Father and the betrayal of Judas), the lens of the narrator orients toward different points on the timeline. In verses 4–5, the lens goes alongside the proceeding of Jesus' preparation. In verses 6–10, the words of Jesus presented in a direct speech also refer to different times, in which the focalization projects. For example, Jesus said to Peter, "What I am doing, you do not understand now, but you will understand later." This word refers to a future point in time when the meaning of footwashing can be revealed. The speech of Jesus to the disciples in verses 12–15 is again about what should be done in the future, instead of the present time of the footwashing event.

While remodeled in Chinese versions, the prototype's story-layer aspects as such are adjusted in different ways. Major changes entail three matters: how to introduce the footwashing event in the first place, how to deliver the characters' speeches, and how to focalize the characters and the visions in both spatial and temporal dimensions. Each Chinese version's storyline has its own way to deal with these matters. Some adopt presentational modes of the prototype, while some use opposite techniques. So is the situation of adjusting focalization. Because of the many possibilities for employing presentational modes and focalization principles, the Chinese renditions of story-layer aspects bring about a great variety to rewrite the prototype's story layer. Examples will be demonstrated in later chapters.

Text-Layer Words and Messages

The text layer makes a narrative ready for readers in a linguistic form that is the author's text-layer words. The "author" here may or may not be a biological author who actually writes down the story on paper, but an agent who communicates the message of the narrative text with readers. Understanding the text-layer author of a narrative is crucial to grasp its messages accurately. A likely scenario is that a story-layer narrator reports on an event that he has observed to a text-layer author, and the author notes down what he has been told about the event and tailors a narrative in his words. The text-layer author has final control over the narrative by making decisions on choosing vocabularies, organizing phrases, adopting language styles, and formulating sentences. This control, or, in other words, the art of the author, penetrates through both the fabula and story layers. In any linguistic piece of narrative texts, after all, each narrative component, from fabula-layer elements to story-layer aspects, is expressed in natural language.

John the Evangelist is the text-layer author of the pericope John 13:1–15. Regardless of who actually wrote down the John verses in the historical context of Johannine community, John the story-layer narrator was the first-person who witnessed and reported the footwashing event in the first place. And not a third party or voice is involved in telling the footwashing story through the biblical pericope in the Gospel of John. John, as both the text-layer author and the story-layer narrator, establishes a voice of authority in the Bible. While reading Chinese footwashing narratives, one can find that not every Chinese piece keeps the authorial voice of John. The voice of the text-layer author in individual Chinese texts being John or not is a useful indicator of the Chinese book's genre and readership. Later chapters on each example of a Chinese footwashing text also will illustrate their varying authorial voices.

Identifying the text-layer author's voice helps us grasp how a narrative text's words characterize its story's messages and convey them to readers. In the footwashing case, the prototype is in Latin, but it is featured in Chinese in different language styles and literary forms. Biblical scholars and theologians have been puzzled and made efforts to decode the notoriously complicated footwashing pericope, as I have explained earlier.[6] Not poking linguistic features of the Latin verses, this study needs to tackle what messages each Chinese footwashing narrative conveys and how the wording of each Chinese text expresses its messages.

Again, some Chinese versions conform to the prototype to the extent that they inherit all the equivocal messages of the pericope, and some other versions differ from the prototype as certain meanings of washing feet are lost. While collecting all scenarios, I have reorganized all the messages expressed in the Chinese footwashing narratives as four types.

Four different meanings are associated with washing feet seen in the Chinese Christian texts: two ways to interpret the footwashing event as a symbol and two ways of viewing it as an experience. In terms of expressing symbolic meanings, washing feet can be understood as a symbol of separation, given that it is situated in the farewell discourse and it refers to the ensuing departure of Jesus from his disciples. Alternatively, it symbolizes a soteriological-Christological significance, as Jesus the Savior who, after washing the apostles' feet, would complete the final salvation at the end of the world. The other two messages of the footwashing story underscore that washing feet is empirical. For one thing, washing feet is an earthly event. That Jesus was not supposed to wash the feet of his students but still did so advocates a virtue of being humble and serving others. In addition to the ethic-moral importance and the reverse of social conventions, the event at the Passover dinner highlights a liturgical need. Whose feet after being washed by Jesus would become clean, in contrast to the ones whose feet were not being washed? Hence, washing feet can be interpreted as a prerequisite for receiving the Eucharist, which imposes a ceremonial-sacramental meaning to the footwashing story.

The pericope in Latin entails all of these potential understandings, explicitly or implicitly. The prototype being rendered into another language means opening possibilities to explore all of its spoken and unspoken messages. Every Chinese footwashing narrative's text layer would spell out some meanings of washing feet that cause exegetical effects to

---

6. See "The Footwashing Story in *Situ*" in chapter 1.

its readers' understanding of the biblical story. A few versions take up the four interpretations fully, including the prototype's intrinsic ambiguity. Most of the Chinese texts encompass part of the four messages and convey them to readers. It is the language styles and forms of the twenty-six Chinese texts that are adjusted differently for their audiences, which will be shown in later chapters.

Part I

Equivalent Narratives in Scriptural Books

THE PRECEDING CHAPTERS COLLECT the Chinese footwashing narratives that exactly correspond to the prototype through the three-layer framework. However, they appear different from one another in terms of genres and readerships. They are extracted from three Chinese Christian books: *Shengjing zhijie* 聖經直解, *Misa jingdian* 彌撒經典, and *Guxin shengjing* 古新聖經.

Chapter 3 provides a holistic view on analyzing all the three versions whose narrative components are identical to the prototype. The three texts still vary due to their compositions. The following chapter 4, chapter 5, and chapter 6 take turns to focus on the three books, respectively. Chapter 4 elaborates on the inclusion of Gospel verses and commentaries in the book *Shengjing zhijie* and its reception. Chapter 5 introduces *Misa jingdian*, the ritual manual for the mass in Chinese. Chapter 6 explains the colloquial rendering of Bible verses and commentary writing combined in the famous *Guxin shengjing*.

A common trait of the three books is that their footwashing texts are translations of the Latin Scripture verse by verse. However, the equivalence of narrative, or equivalence of meaning, does not promise equivalence of function. Each book had its destinies in the Chinese context, but none was recognized as a Chinese edition of the Bible in the Catholic Church. Instead, their compositions resonated with the Chinese literary tradition and printing culture of the time.

3

Corresponding Chinese Versions Varying in Words

WHILE ANALYZING ALL TWENTY-SIX Chinese footwashing narratives with the same three-layer framework, these three versions stand out—the versions in the texts of *Shengjing zhijie*, *Misa jingdian*, and *Guxin shengjing*. They have narrative components equivalent to the prototype in the Latin Vulgate. Compared with the other two parts that demonstrate a great variety of renditions of the prototype, the presentation here has to be dull, because the three versions' narrative components are all the same corresponding to the original pericope, John 13:1–15.

Perhaps one could assume that they are just Chinese sentences translated verse by verse from the Latin Vulgate. At first glance, this might appear to be the case. A more in-depth exploration of these three versions' fabula layers, story layers, and text layers reinforces that the transfer of the biblical account to the Chinese texts was accurately done but in diversified ways of expression. Moreover, the three-layer analysis displays the Chinese versions' similarities and differences in a comparative manner, which gives a boost to our understanding of their textual connections and distinct readerships, more than just describing their linguistic surface.

Fabula-Layer Elements

According to the pericope John 13:1–15, the footwashing event took place at the table that was set for the Passover dinner, which is the background setting of the event. The role of Jesus functions as a protagonist. As the names of Peter and Judas are called upon, they are recognizable as main actors, distinguished from the rest of the disciples. The main plot consists of Jesus' actions for preparing to wash his disciples' feet, the conversations between Jesus and Peter, and the final speech of Jesus giving instructions to his disciples.

These fabula-layer elements of the footwashing prototype change while being rendered into Chinese texts. For instance, the event can be situated in different ways. Sometimes its setting is missed out; but in some other texts, extra descriptions are added to create a background different from the original account. It is in the versions incorporated in *Shengjing zhijie*, *Misa jingdian*, and *Guxin shengjing* that all the prototype's fabula-layer elements remain the same without anything omitted or added.

Settings

The original footwashing story's setting covers its specific timing and location, in combination with the fact that Jesus knew his return hour approaching. In John 13:1–3, the event was about to take place on the day of Passover (*diem festum Paschæ*) and when the supper was done (*cœna facta*) at the dining table. The backdrop nuances involve Jesus knowing (*sciens Jesus*) about the departure and devil entering the heart of Judas who would betray Jesus (*diabolus jam misisset in cor ut traderet eum Judas*). The overall background highlights a farewell discourse foretelling that Jesus would leave the world and his disciples.

The footwashing versions in *Shengjing zhijie* and *Misa jingdian* contain the same fabula-layer setting as the prototype does. The text of *Shengjing zhijie* starts:

> 巴斯卦大瞻禮前一日。耶穌知其謝世歸父。定期已至。雖向愛厥世人。臨終尤特愛。夕飱畢。魔既入茹答西滿夷斯加畧大心。引付厥師。知天主聖父。託掌萬有柄。更知厥昔出于天主。今將復歸。

The day before the grand feast of Passover, Jesus knew that he (should) pass away from the world to return to the Father, the destined time had come. Even if having always loved his own world and people, till the end (he) especially loved them very much. The dinner was done, the devil had already entered the heart of Judas Simon Iscariot, seducing (him) to hand over his teacher. (Jesus) knew that the Heavenly Lord Holy Father had put all things into (him) with power, (he) further knew that his (life) from the beginning had come from the Heavenly Lord. Today (he) should again return.[1]

This writing of *Shengjing zhijie* includes the Passover dinner, the inner thought of Jesus, his love and his hour to leave, his origin from the Heavenly Lord Father and his return back to the Father, and everything else incorporated in the prototype. Even the part about Judas and his

---

1. BnF Chinois 6723, vol. 9, ff. 49a–54a.

potential betrayal are implied too. The version of *Misa jingdian* follows *Shengjing zhijie* in the same way.

The version in the text of *Guxin shengjing* also unfolds according to the prototype, similar to the version in *Shengjing zhijie*. It encompasses the Passover dinner, the inner mind of Jesus, and the devil entering Judas' heart, but with different wording. The text-layer wording is not the concern here, despite the fact that the following English translation of the Chinese source is intended to demonstrate its language style and the difference between the two versions. The beginning of the footwashing text in *Guxin shengjing* reads:

> 巴斯卦瞻禮前一日。耶穌知他要從世回父。此時也剛到在世愛的那些切近人。至終還更爱他們。晚餐畢。魔動了依西加里約得。西滿的子如達斯的心。賣師與仇。耶穌還知聖父。交諸物在他手。又知已從父出。如今回父。

> The day before the feast of Passover, Jesus knew that he (should) from the world return to the Father, this time had just arrived. In the world (that he) had loved those people who were close, at the end (he) still loved them more. The dinner was done, the devil had already moved the heart of Judas the son of Simon Iscariot, (making him) sell his teacher to the enemy. Jesus also knew that the Holy Father had put everything into his hands, (he) again knew that himself had come from the Father, as today (he should) return to the Father.[2]

Preparations

The main plot of the footwashing prototype in the Gospel of John consists of several sections. At first, a series of moves by Jesus leads toward preparing the washing. In the Latin pericope, the preparation unfolds with verbs in succession: *surgit a cœna, et ponit vestimenta sua, et cum accepisset linteum, præcinxit se. Deinde mittit aquam in pelvim, et cœpit lavare pedes discipulorum, et extergere linteo, quo erat præcinctus.* It is recorded that Jesus rose from supper and took off his outer garments, he took a towel and tied it around his waist, then he poured water into a basin and began to wash the disciples' feet and dry them with the towel around his waist.

There are in total six movements: namely, to rise from the table, to take off his coat, to take a towel, to gird the towel around his waist, to pour water into a basin, and, in the end, to begin to wash and to wipe the feet

---

2. *CCT ZKW XB* vol. 33, 624–25.

of his disciples. Not every Chinese version documents all of these actions. Some simplify the preparation process, while some add exaggerations to portray Jesus. Also, some twist certain nuances to provide a different portrayal for preparing the washing.

However, the three versions developed in the texts of *Shengjing zhijie*, *Misa jingdian*, and *Guxin shengjing* fully and exactly adopt these actions from the Latin pericope. For example, the text of *Misa jingdian* reads:

因起離席。卸表衣。白帨纏腰。持盆盛水。濯拭徒足。

Hence (Jesus) rose and stepped away from the feast, took off (his) cover garment, (took) a white cloth to gird around (his) waist, held a basin and poured water (into it), washing and wiping the feet of (his) disciples.[3]

The version in *Guxin shengjing* also follows the prototype, only that its language use is much simpler and colloquial. Again, the linguistic issue is not a fabula-layer concern, and I present the text here just as an example for one to taste different expressions that portray the same scene in the Chinese texts. The words of *Guxin shengjing* on the preparation of Jesus read:

餐畢站起。脫己外衣。取圍巾寄。後滿水於盆。要洗諸徒的足。用寄的巾擦。

After the meal, (he) stood up, took off his outer clothes, fetched a cloth to gird around. Then (he) filled water into a basin, began to wash every disciples' feet, to wipe (them) with the cloth that was girded.[4]

Three Conversations

Another section that makes up the prototype's plot is three dialogues between Jesus and Peter as recorded in John 13:6–10. In the Latin pericope, Peter in verses 6–7 asked, "Master, are you going to wash my feet?" (*Domine, tu mihi lavas pedes?*) Jesus then responded, "What I am doing, you do not understand now, but you will understand later." (*Quod ego facio, tu nescis modo: scies autem postea.*) Peter kept on refusing Jesus by saying in verse 8, "You will never wash my feet." (*Non lavabis mihi pedes in æternum.*) Jesus replied, "Unless I wash you, you will have no inheritance with me." (*Si non lavero te, non habebis partem mecum.*) In verses 9–10, Peter

3. *CCT ZKW XB* vol. 15, 286–95.
4. *CCT ZKW XB* vol. 33, 624–25.

reversed his attitude and requested, "Master, then not only my feet, but my hands and head as well." (*Domine, non tantum pedes meos, sed et manus, et caput.*) Then Jesus said to him, "Whoever has bathed has no need except to have his feet washed, for he is clean all over; so you are clean, but not all." (*Qui lotus est, non indiget nisi ut pedes lavet, sed est mundus totus. Et vos mundi estis, sed non omnes.*)

The wording of these lines that involve multiple interpretations through linguistic expressions belongs to text-layer matters. As far as the fabula-layer plot is concerned, what matters is the completeness of these conversations. The focus is whether all the three dialogues are included and whether the contents of each conversation are retained. In many Chinese versions, one or two dialogues remain but not all the three sets. Even if a full dialogue is there, its talking points are lost at least in part; sometimes, new content beyond the prototype is added. Cases as such can be identified later in other texts.

In the versions extracted from *Shengjing zhijie*, *Misa jingdian*, and *Guxin shengjing*, all the three dialogues are contained the same as in the Latin pericope. For instance, the text of *Shengjing zhijie* corresponding to these conversations between Peter and Jesus reads:

徒曰。主爾乃欲湔吾足。耶穌語之云。予茲攸行。爾今莫知。然後乃知。對曰。無竟于今。弗諸師湔弟足。曰。儻予蔑濯汝。竟弗能享予。曰。若茲。奚翅弟足。手首憑師欲洗。不敢方命。耶穌曰。潔人但須濯足。爾已淨甚。暨列弟偕淨。嗟。惟一弗淨者。[5]

The apostle said, "Lord, so do you want to wash my feet?" Jesus spoke to him, saying, "What I am doing right now, you do not know today. After that, you know then." (Peter) responded and said, "Not till the end from today, (I) will not allow (you) the teacher to wash your student's (which is my) feet." (Jesus) said, "If I do not wash you, (you) cannot have me in the end." (Peter) said, "If so, why only my feet, (my) hands and head, let (them) be washed as the teacher's wish. (I) dare not to disobey (your) command." Jesus said, "Whoever clean only needs to wash feet. You are already very clean. And all the brothers together are clean, well, only one who is not clean."

The text of *Misa jingdian* follows the text of *Shengjing zhijie* with similar wording. It reads:

---

5. BnF Chinois 6723, vol. 9, ff. 49a–54a.

曰。主。爾乃欲涮吾足。耶穌語之云。予茲攸行。爾今莫知。然後乃知。對曰。無。竟于今弗諾師涮弟足。曰。儻予蔑濯。汝竟弗能享予。曰。若茲。奚翅弟足。手首憑師欲洗。耶穌曰。潔人但須濯足。爾巳淨甚。暨列弟偕淨。嗟。惟一弗淨者。

(Peter) said, "Lord, so do you want to wash my feet?" Jesus spoke to him, saying, "What I am doing right now, you do not know today. After that, you know then." (Peter) responded and said, "No, till the end from today, (I) will not allow (you) the teacher to wash your student's feet." (Jesus) said, "If I do not wash, you cannot have me in the end." (Peter) said, "If so, why only my feet, (my) hands and head, let (them) be washed as the teacher's wish." Jesus said, "Whoever clean only needs to wash feet. You are already very clean. And all the brothers together are clean, well, only one who is not clean."[6]

Several minor but helpful revisions to the text in *Shengjing zhijie* are done in the version of *Misa jingdian*. For instance, four characters from the version in *Shengjing zhijie* are missing in the text of *Misa jingdian*. When Peter agreed to accept the washing of his feet, the version in *Shengjing zhijie* adds an extended line to him, that is "bu gan fang ming" (不敢方命), in Chinese meaning "(I) dare not to disobey (your) command." This sentence reinforces the confirmation of Peter's change of attitude. However, the original Latin pericope does not assign this line to Peter. And, the text of *Misa jingdian* leaves it out. The book of *Misa jingdian* was prepared on the basis of *Shengjing zhijie* in a later period by selectively reproducing and revising the text of *Shengjing zhijie*. The variances at the fabula-layer stand for a great example to indicate the intertextual connection and development from the book of *Shengjing zhijie* to the book of *Misa jingdian*, which can be elaborated from a textual history perspective in later chapters.

Regarding the fabula-layer conversations, the text of *Guxin shengjing* also contains all the three dialogues fully. The language used therein is just more colloquial. It reads:

西滿伯多祿向他說。主。你要洗我足麼。耶穌說。我行的。你如今不知。後纔明白。伯多祿望他說。永不許你濯我足。耶穌說。若我不洗你。你與我無干。西滿伯多祿說。主。若如此。不单洗我足。還連我手。我頭。耶穌說。洗澡的人。单該洗足。因渾身乾净了。你們是乾净的。但都不是。

6. *CCT ZKW XB* vol. 15, 286–95.

Simon Peter said to him, "Lord, are you going to wash my feet?" Jesus said, "What I am doing, you do not know as today. Later, (you) will just understand." Peter, looking at him, said, "Never allow you to wash my feet." Jesus said, "If I do not wash you, you and I will have no interference." Simon Peter said, "If so, not only wash my feet, also include my hands, my head." Jesus said, "Whoever has bathed, only should wash (their) feet, because the whole body is clean. You people are clean, but all is not."[7]

Final Speeches

The last section of the prototype's plot is the final speech of Jesus that concludes the footwashing event. Jesus instructed the disciples in four sentences in John 13:12–15. According to the Latin pericope, Jesus said, "Do you realize what I have done for you? You call me 'teacher' and 'master,' and rightly so, for indeed I am. If I, therefore, the master and teacher, have washed your feet, you ought to wash one another's feet. I have given you a model to follow, so that as I have done for you, you should also do." The four sentences constitute the lessons that Jesus left to the apostles in his own words.

Again, not all of them are taken in by individual Chinese versions; some omit the first two sentences, which happens very often; some alter the contents of the final speech. Sometimes, even the whole instruction as a fabula-layer element is missing. Nevertheless, in the texts of *Shengjing zhijie*, *Misa jingdian*, and *Guxin shengjing*, the four lines are fully retained.

For example, in the version incorporated in the text of *Misa jingdian*, Jesus said:

爾其知予茲攸行。爾皆稱予爾師。暨主。是。予主暨師。猶洗爾足。爾然宜相洗足。予今竪表。爾視以師。

"You know I have done just now? You all call me your Teacher and Lord. Yes, I am Lord and Teacher, still wash your feet. You certainly had better wash feet for each other. Today I have set an example, you have watched that as a means to imitate that."[8]

In the version of *Guxin shengjing*, the style of speech appears different, which is chatty and less formal. But the words of Jesus in the Latin pericope are fully included. Jesus in the text of *Guxin shengjing* said:

---

7. *CCT ZKW XB* vol. 33, 624–25.
8. *CCT ZKW XB* vol. 15, 286–95.

我望你們行的。你們懂得明麼。你們稱我為師。為主。說
的好。我本是。若我雖是你們的主。你們的師。尚且洗了
你們的足。你們彼此也該相濯足。我留表與你們。為我望
你們怎行。你們望別人也怎行。

"What I expect you to do, do you understand? You call me as Teacher, as Lord, well said, I inherently am. If I, although as your lord and your teacher, still have washed your feet, you should also wash feet for each other. I leave an example to you, because what I expect you to do, you (should) also expect others to do so."[9]

Story-Layer Aspects

The prototype's story-layer aspects shape the storyline through the eyes of John the narrator. Two measures are incorporated in John 13:1–15: presentation manners and focalization principles. In the original pericope, the narrator John's presentational modes introduce the footwashing event's setting, the actions, and speeches. Its focalization mainly deals with the protagonist Jesus but also encompasses the apostles on the stage; meanwhile, it moves along the actions and speeches of Jesus by making references to certain points.

It is relatively more difficult to grasp these aspects than to identify the fabula-layer elements, especially in the Chinese versions. What is interesting is to see how a Chinese rendition reframes the prototype's presentation mode or focalization method so that the original storyline of the biblical pericope is molded into a variety of versions. Examples showing such great creativity will be presented later in other Chinese Christian texts. The versions featured in *Shengjing zhijie*, *Misa jingdian*, and *Guxin shengjing* still correspond to the prototype as the story-layer aspects in these versions remain the same as the Latin pericope.

Presentational Modes

Presentational modes organize fabula-layer elements at a higher level by involving techniques to make a story. There are two presentational techniques involved in the story layer of the footwashing narrative in the Latin pericope: one is prolepsis to introduce the event's setting, and the other is presenting the lines of characters in a direct speech.

9. *CCT ZKW XB* vol. 33, 624–25.

Prolepsis is also called "flash-forward." At the Passover dinner, the original setting, the narrator's presentation of all fabula-layer matters alludes to what would occur only after the footwashing event. The return of Jesus to his Father was going to happen in a future time after the moment of Passover dinner, and so was the betrayal of Judas. These scenes are presented through the narrator spelling out the inner thought of Jesus and describing the devil's act. Situating the footwashing event by presenting what would happen next can influence the interpretation of the footwashing narrative's discourse. The prolepsis technique serves the story-layer narrator's agenda.

The version in *Shengjing zhijie* uses the same device by inserting what would happen afterward. It reads:

魔既入茹答西滿夷斯加畧大心。引付厥師。

The devil had already entered the heart of Judas Simon Iscariot, seducing (him) to hand over his teacher.[10]

In the text of *Guxin shengjing*, the narrator also refers to other events in near future while reading the inner thought of Jesus. It reads:

耶穌知他要從世回父。

Jesus knew that he (should) from the world return to the Father.[11]

The other involvement of the narrator's maneuver of presentation is about how to assign lines to the characters Jesus and Peter. Speech is a fabula-layer element, but presenting the speech is a story-layer decision, which can be quotation without intermediate interference in a direct manner or reporting speech and paraphrasing in an indirect manner. In the Latin pericope, all the speech is presented in direct quotations. When Jesus and Peter were having three dialogues back and forth, when Jesus gave the final instruction in the end, it is the story-layer narrator who let them speak.

Despite a lack of quotation marks—because modern punctuation system had not become a convention yet in Chinese writings at that time—one can still use word indicators to sort out the presentational mode of speech in the Chinese texts. Again, each Chinese version has its arrangement. Sometimes, a version adopts both direct speech and indirect speech. In the texts of *Shengjing zhijie*, *Misa jingdian*, and *Guxin shengjing*, all the characters' lines are cited directly, in accordance with the prototype.

---

10. BnF Chinois 6723, vol. 9, ff. 49a–54a.
11. *CCT ZKW XB* vol. 33, 624–25.

For example, the text of *Misa jingdian* adopts a self-referencing pronoun "yu" (予) meaning "I" in classical Chinese when Jesus referred to himself. The pronoun is a useful signal in the absence of quotation marks. In this version, Jesus responded to Peter by calling him in "er" (爾) in a literary style of "you" in Chinese. The text reads:

耶穌語之云。予茲攸行。爾今莫知。

Jesus spoke to him, saying, "What I am doing right now, you do not know to-day. After that, you know then."[12]

With different word indicators, the text of *Guxin shengjing* also presents the conversations in a direct speech. Therein, Jesus called himself "wo" (我) meaning "I" and Peter "ni" (你) meaning "you." These words are close to modern Mandarin Chinese, which is more accessible than the literary writings of classical Chinese. The same line in the text of *Guxin shengjing* reads:

耶穌說。我行的。你如今不知。

Jesus said, "What I am doing, you do not know as today."[13]

Focalizations

Presentation is about the narrator's output, for presenting what fabula elements that the narrator "sees." In comparison, focalization is about the narrator's lens, to determine which fabula elements the narrator "sees" at first, which second, and how the narrator "sees" those elements. Focalization adjusts the distance and timing between the narrator who sees and what is seen by the narrator. As for the footwashing prototype, its story-layer focalization can be divided into two dimensions: focalization in space and focalization in time.

The spatial focalization employed by the story-layer narrator John in the Latin pericope can be described with two specific measures: the spotlight and the narrator' vision. Jesus, as the protagonist, always occupies the spotlight. Peter and Judas also join in the public eye because their names are called upon throughout the storyline, particularly in John 13:2 and John 13:6–11. In the meantime, the narrator's vision is overall panoramic since it encompasses the whole group of apostles. According to the verses, Jesus addressed the apostles

---

12. *CCT ZKW XB* vol. 15, 286–95.
13. *CCT ZKW XB* vol. 33, 624–25.

in plural pronouns, as in John 13:15 (*Exemplum enim dedi vobis, ut quemadmodum ego feci vobis, ita et vos faciatis*).

In all Chinese versions, Jesus is placed at the center of the stage; yet, the spotlight is not always exclusive. Sometimes, other roles occupy the narrator's lens too. For instance, a series of Chinese texts include long expositions just on feet. The combination of the spotlight and the narrator's vision, at any rate, can bring about varied manners to play with spatial focalization. Not a surprise, the versions in the texts of *Shengjing zhijie*, *Misa jingdian*, and *Guxin shengjing* still keep consistent with the prototype, without changing anything of the spatial dimension of the focalization used in the biblical pericope.

The temporal focalization of the prototype's story layer involves movement. It shoots different moments and delivers them with a time sequence. From the Passover dinner to Jesus rising from the dining table to his preparation, his conversations with Peter, and then to the completion of washing the disciples' feet, the story develops in time. One signal is that Jesus first stepped away from the dinner (*surgit a cœna*) and reclined at the dining table again (*cum recubuisset iterum*) in the end.

Most Chinese versions unfold with a time sequence as well, although a few versions only present the event as one scene that requires no engagement with time changing. The three versions in the texts of *Shengjing zhijie*, *Misa jingdian*, and *Guxin shengjing* have storylines moving forward. They all stream the ongoing process of the footwashing event precisely as the prototype does, from Jesus raising from the dinner to his preparation, and eventually to the end when he sat back at the table and gave the final speech.

Text-Layer Words and Messages

A narrative text's surface is its text layer, which is also a medium between author and reader as this is what a reader of the narrative can immediately access. The text-layer author has ultimate control over how the story is delivered to its readers. In the John verses, there is no third party to intervene in the delivery. No one stands in-between the text layer and readers of the Gospel of John. It is to say that the story-layer narrator John and the text-layer author John can be considered the same without involving another authorial voice. The authority of narrating the footwashing story is established by the narrator and the author John's voice.

When the footwashing narrative is transformed into various shapes in all sorts of Chinese Christian texts, the role of the text-layer author in different texts also becomes multiplied. The author's voice in each text would be adjusted for their respective readerships. If a Chinese text does not engage with any other authorial voice to address its audiences but only adopts the tone of the narrator/author John, the same as the prototype, its text layer suggests a signal that this version is made in imitation of the original pericope. In other words, when a Chinese footwashing narrative's text-layer author only and exclusively corresponds to the role of John in the Gospel, it is in a position to claim authority for telling the biblical story in Chinese. There are indeed several Chinese texts of the footwashing narrative being fabricated in this way. Given the absence of a Chinese Bible of that time, those texts could fill in the category of a parallel status. The versions extracted from the texts of *Shengjing zhijie*, *Misa jingdian*, and *Guxin shengjing* are just adopting this approach.

What executes the author's voice for telling a narrative is words. Words are primarily concerned with the text layer but have penetrated through both of the fabula and story layers by expressing the fabula-layer elements and story-layer aspects. The purpose of choosing and organizing particular words is to convey particular messages of the author to readers of the narrative text. In the Bible, the footwashing prototype embodies not only messages but also vagueness. As Erich Auerbach says, "While on the one hand Scripture speaks very simply, as if to children, on the other hand, it contains secrets and riddles which are revealed to very few."[14] The footwashing pericope is not that complicated in terms of its narration, but as part of the Bible verses, its words incorporate intrinsic complexity that can always generate multiple interpretations.

The Chinese versions that are already diversified have developed the footwashing account in their texts to varying discourses. Each can take its readers in different directions. To display all messages spotted in the Chinese footwashing versions, I have listed them as four types of understandings. They can all be read through the prototype narrative's inherent implications, as the previous chapter has briefed. Each of the three versions expressed in the texts of *Shengjing zhijie*, *Misa jingdian*, and *Guxin shengjing* suggest the four interpretations fully. They contain therein the prototype's certain ambiguity too. Nevertheless, the same meaning still is worked out through different words in each text.

To take one example, the text of *Shengjing zhijie* lays stress on all four interpretations. It first points out the departure of Jesus in both an empirical and theological sense. The text states:

耶穌知其謝世歸父。定期已至。

14. Auerbach, *Mimesis*, 154.

Jesus knew that he (should) pass away from the world to return to the Father, the destined time had come.¹⁵

This description of the inner world of Jesus echoes the Latin verse (*sciens Jesus quia venit hora ejus ut transeat ex hoc mundo ad Patrem*) word by word, the order of the Latin words being rearranged for making a Chinese sentence read more smoothly and more literary. The very same verse in the text of *Guxin shengjing* is translated into another one, in a totally different style with different word expressions. The text of *Guxin shengjing* also situates the footwashing narrative in the context of the departure of Jesus by starting with:

耶穌知他要從世回父。此時也剛到。

Jesus knew that he (should) from the world return to the Father, this time had just arrived.¹⁶

In addition, the version in *Shengjing zhijie* assigns the footwashing event another symbolic meaning that associates with the role of Jesus as the Savior. This meaning is highlighted during the conversations between Jesus and Peter. According to what Jesus said, salvation is to be completed only after the footwashing is done. The words to fill the line of Jesus used in *Shengjing zhijie* are:

儻予蔑濯汝。竟弗能享予。

"If I do not wash you, (you) cannot have me in the end."¹⁷

The version in the text of *Misa jingdian* follows the version in *Shengjing zhijie* by using "xiang" (享) to resonate the Latin words "*habebis partem mecum*" to translate the "part" of Jesus Christ. This "part" is crucial for working on theological hermeneutics of the footwashing narrative. The Chinese character used in *Shengjing zhijie* and *Misa jingdian* perfectly matches the need to create a room for sitting in ambiguities of the "part" of Jesus Christ, as "xiang" (享) means to eat, to have, to receive, to enjoy, and to share. This character can convey meanings of the "part" without losing its potential soteriological-Christological significance. The abundant connotations of the Chinese character already create a linkage between the footwashing event and the liturgical aspect regarding the Eucharist.

In comparison, the "part" is spelled out as "interference" in the version of *Guxin shengjing*. The same line of Jesus in *Guxin shengjing* appears to be:

---

15. BnF Chinois 6723, vol. 9, ff. 49a–54a.
16. *CCT ZKW XB* vol. 33, 624–25.
17. BnF Chinois 6723, vol. 9, ff. 49a–54a.

若我不洗你。你與我無干。

"If I do not wash you, you and I will have no interference."[18]

The "interference" here does not have a negative tone but more of expression about relations and influences. This word does convey certain ambiguity too but not as rich as the character "xiang" (享) as it lacks the meaning of eating and sharing. "To have" Jesus in *Shengjing zhijie* and *Misa jingdian* hence becomes "to have interference" with Jesus in *Guxin shengjing*. What is lost here is a touching on the aspect of the Eucharist.

Moreover, all of these three versions speak of the virtue of humility and service, which is also the most obvious and frequently highlighted message in almost every Chinese footwashing text. In line with the prototype, this lesson on virtue is highlighted in the final instruction of Jesus. The text of *Shengjing zhijie* gives the line of Jesus in the following:

爾其知予茲攸行。爾皆稱予爾師。暨主。是。予主暨師。猶洗爾足。爾然宜相洗足。予今豎表。爾視以師。

"You know I have done just now? You all call me your Teacher and Lord. Yes, I am Lord and Teacher, still wash your feet. You certainly had better wash feet for each other. Today I have set an example, you have watched that as a means to imitate that."[19]

The same line of Jesus in *Guxin shengjing* is less sophisticated or literary but speaks for the same lesson. The text reads:

我望你們行的。你們懂得明麼。你們稱我為師。為主。說的好。我本是。若我雖是你們的主。你們的師。尚且洗了你們的足。你們彼此也該相濯足。我留表與你們。為我望你們怎行。你們望別人也怎行。

"What I expect you to do, do you understand? You call me as Teacher, as Lord, well said, I inherently am. If I, although as your lord and your teacher, still have washed your feet, you should also wash feet for each other. I leave an example to you, because what I expect you to do, you (should) also expect others to do so."[20]

Through the three-layer framework, I have demonstrated that the texts of *Shengjing zhijie,* *Misa jingdian,* and *Guxin shengjing* feature their own footwashing narratives exactly following the prototype. The prototype's

---

18. *CCT ZKW XB* vol. 33, 624–25.
19. BnF Chinois 6723, vol. 9, ff. 49a–54a.
20. *CCT ZKW XB* vol. 33, 624–25.

narrative components remain unchanged in the three versions, from its fabula-layer elements and story-layer aspects to text-layer messages. Still, the three Chinese texts' wordings vary.

Besides, if only speaking from the textual surface, the footwashing texts in *Shengjing zhijie*, *Misa jingdian*, and *Guxin shengjing* represent verse-by-verse translations of the Latin pericope of John 13:1–15, although in different styles of translation. The text of *Shengjing zhijie* adopts erudite Chinese, the written language of scholars and officials in the early seventeenth century; in contrast, the text of *Guxin shengjing* uses colloquial Chinese, the language of commoners for daily use in the eighteenth century. The footwashing narrative of *Misa jingdian* is somewhat of a copy of the corresponding text extracted from *Shengjing zhijie*, with revisions and adjustments. However, none of these texts promises a single compromised version of the Bible. Each was shaped in specific contexts for particular readerships and purposes. The following chapters will continue presenting the three books in their own terms.

4

Shengjing zhijie: Straight Explanation of Sacred Scriptures

THE BOOK *SHENGJING ZHIJIE*, composed and published during the years 1636 and 1642, has become increasingly known in recent years; issues regarding its authorship and readership are not yet fully resolved, though.[1] The footwashing fragment found in this book indicates certain textual features regarding its composition and intended readership. In this new light, I revisit the book of *Shengjing zhijie* with a focus on its textuality, in order to understand better its role among other Chinese Christian texts for spreading biblical content in the absence of a Chinese Bible.

The copy of *Shengjing zhijie* that I examine is currently preserved in the National Library of France. It is a reprint of a woodblock carved in 1739 Beijing. The whole set contains eight fascicles, or physical copies, so to speak. Seven fascicles bring in fourteen volumes of the body part of this book, for every two volumes are bound as one fascicle. Another fascicle contains paratexts that are designed to assist readers' use and experience of this book. The name of Manuel Dias, SJ (junior) (1574–1659), as its author is indicated on the first page of every volume.

Paratexts Planned for Practical Uses

The paratexts include one preface, two lists of Sundays and major feast days respectively in a liturgical year, and one index of subjects elaborated throughout the book. They are compiled in the separate booklet called "mulu juan" (目錄卷), the volume of a table of contents in Chinese.

In the preface, Dias explained his motivation for making this book. He said:

---

1. Standaert, "The Bible in Early Seventeenth-Century China"; Shioyama, "カソリックによる聖書抄訳 ディアスの 『聖経直解』"; Chen, "The *Shengjing zhijie*"; Marchioron, "An Example of Exegesis in the Late Ming Dynasty."

不佞忘其固陋，祖述舊聞，著為直解，以便玩繹。大率欲人知崇天主，從其至真至正之教。... 至於文詞膚拙，言不盡意，所不敢諱。觀者取其意而略其詞，可矣。

(I) the untalented, forgetting that I am ill-informed and ignorant, follow the ancestors to tell anecdotes in the past, (and so) compose them as this *Direct Explanation*, in order to explore and to interpret (the scriptures). Generally, (I) desire to let people know about worshiping the Heavenly Lord and following his extremely true and the most orthodox teachings. . . . As for (my) superficial and clumsy words and expressions, the language does not fully express meaning, that is what I dare not to conceal. (Therefore,) readers should take out the meanings and ignore the words, (that would be) fine then.[2]

This piece is full of modesty, a default convention for Chinese literary scholars. What is more interesting is the author's concern about delivering messages to its readers. Dias spoke of the readers in his mind and his expectations from them. He wrote:

蓋聖經載吾主之聖德，述吾主之聖行，并紀從主諸聖之奇節。故其言皆至言，雖多不厭。學者習覽習聽而習玩之。庶幾知其真，嗜其味，而收其益矣。

Generally speaking, Sacred Scriptures wrote down the holy virtues of our Lord, accounted the sage deed of our Lord, and recorded the marvelous conduct of every saint who followed the Lord. Therefore, the words (of the Sacred Scriptures) are the best of all, while numerous but not tiring. Whoever study (the Sacred Scriptures) should frequently look at, listen to, and ponder over it. Hopefully, they may know the authenticity of it, be fond of its taste, and receive benefit from it.[3]

According to Dias, whoever studies *Shengjing zhijie* should frequently look at, listen to, and ponder over it. The three verbs—"to look," "to listen," and "to ponder"—collectively request how readers of *Shengjing zhijie* should be reading it. To Chinese minds, a learned scholar should read a good book as a real gourmet enjoys a delicious plate, knowing the texture of the dish, savoring it critically but also joyfully, and continuing to perceive its aftertaste. Dias proposed the same approach to his readers for reading *Shengjing zhijie*.

2. BnF Chinois 6722, vol. mulu, f. 2b.
3. BnF Chinois 6722, vol. mulu, f. 5b.

In a likely scenario, a lettered man could read this book in private at his desk, perhaps quietly. Otherwise, he could read it aloud to a less educated group and explain what was written in the book to the group so that fellows incapable of reading this book could listen and communicate about its content. The group may consist of Chinese clergy, laypersons, and sympathizers who were friendly toward Christian believers. A European priest may be present too at the group reading. After studying specific passages, some readers would like to meditate upon them on a liturgical day, as the readings on liturgical days were already regulated in this book with the two lists of liturgical days.

One list gives Sundays in a liturgical year, and it is named "zhousui zhuri zhi mulu" (周歲主日之目錄). Each Sunday is associated with a page number—which folio in which volume—with which one can find the Gospel readings on that day in the body part of *Shengjing zhijie*. The readings for Sundays are collected in the first through the eighth volumes. The other list in a similar manner works for the major feast days and is named "zhousui zhanli zhi mulu" (周歲瞻禮之目錄). It includes fixed and movable feast days; also, it indicates where to locate Gospel readings. The readings for feast days are provided in the ninth through the fourteenth volumes.

The two "tables of contents" are practical tools to mediate the relations between *Shengjing zhijie* and its readers in the first place. The names of Sundays and feast days are in accordance with the Roman Missal of that time; meanwhile, the order of feast days is adapted to the Chinese lunar calendar, the primary timetable for Chinese agriculture and traditional rituals. By following the page numbers to the passages for the Gospel readings, readers could find Gospel readings for each Sunday and feast day as the Roman Missal prescribed; they could familiarize themselves with the calendar as well due to the adaptation to the lunar calendar. Before mass, priests—either European or Chinese priests—also could use this book to prepare sermons, and after mass, Chinese converts also could study readings together with the help of this book. They could be assisted with abundant sources of exegesis to Gospel verses, which I will explain later.

The index is another "table of contents," called "zashi zhi mulu" (雜事之目錄), meaning "a table of miscellaneous matters" (figure 1). It is, in fact, a functional subject index with careful design.[4] It exhibits about one hundred and forty-four subjects pertaining to Christianity.

---

4. Chen, "The *Shengjing zhijie*," 175–79.

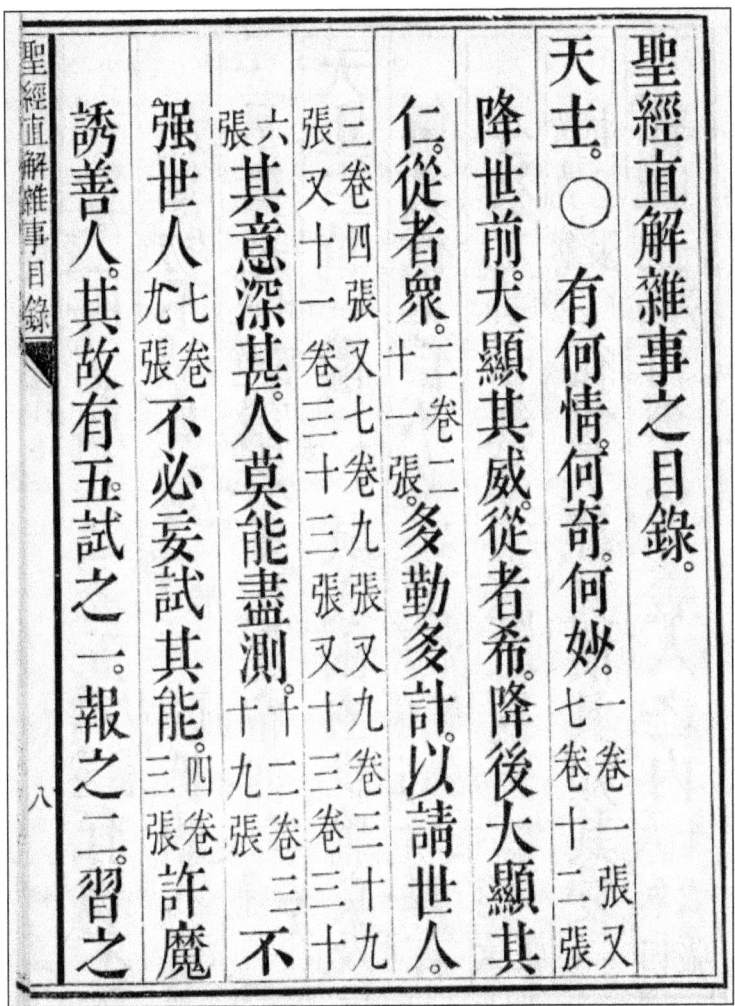

Figure 1

These themes overall entail fundamental Christian teachings, doctrines, major terms of Christianity, and theological concerns that interested Chinese audiences the most at that time. Each subject matter is printed as a thematic heading in a new column. Like an entry, the heading is followed by modifications to define or to describe it more precisely.[5] Modifications are indented one-character lower. Together, they form supporting arguments and specifics to demonstrate each subject. Referencing numbers also are provided for locating each modification throughout the body text of

5. Borko and Bernier, *Indexing Concepts and Methods*, 20–21.

Shengjing zhijie. The selection and organization of the subjects and their modifications seem to be following a systematic editorial principle. Nevertheless, it has not yet been identified whether this index directly conforms to any European or Chinese source.

The subject index usually functions as a shortcut for readers to efficiently flip through an entire book and to precisely locate the passages as needed.[6] This piece could aid readers of *Shengjing zhijie* to use it as a versatile reference for different purposes. If leaders of a congregation (such as "huizhang" 會長) were to explain certain concepts or beliefs to fellows during communal reading activities, they could use this index to quickly find full elaboration of a variety of subject matters. Catechumen, coadjutors, and outsiders who are eligible to read this book also could select proper themes to study in private or groups. This index can help readers to access materials in *Shengjing zhijie* more efficiently. Also, it can create linkages between passages scattered throughout the book.

The Footwashing Text and Commentary with Layout Design

The body text of *Shengjing zhijie* is generally arranged according to Sundays and feast days in a liturgical year. The materials for each day consist of two sections. One section is called "Scripture," that is "jing" (經) in Chinese. It contains the Gospel readings on Sundays and major feast days, and the readings are filled with running interlinear annotations. The other section is called "zhen" (箴), meaning "exegesis." It provides long commentaries upon verses selected from the Scripture section ahead of it.

As of the footwashing case in the text of *Shengjing zhijie*, the fragment previously analyzed with the three-layer frame is found in the reading on the feast day of Jesus establishing the Eucharist, in the ninth volume. An entire page explains the feast day (figure 2).

---

6. Wheatley, *What Is an Index?*

SHENGJING ZHIJIE: STRAIGHT EXPLANATION OF SACRED SCRIPTURES

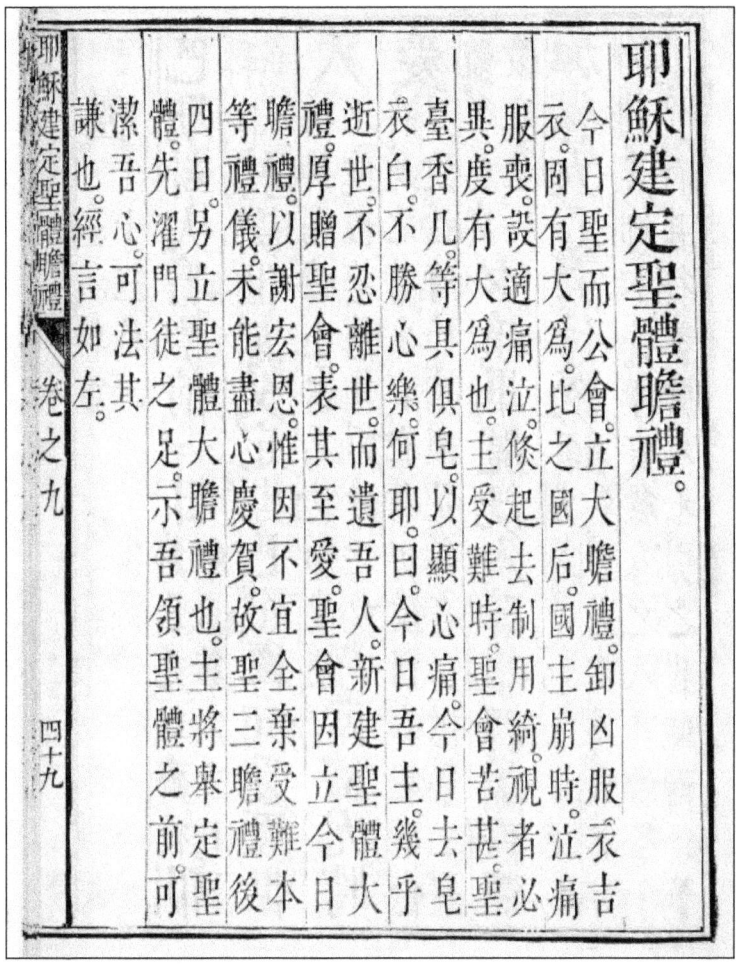

Figure 2

On the next page, the Gospel reading starts in the Scripture section (figure 3). Subsequent to the Scripture section is the exegesis section on the foot-washing pericope, including commentaries on several verses and moral admonitions (figure 4).

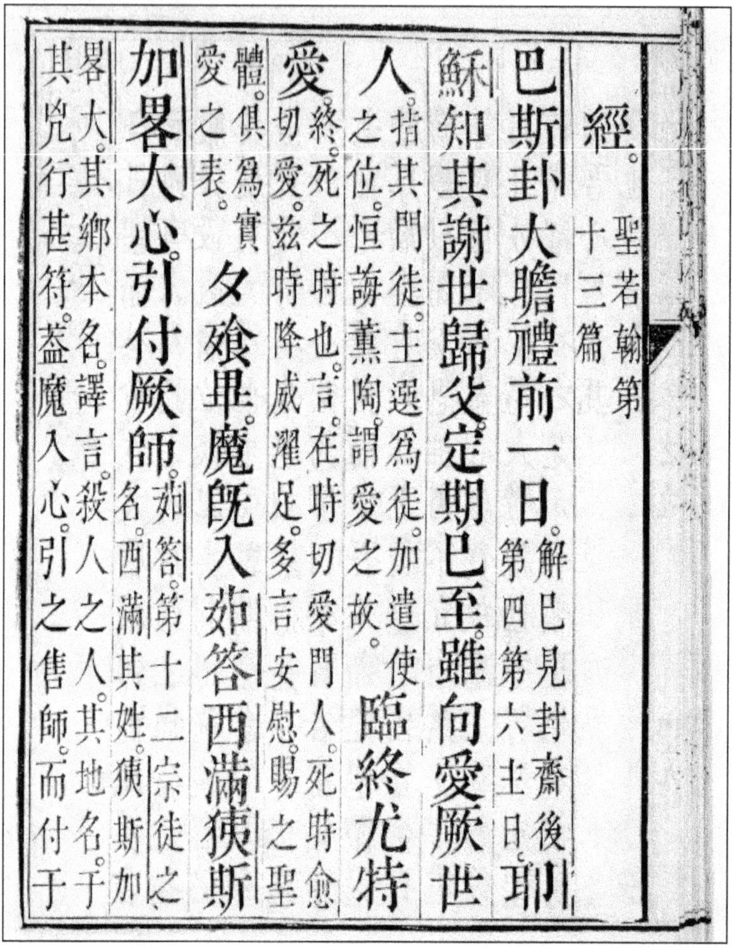

經。聖若翰第十三篇

巴斯卦大瞻禮前一日。解巳見封齋後第四第六主日。耶穌知其謝世歸父定期巳至。雖向愛厥世人。指其門徒。主選爲徒。加遣使之位。恒誨薰陶。謂愛之故。臨終尤特愛。終。死之時也。言在時切愛門人。死時愈切愛。茲時降威濯足。多言安慰。賜之聖體。俱爲實愛之表。夕飧畢。魔既入茹答西滿猶斯加畧大心。引付厥師。茹答。第十二宗徒之名。西滿其姓。猶斯加畧大。其鄉本名。譯言。殺人之人。其地名。于其兇行甚符。蓋魔入心。引之售師。而付于

Figure 3

SHENGJING ZHIJIE: STRAIGHT EXPLANATION OF SACRED SCRIPTURES

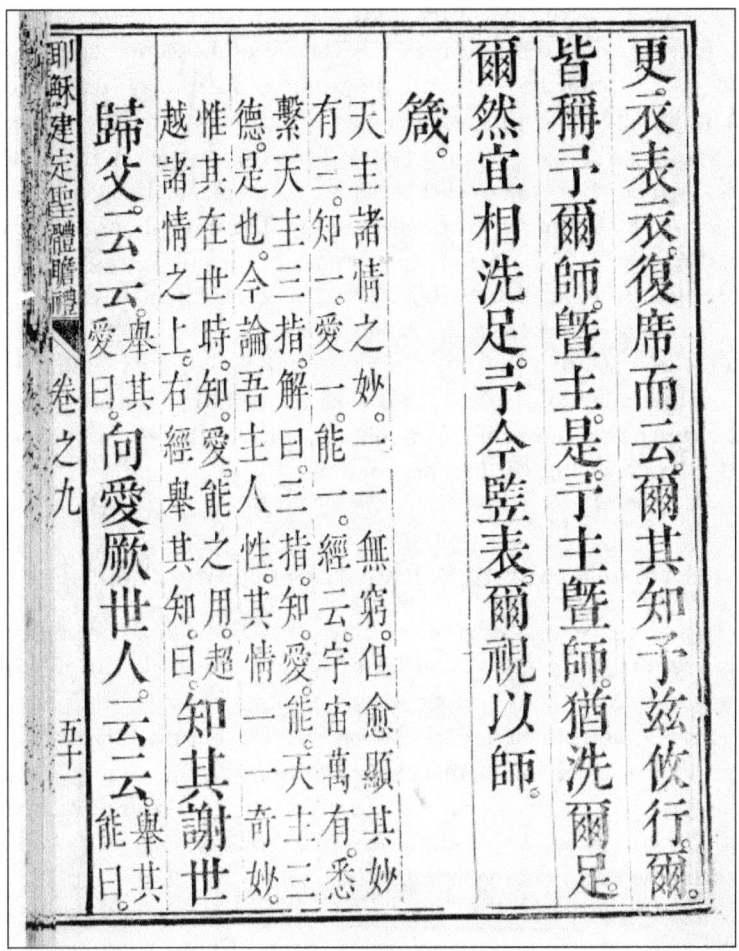

Figure 4

The pages extracted from the book of *Shengjing zhijie* show graphic marks. In general, words corresponding to the Bible verses are printed in large characters, and the rest are in small characters. The Scripture section consists of the Gospel verses of John 13:1–15 in larger size and interlinear annotations that are printed smaller, so two characters in one column. In the exegesis section, the Bible verses are still printed in larger characters as opposed to the smaller-sized commentary. Without color printing, using different character sizes to frame contents in woodblock cutting is an impressive design. More importantly, the page layout can guide readers during their reading of this book. For instance, the contrast between larger and smaller characters illustrates the dominant role of the Gospel verses.

The overall structure of the body text of *Shengjing zhijie* follows the same pattern as the footwashing case. The Scripture section and exegesis section are combined to complete the readings on Sundays or feast days. Each liturgical day starts from a new page with a short introductory passage that indicates where the ensuing Gospel verses are located in the Bible. In the Scripture section, the Gospel verses are accompanied by interlinear annotations to make the verses comprehensible. The annotations add various biblical references and provide explanations for difficult words, terms, and expressions that were alien to Chinese readers of that time. The exegesis section offers long commentary in persuasive writing, by way of first repeating certain verses selected from the Scripture section and then adding moral lessons regarding those verses. The Gospel verses throughout are printed in large characters with one line per column, whereas the rest are printed in small characters with two lines per column.

Gospel Verses Claiming Authority in Erudite Chinese

The Scripture passages in large characters are arranged according to the Gospel readings on Sundays and feast days in a liturgical year prescribed in the Roman Missal. To the first generation of missionaries in China, preparing Bible verses for liturgical use was more urgent than translating the entire Bible.[7] It seems logical that Dias gave priority to the reading in liturgical contexts. Given the canonical status of the liturgical reading during the mass, this arrangement also empowered the book of *Shengjing zhijie* as a representative of the church authority in China.

As a sign of making Christian Scripture words for Chinese readers, the Gospel verses appear to be composed in literary Chinese and in the form of classics. Rendering Bible verses into another language always involves language and writing issues, such as adopting styles of vernacular or literary language and framing the verses in prose or rhymed lines.

As the footwashing text extracted from *Shengjing zhijie* has shown, the biblical account is featured in erudite Chinese in a sophisticated way. For instance, it converts part of John 13:1 from the Latin verse "*cum dilexisset suos, qui erant in mundo, in finem dilexit eos*" into the Chinese sentence "sui xiang ai jue shi ren, lin zhong you te ai." (雖向愛厥世人。臨終尤特愛。) This Chinese sentence, meaning "although having always loved his people in the world, near the end (he) particularly loves (them) very much," has the syntax and grammatical structure of classical Chinese. The character "jüe" (厥), meaning "his" as a possessive pronoun, is a good example. The phrasing is a

---

7. Dehergne, "Travaux des jésuites sur la Bible en Chine," 213.

Chinese equivalent to the Latin word *suos*, precisely retaining the accuracy. This usage is no longer seen in modern mandarin Chinese.

Besides, the Gospel verses are refined in a form that can be traced to the Confucian *Classic of Documents* or just the *Documents*, in Chinese *Shangshu* 尚書. Chen Yuan 陳垣 (1880–1971), a Chinese historian and classical scholar, once commented that *Shengjing zhijie* was an imitation of the *Documents*, similar to other works composed by Dias.[8] The *Documents* is one of the Five Classics in the Confucian tradition. It was valued as the earliest collection of historical records of antiquity before Confucius and thus was considered one of the most prominent sacred texts in Chinese.[9] Its composition also was considered the origin of Chinese literary writing.[10] Emperors through the Ming Dynasty were particularly fond of this book because of its classical and historical strengths, its brevity, its antiquity, and its didactic function.[11] A genre of writing official documents called "tiben" (題本) also was based on its model of recounting state affairs and moral disciplines in elegant Chinese.[12] Hence, not only well-educated officials but also lower degree holders would be very familiar with the literary features of the *Documents*. The Jesuits must have studied this book because it was part of study materials in their own *ratio studiorum*, together with the Four Books.[13] Some collaborators who jointly revised *Shengjing zhijie* actually participated in planning this *ratio studiorum* in the years around 1620.[14] Preparing the Gospel verses based on the writing model of the *Documents* not only advocates the tradition of Christianity but also reinforces the influence of *Shengjing zhijie*.

In addition, the writing style of Gospel verses in the Scripture section may have assimilated syntactic constructions from Buddhist sacred texts as well. For instance, the reading on a liturgical day often begins with a fixed phrase "weishi" (維時), meaning "at that time," although it does not occur

---

8. Chen, "Zailun *Zunzhu shengfan* yiben," 204, 206, 211–12.

9. Henderson, *Scripture, Canon and Commentary*, 50–52; Elman, "Philosophy (I-LI) versus Philology (K'ao-Cheng)," 185–86, 199.

10. This comment was made by a Ming literary critic in the sixteenth century. See Huang, *Liuyi bieliu*.

11. For instance, three emperors of the Ming Dynasty commanded the publication of commentaries on *Shangshu*: Hongwu Emperor (reign: 1368–1398), Hongxi Emperor (reign: 1424–1425), and Jiajing Emperor (reign: 1521–1567).

12. Chen, "The *Shengjing zhijie*," 182.

13. Golvers, *Libraries of Western Learning for China*, 12–13.

14. Giulio Aleni, Gaspar Ferreira (1571–1649), and Niccolò Longobardo (1559–1654), among others, were part of the planners. See Brockey, *Journey to the East*, 256–57, 263–64.

in the footwashing text. This introductory note corresponds to the indicator of the liturgical setting in the Missal, such as "*in illo tempore dixit Jesus ad discipulis suis*" in Latin.[15] It also is close to a conventional opening in Buddhist sutra, which often starts with a phrase, "thus have I heard," that is "rushi wowen" (如是我聞) in Chinese, and an adverb expressing "at that time" often follows. The Chinese wording of "at that time" can vary, such as "yishi" (一時), "ershi" (爾時), and "nashi" (那時). This expression has more significance in formatting than semantic meaning. Adopting such a format to start the Gospel reading on a liturgical day could immediately attract Chinese audiences, especially the ones who were familiar with the Buddhist sutra, so that they may generate interest in ensuring Christian verses.

Corresponding to its language style or writing form, the Gospel verses in the Scripture section of *Shengjing zhijie* were highly regarded among missionaries and Chinese Christians. At least, they appeared again in another two major works of Chinese Christianity: one is *Misa jingdian* by Lodovico Buglio, SJ (1606–1682), which is involved in this study; and the other is a book for spiritual exercises, *Shengjing guangyi* 聖經廣益 (1740), by Joseph M.A. de Moyriac de Mailla, SJ (1669–1748).[16] The Gospel readings on liturgical days in these two books were taken from the Scripture section of *Shengjing zhijie*, with minor revisions. This use confirms that the Chinese rendition of the Gospel verses in *Shengjing zhijie* was considered accurate and trustworthy years after this book was published.

Broad and Positive Reception within and beyond Christians

Even before a complete set was published between 1636 and 1642, this book already had started circulating in forms of manuscripts and handwritten copies. After its first publication, many reprints followed. The reproduction of *Shengjing zhijie* continued through the late eighteenth and the early twentieth centuries.[17] An abridged edition also was available in simplified Chinese, Manchu, and Korean.[18] Parts of this book were even translated back to Latin when missionaries debated upon Chinese Christian terms.[19]

15. Lampe, *The Cambridge History of the Bible*, 226.
16. Standaert, "The Spiritual Exercises of Ignatius of Loyola."
17. See CCT Database.
18. Baker, "A Note of Jesuit Works in Chinese," 32.
19. Dehergne, *Répertoire*, 219. Antoine Thomas, SJ (1644–1709) defended *Shengjing zhijie* in his letter from Beijing in 1708, and the letter is preserved in Biblioteca da Ajuda (série da Província da China. Cód. Ms. 49–V–26).

The wide reception of *Shengjing zhijie* also can be witnessed in other contemporaneous and later Chinese Christian books, as they continuously recommend *Shengjing zhijie* as a compulsory book for priests to address Chinese audiences and for Chinese readers to study Christian teachings. The book, *Shengxin guitiao* 聖心規條 (ca. 1744) by Joseph M. A. de Moyriac de Mailla, has a reading list of titles that Christians should read and learn by heart. *Shengjing zhijie* is the first on this list.[20] More evidence confirming the classic status of *Shengjing zhijie* is *Chuxue zhinan* 初學指南 (after 1860), a Chinese instruction for novices in the Society of Jesuits. In this book, *Shengjing zhijie* is assigned as one of five books that Chinese priests had to read every day.[21]

Through other Chinese Christian books, *Shengjing zhijie* was circulated beyond the circle of converts too. Readers outside of the Christian Church could easily come across *Shengjing zhijie*, as many Christian books elaborating on theological matters refer their readers to it as a reference work. These books have their own readerships but are mainly for outsiders such as sympathizers and religious opponents. For instance, a book, *Wenda huichao* 問答彙抄 (ca. 1670s), compiled by Chinese Christian scholar Li Jiugong 李九功 (?–1681), contains a large number of passages from *Shengjing zhijie*.[22] While *Wenda huichao* was distributed widely, the passages cited from *Shengjing zhijie* reached readers who had not yet read *Shengjing zhijie*. Anti-Christian audiences may have read this book too. In response to the Muslim adversary Yang Guangxian's attack on Christianity at court, Lodovico Buglio suggested he read *Shengjing zhijie*.[23] As such, *Shengjing zhijie*, or at least part of it, was brought to a broader audience beyond insiders.

Not only was the title of *Shengjing zhijie* recommended, but the book also was actually studied by both Christians and non-Christians. Local communities of Chinese Christians must have had this book at their disposal because many copies of *Shengjing zhijie* were confiscated all over the country when Christianity was banned.[24] The famous mathematician, Mei Wending 梅文鼎 (1633–1721), in the Qing Dynasty, also had *Shengjing zhijie* at his desk. He was not a convert, but he had interests in calendar making and consulted *Shengjing zhijie* to look for the biblical chronology

---

20. *CCT ZKW XB* vol. 17, 312.
21. *CCT ZKW XB* vol. 22, 293.
22. *CCT ARSI* vol. 8, 251, 390.
23. *WX*, 284–86.
24. Zhang, "Kanshu chuanjiao," 108–16.

recorded therein. In this case, Mei Wending used *Shengjing zhijie* as a reliable source for his scientific pursuits.[25]

As seen from multiple angles, *Shengjing zhijie* had a broad and positive reception. The footwashing story, as part of its composition, was delivered to readers who used this book to serve their different purposes. Individuals or groups who read *Shengjing zhijie* could encounter the biblical narrative in a liturgical context. They may have heard the story during sermons. It also could be brought up in the course of conversation between Christians and non-Christians. To both insiders and outsiders, *Shengjing zhijie* was a comprehensive Christian book that could facilitate their exploration of theological or other matters concerning Christianity.

---

25. Dudink, "Biblical Chronology and the Transmission of the Theory of Six 'World Ages' to China."

5

Misa jingdian: Classic and Canon on the Mass

*M*ISA JINGDIAN WAS PART of a project to prepare native Chinese priests for performing the liturgy. Among other Chinese liturgical works, the mission of *Misa jingdian* was to provide guidance in Chinese for native priests to celebrate mass. Studies on *Misa jingdian* have been rare but fruitful.[1] It is known that *Misa jingdian* is a Chinese Missal translating the mass prescribed in the Roman Missal into a ritual that Chinese priests could perform.

The Roman Missal was promulgated by Pope Pius V (papacy: 1566–1572) after the Council of Trent; it was *Missale Romanum* (1570). This authentic edition was accompanied by a bull to forbid anyone to change any part of the missal in any way. The uniformity in celebrating the mass was thereby established. Although several revisions were made to the Pius V edition, such as the one by Pope Clement VIII (papacy: 1592–1605) in 1604 and by Pope Urban VIII (papacy: 1623–1644) in 1634, the main body of the 1570 version always remained, and it was in use in the church until the Second Vatican Council. With the Roman Missal as a foundation, this chapter explores the representation of the footwashing rite and the mass in the book of Chinese Missal, *Misa jingdian*.

Reading the Footwashing Pericope as Part of the Mass

The copy of *Misa jingdian* that I examine is a facsimile compiled in *CCT ZKW XB*. The book was originally printed in 1670 in Beijing. Its front matter is particularly interesting as both Latin words and Chinese characters were carved in woodblock printing. The first page bears a Chinese title (figure 5).

---

1. Bontinck, *La lutte autour de la liturgie chinoise*, 181–82; Seah, "The 1670 Chinese Missal."

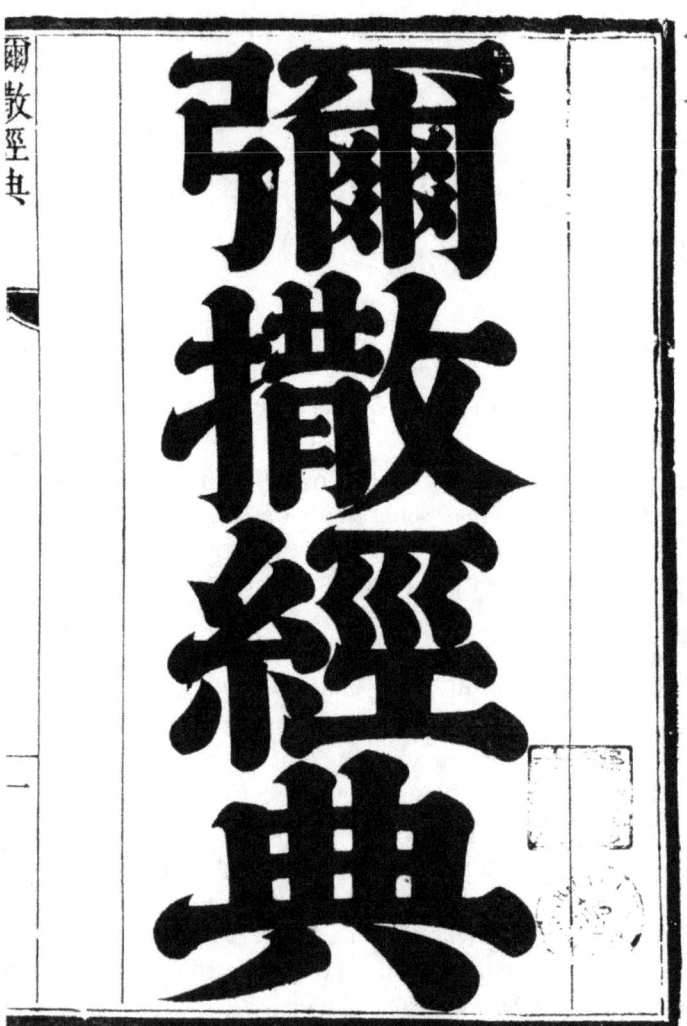

Figure 5

There are also two stamps: a square one for China Vice-Provincial that is carved in Chinese characters "yesuhui zhonghua sheng" (耶穌會中華省); and a round one of the Society of Jesus carved as "IHS." The frontispiece has the four evangelists illustrated with their respective apocalyptic creatures (figure 6).

Figure 6

The Latin inscription indicates that this book is a Chinese edition of the Roman Missal endorsed by Pope Paul V. What follows is the information on its author, Lodovico Buglio, the Society of Jesus, and its publication date and time. The front matter mirrored in a Chinese-Latin pair underscores the authority of the Chinese Missal that could be traced back to the European church and the reliability of this book as it was approved under the supervision of the China mission.

With regard to the rite of washing feet, Pope Pius V, who reformed the 1570 Roman Missal, included the washing of feet in a section following the mass of the Lord's Supper, "Feria V: In Cœna Domini." When celebrating the ritual of footwashing on Holy Thursday in Chinese during the late seventeenth and eighteenth centuries, the priest would turn to the Chinese Missal, *Misa jingdian*. The mass on the feast day when the ceremony of washing feet is supposed to take place starts from folio 78b (figure 7) through folio 83a.[2]

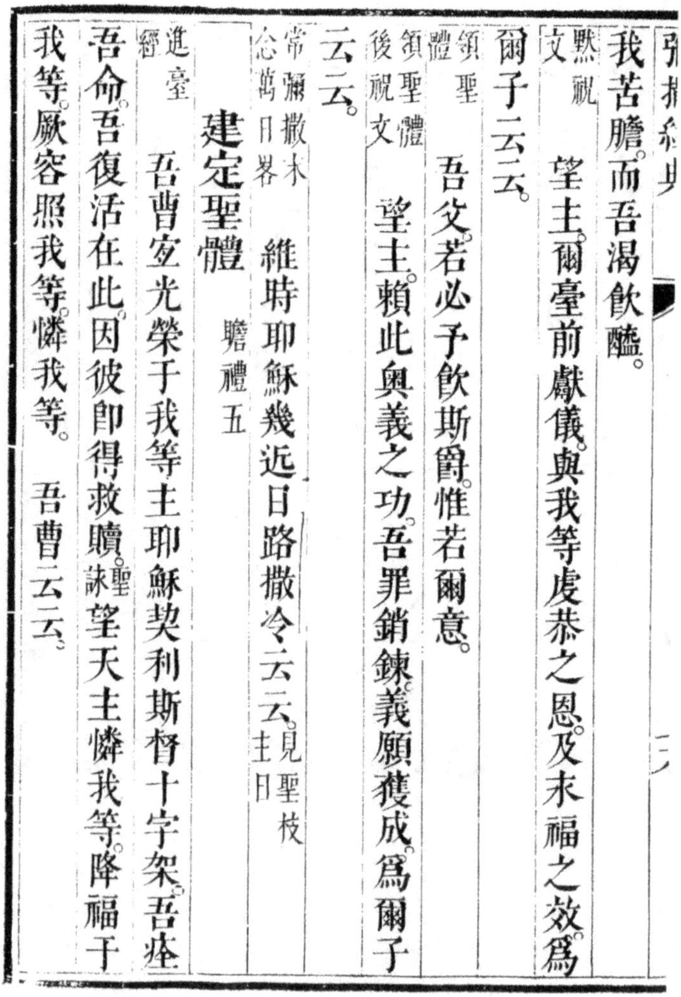

我苦膽。而吾渴飲醯。
默祝文 望主爾臺前獻儀。與我等虔恭之恩。及永福之效。爲爾子云云。
領聖體 吾父若必予飲斯爵。惟若爾意。
領聖體後祝文 望主賴此輿義之功。吾罪銷鍊。義願獲成。爲爾子云云。
常彌撒末公念萬日畧 維時耶穌幾近日路撒冷云云。見聖枝主日
建定聖體 瞻禮五
進臺經 吾曹宜光榮于我等主耶穌契利斯督十字架。吾主吾命。吾復活在此。因彼即得救贖。聖詠 望天主憐我等。降福于我等。厥容照我等。憐我等。 吾曹云云。

Figure 7

2. *CCT ZKW XB* vol. 15, 286–95.

In Chinese, the mass on that day is titled "jianding shengti" (建定聖體), meaning "establishing the Eucharist." The introductory rites begin with introit as the liturgical text represents. The characters "jintai jing" (進臺經), meaning "introibo ad altare dei," are set in a small size as an indicator; this is followed by large-character texts that indicates what to be said while the priest approaches the altar. In general, large characters on the page layout are meant to be read, either aloud or silently, according to the instructions printed in small characters. The procession also is regulated in small-size characters. In contrast, the liturgy of words appears in large-size characters.

The footwashing text in *Misa jingdian* that has been analyzed earlier is extracted from the liturgy of words for the mass. On Holy Thursday, the epistle passages are from 1 Corinthians 11:20–32, in accordance with the Roman Missal. The Gospel reading also is consistent with the Roman Missal, which corresponds to the pericope of John 13:1–15. As the previous analysis shows through the three-layer framework, the footwashing story in *Misa jingdian* equals the prototype in the Latin Vulgate, and its textual surface is based on the Gospel verses in the Scripture section of *Shengjing zhijie*.

To be more specific, Buglio's use of the translation in *Shengjing zhijie* was combined with revision. If comparing the two footwashing texts word by word, one can find that one sentence from the text in *Shengjing zhijie* is missing in the version in *Misa jingdian*. At Peter's reception of the footwashing gesture, the version in *Shengjing zhijie* has an additional line to Peter, "not daring to rebel against (your) command." In Chinese, the sentence is of four characters: "bu gan fang ming" (不敢方命). Although this sentence shows Peter's verbal confirmation, the original pericope does not have it in Latin. While taking the Gospel reading on Holy Thursday from *Shengjing zhijie*, Buglio left it out. The discretion was in line with his other efforts to maintain the Roman Missal unchanged as much as possible in its Chinese version, *Misa jingdian*.

Performing the Footwashing Rite through Textuality

Except for the liturgy of words, the liturgy of the Eucharist, and other generic rituals during the mass, the footwashing rite was prescribed at the end of the mass on that particular day. In *Misa jingdian*, the Chinese phrase indicates "misa bi" (彌撒畢), meaning the mass being completed. Afterward, a two-page-long instruction unfolds to move on to the footwashing rite (figures 8 and 9).

在此世攸行賴爾無滅之恩即得常行爲爾子云云

念彌撒畢降福念聖若望萬日畧經起

今日堂內小堂備具供聖爵偕聖體之處修飾點燭等項彌撒畢點多大燭照常引行下副祭者持十字偕二鐸德穿白表衣立臺前著乳香于兩吊爐不降福鐸德偕輔祭者三次立臺前著乳香于兩吊爐不降福鐸德偕輔祭者三次奉香于聖體由副祭者披方帕邊遞兩肩偕別輔祭者跪接聖體立申時歌聖詠請吾副祭者在左副祭者至于鐸德之所引聖體立先置吾兩位亞歌德多時常祭奉香後置之匣內奏樂所念吾兩位亞歌德多時常祭奉香後置之匣內奏樂所

舌詠云云至其所副祭者跪奉香後置之匣內奏樂所念全天主分予衣而予衣拈鬮聖詠畢

子天主盻覩予云云

撒臺惶等項齊集臺惶致或值會者穿白衣侍側誦經值會者會前跪請降福經畢副祭者會前跪請降福

掛紫色表帶于吊爐乳香偕副祭利多侍禮者手持經本如前奉香祭後

受福訖兩位雅偹具巴斯卦大瞻禮

者手持經本畫如前奉香祭後值會者脫大表衣白悅鐸

前一日云云祭者如常奉副祭後值會者

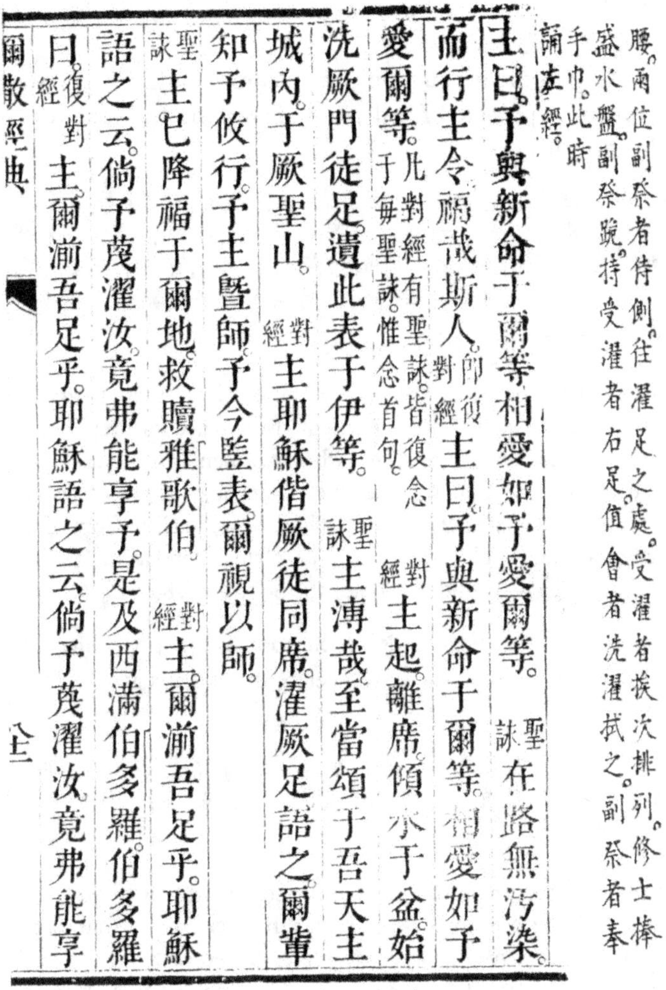

腰。兩位副祭者侍側。往濯足之處。受濯者挨次排列。修士捧
盛水盤。副祭跪。持受濯者右足。值會者洗濯拭之。副祭者奉
手巾。此時
誦左經。
主曰。予與新命于爾等相愛如予愛爾等。聖詠在路無汚染。
而行主令。爾哉斯人。即復對經主曰。予與新命于爾等。相愛如予
愛爾等。凡對經有聖詠。皆復念于每聖詠。惟念首句。對經主起。離席。傾水于盆。始
洗厥門徒足。遺此表于伊等。聖詠主溥哉。至當頌于吾天主
城內。于厥聖山。對經主耶穌偕厥徒同席。濯厥足語之。爾輩
知予攸行。予主暨師。予今豎表爾。視以師。
聖詠主已降福于爾地。救贖雅歌伯。對經主。爾湔吾足乎。耶穌
語之云。倘予蔑濯汝。竟弗能享予。是及西滿伯多羅。伯多羅
曰。復對經主。爾湔吾足乎。耶穌語之云。倘予蔑濯汝。竟弗能享
彌撒經典

Figure 9

These pages in *Misa Jingdian* meticulously prescribe how a footwashing rite should be done. The text would guide the celebrants to practice the footwashing in imitation of Jesus in the Bible.

In the Roman Missal, Pope Pius V placed the footwashing rite after the mass. He did not make it part of the mass but indicated that it was to take place at a suitable hour after the stripping of the altars. Correspondingly, the text of *Misa jingdian* situates the footwashing rite right after the mass. The separate footwashing ceremony is about to start "after the completion of stripping of the altars and so forth, when the time comes the wooden rattle strikes" that in Chinese reads "che taiwei deng xiang bi, zhi qishi jibang" (撤臺帷等項畢 至其時擊梆).

According to the instruction, the celebrant and his assisting concelebrants should be prepared for the rite of washing feet. The text in *Misa jingdian* reads:

> 眾修士齊集。主教。或值會者。于領及白衣上掛紫色表帶。于備具之所。副祭者。下副祭者。穿白衣侍側。着乳香于吊爐。後副祭者。胸前懷萬日略經。值會前跪。請降福。. . . 兩位雅歌利多侍側。持點燭。下副祭者。手持經本。畫經本。

> All the prelates gather. Bishop or the on-duty priest wears the purple outer belt on white vestment at the place for preparation. Deacons and sub-deacons wear white vestments and attend aside, putting incense into the thurible. Then, a deacon carries the Scripture of Gospels at the front of his chest, kneels in front of the priest, asking for blessings. . . . Two acolytes attend aside, holding candlesticks. A sub-deacon holds the book and signs it.[3]

After reciting the beginning of the John pericope, remembering the setting of the footwashing event, the celebrant and his assistants first need to walk to a special spot for the washing. The text continues:

> 如前畢。下副祭者。遞開經本。親于值會者。副祭者如常奉香。後值會者。脫大表衣。白帨纏腰。兩位副祭者侍側。往濯足之處。

> As the proceeding ends, the sub-deacon hands the open Scripture to the priest. The deacon burns the incense as usual. Later, the priest takes off the outer vestment, girded with a white cloth around his waist. Two deacons attend aside. They walk to the spot of washing feet.[4]

At the spot, the footwashing practice is jointly performed by the priest, his assistants, and the receivers. Whoever should be selected to receive this ritual is not clarified in the text, but they ought to sit down. The text reads:

> 受濯者挨次排列。修士捧盛水盤。副祭跪。持受濯者右足。值會者洗濯拭之。副祭者奉手巾。

---

3. *CCT ZKW XB* vol. 15, 292.
4. *CCT ZKW XB* vol. 15, 292–93.

The receivers of the washing sit one by one, side by side. A clergy holds up the water basin in two hands. A deacon kneels, holding each receiver's right foot. The priest washes and wipes it. A deacon offers hand towel.[5]

In the meantime, walking to the spot of washing and the process of washing are all accompanied by the readings of some parts of the footwashing pericope in the Gospel of John. In *Misa jingdian*, these readings are all printed in large characters, and they do correspond to the antiphons that are in the "antiphona" section in the Roman Missal. The Latin text of antiphons accompanying the footwashing rite consists of fragmented texts from the Gospel of John, Psalms, and others. So do the Chinese words to recite for the footwashing rite. While the practice itself echoes what Jesus did in the Bible, these words being read aloud bring the moment of Jesus washing his disciples' feet back to the current community and the practice.

Page Layout Design Defining the Structure of Mass

As has been noticed, the printing of large characters and small characters distinguishes the liturgy of words from the rest. The different formats consisting of different sizes of characters and symbols collectively indicate what to say, what to do, and how to say or do it during the mass. This design appears on the page layout throughout the book of *Misa jingdian*.

A Latin edition of the Roman Missal can help shed light on how the elements of a mass are presented in the Chinese ritual manual, *Misa jingdian*. From two sample pages, one can observe the formal rules of text composition in the Roman Missal (figure 10) and the Chinese Missal (figure 11).

---

5. *CCT ZKW XB* vol. 15, 293.

RVBRICAE GENERALES MISSALIS.

MISSA quotidie dicitur secundum ordinem Officij de festo Duplici, vel Semiduplici, vel Simplici: de Dominica, vel Feria: de Vigilia, de Octaua, & extra ordinem Officij, Votiua, vel pro Defunctis.

De Duplici.

MISSA dicitur de Duplici illis diebus, quibus in Calēdario ponitur hæc nota, Duplex: & in Festis mobilibus, quandocunque Officium fit.

¶ IN Duplicibus dicitur vna tantùm Oratio, nisi aliqua Commemoratio fieri debeat. Alia omnia dicuntur vt in proprijs Missis assignatum est. Quando dici debet, Gloria in excelsis, & Credo, inferius dicitur in proprijs Rubricis.

De Semiduplici, & Simplici.

MISSA de Semiduplici dicitur, quando in Calendario ponitur hæc vox, Semiduplex. Præterea, in Dominicis, & diebus infra Octauas.

¶ IN Semiduplicibus, tam festis quàm Dominicis, & infra Octauas dicūtur plures Orationes, vt infrà dicetur in Rubrica de Oratione: Infra Octauam dicitur Missa sicut in die Festi, nisi propriā Missam habuerit: In Dominicis verò, sicut in proprijs locis assignatur.

¶ DE Simplici, dicitur Missa sicut de Semiduplici, vt suis locis ponitur.

De Feria & Vigilia.

MISSA de Feria dicitur, quando non occurrit Festum, vel Octaua, vel Sabbathum, in quo fit Officium beatæ Mariæ.

¶ IN Feriis tamē Quadragesimæ, Quatuor Temporum, Rogationum, & Vigiliarum, etiam si Duplex vel Semiduplex festum, vel Octaua occurrat, in Ecclesiis Collegiatis dicuntur duæ Missæ, vna de Festo, altera de Feria.

¶ IN Vigiliis autem quæ veniunt infra Octauam, Missa dicitur de Vigilia, cum Commemoratione Octauæ. Si Festum habens Vigiliam celebretur Feria secunda, Missa Vigiliæ dicitur in Sabbatho, sicut etiam fit Officium.

¶ MISSA Vigiliæ in Aduentu occurrentis, dicitur cum Commemoratione de Aduentu, licet de ea non sit factum Officium, excepta Vigilia Natiuitatis, & Epiphaniæ Vigilia.

¶ SI in Quadragesima, & Quatuor Temporibus occurrat Vigilia, dicatur Missa de Feria, cum Commemoratione Vigiliæ. Toto tempore Paschali nō dicitur Missa de Vigilia, nisi in Vigilia Ascensionis, quæ tamen non ieiunatur, sicut nec Vigilia Epiphaniæ.

De Missis Votiuis S. Mariæ, & alijs.

IN Sabbathis non impeditis Festo Duplici, & Semiduplici, dicitur Missa de sancta Maria secundùm varietatem temporum, vt in fine Missalis ponitur. Si Sabbathū fuerit impeditū Festo Duplici, Semiduplici, Octaua, Vigilia, Feria Quatuor Temporū & Quadragesimæ, Missa principalis dicitur secundum Officium diei.

¶ IN Aduentu autem, licet Officium non fiat de S. Maria in Sabbatho, dicitur tamen Missa principalis de ea cum Commemoratione de Aduentu, nisi fuerint Quatuor Tempora, vt suprà. Aliis diebus infra Hebdomadam, quando Officiū fit de Feria (exceptis Feriis Aduentus, Quadragesimæ, Quatuor Temporum, Rogationum, & Vigiliarum) dici potest aliqua Missa Votiua etiam in principali Missa, quæ dicitur Conuentualis, secundum ordinem dierū in fine Missalis assignatum. Quæ tamen Missæ, & aliæ quæcunq, Votiuæ,

Figure 10

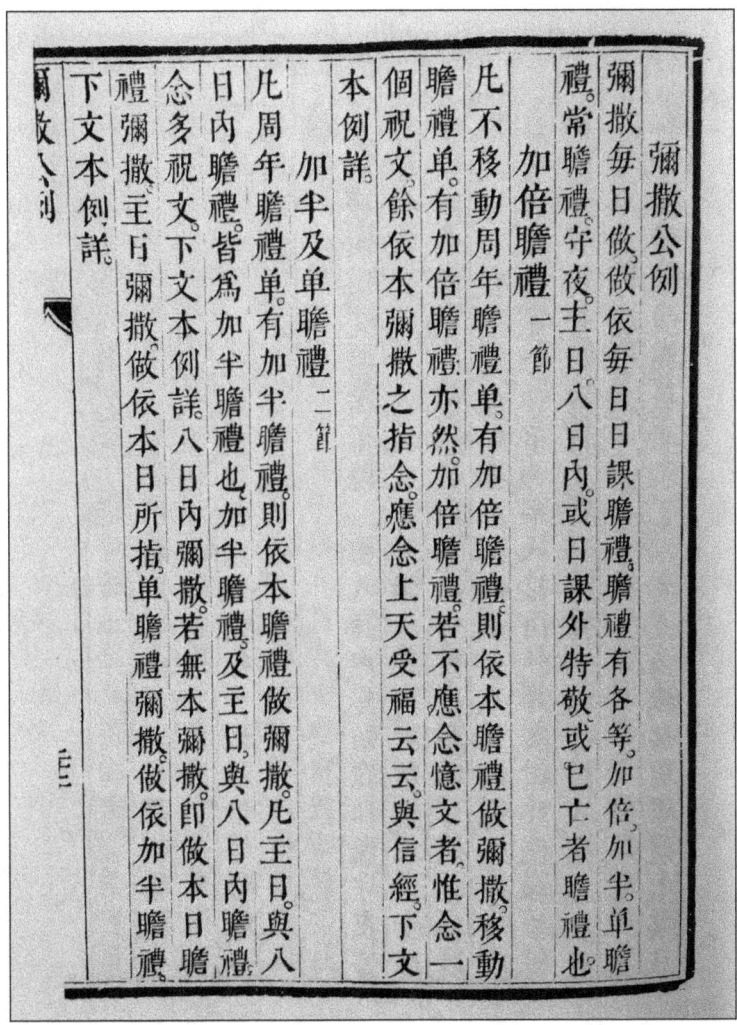

Figure 11

The Latin edition has headings printed in red, which serves as a rubric to guide its users, in contrast to engravings of the rest in black. It prescribes what to say (do) and how to say (do) it with typographical design in letterpress. It uses the rubric—an iconic element printed in red with symbols—to regulate the ritual manual. This principle is adopted in the Chinese book but expressed alternatively. As a woodblock-printed Chinese book, *Misa jingdian* translates the rubrics into another design of rubric marks. It uses different sizes of Chinese characters and purposeful arrangement of those characters to indicate the different roles of the texts. The distinction of character sizes and their positions on a page layout together designate different functions of the texts printed in the body part of *Misa jingdian*.

As for more specifics of *Misa jingdian*, the large-sized characters are set in one column, and they provide the words to recite during the mass. The readings include passages from the epistles that are called "jingshu" (經書) in *Misa jingdian* and those from the Gospels that are called "wanrilüe jing" (萬日略經) herein, hymns and prayers of different kinds, such as the offertory prayers that are generally referred to as "zhuwen" (祝文) and psalms "shengyong" (聖詠). These were also the major difficulties for rendering the Roman Missal into this Chinese book, as Lodovico Buglio expressed in his letter.[6] The small-sized characters are set with two lines in one column, and they instruct what to say and what to do (or not to do), how (and when) to say it, and how (and when) to do it during specific phases of a mass. To priests who could use this book, these texts were purely instructive, and they were not supposed to be spoken. They accompany the large-sized readings by making transitions between what to say and how to say those words.

Except for the page layout that visualizes elements of every part of the mass, the paratexts of the book of *Misa jingdian* provide meticulous rules for performing the mass. The organization of body content also guides different stages of the mass, in accordance with the Roman Missal. At the risk of running into details, the following demonstrates formal aspects of the paratexts and the organization of body text in *Misa jingdian*.

The paratexts at the beginning of *Misa jingdian* prescribe basic rules for performing the mass. The paratextual elements include a detailed table of contents, an ecclesiastic calendar with movable feast days, "linian yidong zhanli biao" (歷年移動瞻禮表), and general regulations that define terms, rules, and material objects involved in the mass. The prefixed introductory regulations echo the Missal in Latin, such as "misa gongli" (彌撒公例) corresponding to "Rubricae generales Missalis," "misa lijie" (彌撒禮節) being "Ritus celebrandi Missam," and "zuo misa huoquezhe" (做彌撒或缺者), equivalent to "De Defectibus circa Missam occurrentibus."

These paratextual pieces are designed in a manner distinct from the body part of *Misa jingdian*, with smaller characters and more columns on a page layout than the body text. In other words, these paratexts and the main body of *Misa jingdian* may have been carved with different sets of woodblocks. The explanations and regulations printed in this section are not often consulted in practice since trained priests who are expected to use the missal already should have known the rules by heart. Moreover, these texts do not directly engage with ritual performances. Unlike the texts in the body part, they are not supposed to be read or referred to during the mass.

---

6. Bontinck, *La lutte autour de la liturgie chinoise*, 156–57.

The body part of *Misa jingdian* is structured as a textual presentation of mass. The divisions and the organization of different divisions within the book show different stages of mass, which is indicated by printed marks on every page. To be specific, the body text is divided into divisions and subdivisions, and each subdivision corresponds to a specific section of the mass. The overall dividing is consistently indicated by the characters printed in the block heart on each folio page, which is called a central seam. This design can be seen at the edge of every *Misa jingdian* page. In the body part of this book, one can find one-to-one relations between the Chinese characters in the block heart and the Latin titles of each division in the Roman Missal.

According to the Chinese characters printed as a central seam, the body of *Misa jingdian* consists of two main divisions. The first division has the characters "彌撒經典" in block heart, and the second has different indicators. The first division has more subdivisions providing specifics that can be consulted during different stages of the mass. Using a central seam to show each division's heading inside a book is a convention used for woodblock printing. Such a purposeful design sounds like common sense to modern publishers and readers, yet it is a creative strategy to transfer the structure of the mass from its Latin manual into a Chinese book's divisions.

The organization of different divisions and their indicators in block heart as such could facilitate the book's users to locate texts in the body part. A priest, while using *Misa jingdian* during a mass, could easily flip this book through and arrive at the right section or page as needed. He may go back and forth between the "misa cixu" (彌撒次序) that is "Ordinarium Missae" and other subdivisions. With the movement of the priest's hands turning pages, the ritual goes on.

Performing a mass involves different roles, verbal texts, and body movements, all of which are manifested in the printed presentations of the missal. Both the European and Chinese books of the missal stick to the same principle to visualize these elements respectively in the Roman Missal and *Misa jingdian*. However, the Latin and Chinese editions have distinct formats featured in their own printing cultures. *Misa jingdian* mirrors the colored print of the Roman Missal with its own prints in the form of a Chinese book, and those features indicate a clear structure of the mass. One can see through paper how a mass is structured in *Misa jingdian* corresponding to that in Latin.

Imagine a scenario somewhere in early Qing China when a mass was taking place on a feast day in Chinese. A copy of *Misa jingdian* would be placed at the altar as part of the public display of the mass. During the mass, the celebrant priest ought to flip pages several times with the help of the block heart in the book. At each stage of the mass, he would follow the small-sized texts for instructions. These are the rules to guide the priest for correct performance. The small-sized contents include formulas in the celebration; for instance, "zhuwen" (祝文), the orations, and "bijing" (陛經), the graduals, body movements and postures such as "duode zai taixiazuo buzhuanshen hezhang nian" (鐸德在臺下左不轉身合掌念) that instruct the priest to the left of the altar to close his hands without turning around and to recite the readings that follow. Other regulations such as to read silently or vocally are printed in small-sized characters too. Meanwhile, the words printed in large characters, ought to be read, either silently or vocally, according to the corresponding small-sized instructions. These larger-sized texts to be recited mainly consist of the liturgy of words. Chinese audiences who attended this mass would hear those words through the priest. After turning over the pages in the book of *Misa jingdian* several times, for which the block heart could be of help, the priest would finally give the final blessings with communion and concluding rites. Then, the book of *Misa jingdian* was closed, and so was the mass.

An Afterlife of the Print

Regarding the actual use of *Misa jingdian*, historical evidence is, by and large, missing. Indeed, there is no endorsement from the church in Rome on record. After Buglio finished producing *Misa jingdian*, Philippe Couplet sought the approbation of it during his procuration in Europe.

Couplet presented to the church this Chinese book together with a descriptive summary in Latin, as the theologians and the pope did not read Chinese.[7] Also, he and Daniël Papebrochius, SJ (1628–1714), cited a case that ancient Slavic had been favored to be used in liturgy before, continually arguing for Chinese as a liturgical language.[8] Yet, the mission of Couplet did not succeed.

Couplet then tried to print a new European edition of *Misa jingdian* in Europe, as Alessandro Ciceri, SJ (1639–1703), once encouraged him to do in a letter. Couplet embarked on this project. In another letter written on May 26 in 1686, he first asked Daniël Papebrochius for twenty or more samples of the illustrations contained in the Plantin edition of *Missale Romanum*. He added, "If the illustrations have Latin text on the backside of the page layout, it is not important; the tables of calendars, on which we may stick Chinese prayers in the same amount, are also welcomed."[9] Also, he

---

7. Bontinck, *La lutte autour de la liturgie chinoise*, 155–56.

8. Golvers, "D. Papebrochius, S.J., Ph. Couplet en de Vlaamse jezuïeten in China," 42–43.

9. Golvers, "D. Papebrochius, S.J., Ph. Couplet en de Vlaamse jezuïeten in China," 42.

thought that the movable blocks used to print Chinese characters for *Confucius Sinarum Philosophus* (1687) could be of use for printing a European edition of *Misa jingdian*. Eventually, Couplet received illustrations from the printing house of Plantin, but it was still impossible to reprint *Misa jingdian* in Europe due to the limitations of movable type.[10]

Nevertheless, the afterlife of this book can shed light on the history of Chinese liturgy. The calendar provided in *Misa jingdian* marks the years from 1676 until 1736, which is a timespan commonly designated in several other books of Christian liturgy in Chinese. As late as 1676, another two Chinese Christian books regarding liturgy were produced, namely a Chinese breviary titled *Rike gaiyao* 日課概要 (1674) and a Chinese manual of the ministry of sacraments titled *Shengshi lidian* 聖事禮典 (1675).[11] Both books had illustrated frontispieces with the Latin inscriptions in line with *Misa jingdian* and the same table of fixed feast days in one year. In other words, these books were associated with *Misa jingdian*, preparing ritual manuals for native Chinese priests. The Chinese liturgy did take shape on paper through these printed books. The series of books for Chinese liturgy, including *Misa jingdian*, was produced as an action in line with the church in Europe. As a matter of fact, in 1615 when Nicolas Trigault, SJ (1577–1628), obtained permission for translating the Bible into erudite Chinese, Pope Paul V also gave permission to Chinese priests to celebrate mass and to recite the canonical hours in erudite Chinese.[12] As time passed, the efficacy of the 1615 permission vanished too.

In spite of the fact that it is unknown whether the mass was actually celebrated in Chinese by following *Misa jingdian*, the book itself is a monumental work in the history of Chinese Christianity. For instance, *Misa jingdian* was referenced for other purposes, and it was widely known among missionaries beyond the Jesuits. Francesco da Ottaviano, OFM (1677–1737), in a note written in 1737, made extensive comments on *Misa jingdian*.[13] Jean Basset, MEP (1662–1707), also regarded *Misa jingdian* as a milestone in terms of transmitting the Bible and liturgy in Chinese. He consulted this book while translating the four Gospels into Chinese by himself.[14]

---

10. For printing Chinese characters in Europe, see Golvers, "The Earliest Examples of Chinese Characters."

11. Both can be found in the National Library of France: BnF Chinois 7388 and BnF Chinois 7390, respectively.

12. Bontinck, *La lutte autour de la liturgie chinoise*, 36–44. Dunne, "What Happened to the Chinese Liturgy?," 4.

13. A handwritten copy of this note is preserved in the Roman Archives of the Society of Jesus.

14. Bontinck, *La lutte autour de la liturgie chinoise*, 285. Barriquand, "First Comprehensive Translation," 101–2.

6

Guxin shengjing: Old and New Holy Scriptures

Louis Poirot, SJ (1735–1813), translated the New Testament and part of the Old Testament with commentary in *Guxin shengjing* (ca. 1790–1810). The compilation of *Guxin shengjing* follows the order of books in the Testaments. In terms of portions of translated passages, it is the most complete Chinese-language translation of the Bible in history, although the manuscript was not approved for publication.

Studies on *Guxin shengjing* are mainly published in Asian languages, and the focus of existing scholarship is always on its language style that resonated with the time of Qing China.[1] My examination of *Guxin shengjing* emphasizes its composition as integrating the translation and commentary into one, as the commentary accompanying the Bible verses adds particular features to this book. The edition that I consult is a handwritten copy facsimile in *CCT ZKW XB*.

Paratexts Expressing the Mind of the Author

Louis Poirot was outspoken of his agenda for writing this book. In two prefaces to *Guxin shengjing*, the author explained the editorial norms applied in this book, his motivation, and his choice of a specific language style that was accessible to commoners. These paratexts give us an idea of, on the one hand, how Poirot composed *Guxin shengjing* as a continuation of his predecessor missionaries' efforts to translate part of the Bible into Chinese as Manuel Dias had done so with *Shengjing zhijie* and, on the other hand, how Poirot differentiated *Guxin shengjing* from the rest of Chinese Christian books with readers in mind.

---

1. For recent references in Chinese and Japanese, see Li, "Jindai baihuawen"; Zheng, "Xinchuan yu xinquan"; Zheng, "He Qingtai *Guxin shengjing* yanjiu"; Song, "'Benyi' yu 'tuyu' zhijian"; Yu, "聖書福音書の漢訳をめぐって."

In terms of continuation, at first, *Guxin shengjing* stays consistent with Christian texts before it in translating Christian terms. Similar editorial norms adopted in earlier printed books also appear in *Guxin shengjing*. For instance, the names of biblical figures, locations, and feast days are marked with different formats. Short straight lines, double lines, and triple lines are used to indicate names of persons, locations, and trees respectively.[2] These marks on the printed page layout have been seen in the book of *Shengjing zhijie*. Even though *Guxin shengjing* is a text still in the stage of manuscript and handwritten copies, the purposeful use of symbols to highlight Christian terms shows the author's deliberation to develop the tradition of producing Chinese Christian books in line with earlier printed works.

On the other hand, Poirot drew a clear line between *Guxin shengjing* and other books as far as language style was concerned. He preferred colloquial Chinese as opposed to the erudite language of Chinese scholars and officials. When the Curate Apostolic of Tonkin Occidental proposed to develop it in literary Chinese, Poirot defended his choice of everyday Chinese. He contended that using everyday language was the intention of God and accused sophisticated writings of losing ignorant people and their souls. The preface in *Guxin shengjing* speaks:

為幾個懂文法的人。不忍耽擱了萬萬愚蒙的人。不能懂文深的書。他們的靈魂。也不能得受便益。

For a handful of people who understand grammar, (I) cannot bear losing the hundred million of ignorant people. (They) cannot grasp books of profound writings, (so that) their souls cannot obtain benefits either.[3]

As seen from another angle, the target audience in Poirot's mind was the "ignorant" ones in his words. For these readers, Poirot promoted colloquial Chinese as the only proper language for translating Bible verses. He gave priority to the literal meaning of Bible verses because he believed that the words denoted and kept the original message of God.[4] His concern was more for pastoral needs. This clear preference was executed in his language use for composing *Guxin shengjing*.

The previously analyzed footwashing text is located in the Gospel of John in *Guxin shengjing*. In an effort to translate the New Testament into Chinese, Poirot had the full Gospel translated. John 13:1–15, as part of the Gospel, was also translated verse-by-verse (figure 12).

2. *CCT ZKW XB* vol. 28, 7.
3. *CCT ZKW XB* vol. 28, 10.
4. *CCT ZKW XB* vol. 28, 6.

PART I: EQUIVALENT NARRATIVES IN SCRIPTURAL BOOKS

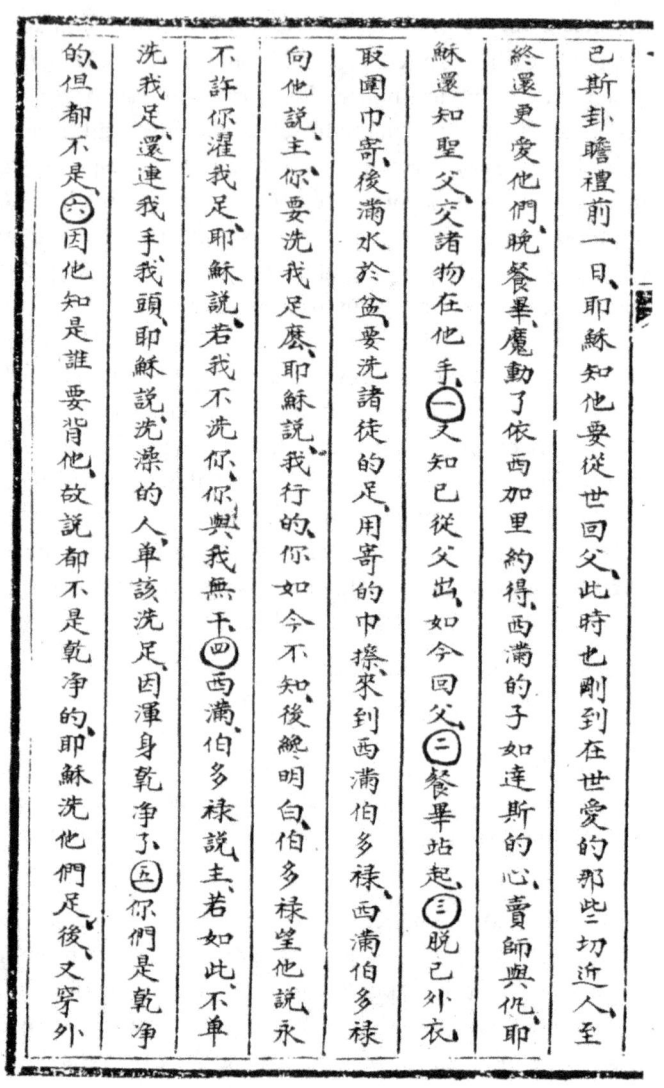

Figure 12

The comparison between the two footwashing versions' text layers—in *Guxin shengjing* and *Shengjing zhijie,* as the earlier chapter has shown—indicates that the wording of *Guxin shengjing* follows a conversational pattern. The writing as of *Guxin shengjing* is more of a spoken version designed to tell the footwashing story verbally. Poirot believed that the words telling the footwashing story could be uttered from mouth to mouth because the Bible verses were translated into the Chinese used in daily conversations by ordinary people.

Another instance can explain this language style clearer. The Latin word "*verbum*" in John 1:1 appears in *Guxin shengjing* in two different ways. Poirot first used three Chinese characters, "wu er peng" (物爾朋), to imitate the Latin word's sound and then explained it in Chinese as "hua" (話), meaning "words."[5] This example often is taken by scholars to show Poirot's literal and exact translation of the Latin Bible.[6] As a matter of fact, the same word "verbum" had been translated into "wu er peng" much earlier in *Shengjing zhijie*. While the "verbum" in *Guxin shengjing* is interpreted in terms of contrast between the emptiness of words and concreteness of objects, the explanation of "verbum" in *Shengjing zhijie* addresses both its literal and figurative meanings. The explanation in *Shengjing zhijie* also touches upon a deeper theological understanding of John 1:1 by drawing on the words and image of the Heavenly Lord.[7] In comparison to the translation and interpretation practice done in *Shengjing zhijie*, Poirot did make the Latin word sound and the verse accessible to Chinese audiences, but at the expense of diminishing the original word's exegetical power.

The only and eventual goal of Poirot was to enable less-educated audiences in China to obtain a literal sense of the Bible verses. He argued the way to do so was to use "suyu" (俗語), the customary, common, unrefined, and understandable language. Poirot said:

> 所以特用俗語。說了一件事。又重說。要高明的。或愚蒙的。都能容易懂得。也深深記得要緊的道理。
>
> So, (the author) particularly uses suyu, having talked about one thing and then says it again. (The author) wants the sophisticated or the ignorant, both to understand easily, and to deeply remember the important teachings.[8]

According to Poirot, allowing less-educated commoners to have access to the Bible verses was not meant to prevent learned minds from reading *Guxin shengjing*. Biblical words can be made accessible to the uneducated and the educated. Using commentary, in the form of endnotes, to accompany the Bible verses can be viewed as taking up the tradition of lettermen.

Commenting on the Footwashing Text

The footwashing text in *Guxin Shengjing* that has been analyzed with the three-layer framework has another text attached to it. Certain verses from

5. *CCT ZKW XB* vol. 29, 559.
6. Song, "'Benyi' yu 'tuyu' zhijian," 40.
7. BnF Chinois 6723, vol. 9, f. 21b–22a.
8. *CCT ZKW XB* vol. 28, 10.

John 13:1–15 are selectively marked with sequential circles, with minuscule characters fitted in the circle indicating sequential numbers. The commentary text follows at the end of the entire chapter 13 of the Gospel of John (figure 13).

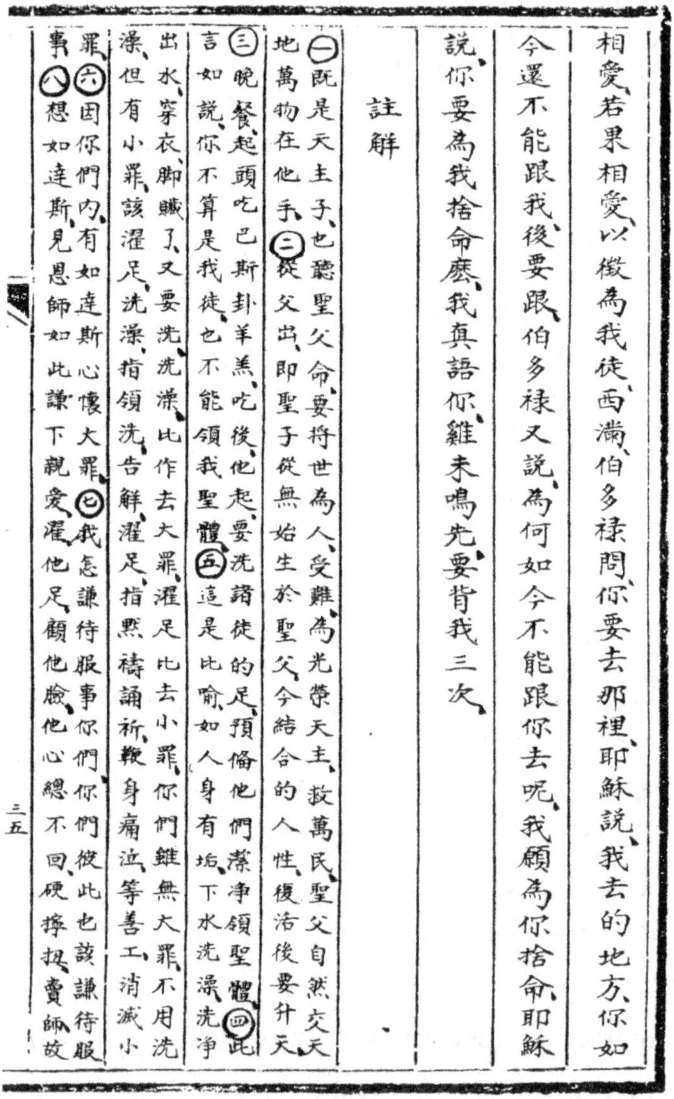

Figure 13

While the Bible verses appear in large characters with each line taking up one column, the commentary is in small characters with two lines in one column. The selected verses to comment upon are not repeated, but the numerated circles link the individually marked verses to corresponding explanations.

Modern readers may be familiar with this format since it functions as endnotes. In the sixteenth to the eighteenth centuries, this was one of many forms of commentary often seen in the Chinese literary tradition. This form was particularly popular insofar as printed vernacular novels often used it. Fictional and lyric writings of that time often had annotations in the end, and that was called "pingzhu" (評註), meaning "comments and notes."[9] Poirot seemed to have a strong opinion regarding the commentary form as well. He defended the choice of endnotes by criticizing interlinear annotations. Poirot believed that the interlinear notes running throughout the main text broke apart the verses, thus making the verses scattered.[10]

About the method and source for preparing commentaries in *Guxin shengjing*, as previous studies have pointed out, Poirot may have drawn inspiration from the reference work, *Commentarii in Scripturam Sacram*, which is also called "Great Commentary of Cornelius Lapide."[11] Cornelius Lapide, SJ (1567–1637), collected existing commentators' exegesis of almost all the sacred books to compile this practically universal commentary. Several editions of this book were printed in Antwerp but arrived in Beijing during the seventeenth and eighteenth centuries, to which Poirot did have access.[12] However, there has not yet been a close look into how the two commentary works bear a resemblance to each other. The footwashing case can open a window for us to compare the commentary on the footwashing pericope developed in *Guxin shengjing* and that in Lapide's book.

There are in total seven circles selecting verses from John 13:1–15 in *Guxin shengjing*. They select verse 3, part of verse 4, part of verse 5, all of verse 10 and all of verse 15. These words are commented upon in the endnotes. But, in Lapide's book of commentaries on the Gospel of John, *Commentarius in Evangelium S. Lucæ et S. Joannis*, the commented verses include verses 1, 3, 5, 6, 7, 8, 10, 11, 13, and 15. Secondly, none of the seven commentaries in *Guxin shengjing* incorporate quotations from any other commentators. What appears in Lapide's book are many quotes from St. Basil, St. Chrysostom, Cyril, St. Cyprian, St. Augustine, St. Thomas, St.

---

9. Zheng, "He Qingtai *Guxin shengjing* yanjiu," 115–17.
10. *CCT ZKW XB* vol. 28, 7.
11. Bontinck, *La lutte autour de la liturgie chinoise*, 383.
12. Verhaeren, *Beitang tushuguan cang xiwen shanben mulu*, numbers 1972–84.

Bernard, Toletus, and so on. Thirdly, the text in *Guxin shengjing* does not introduce a Bible concordance. In the commentaries collected in Lapide's work, some Bible concordances, such as 3 Kings 12:16, Genesis 3:15, Isaiah 52: 7, Matthew 22:10, and Acts 1:1 are provided.

At least at these three aspects, the commentaries in *Guxin shengjing* can hardly find corresponding contents in Lapide's book. However, there is one correspondence between the two works. In the exposition of the first part of verse 10, circled as the fifth commentary under the Chinese character "五" in *Guxin shengjing*, an analogy is adopted to explain what it means that a person after taking a bath is clean thoroughly and only needs to wash his feet. A similar parallel is drawn in the book of Lapide who had summed up several previous commentators and synthesized a commentary that reads:

> Nota, Christum hîc alludere ad eos, qui se lauant in balneis, qui toti quidem loti & mundi ex eis exeunt; sed quia pedibus nudis terram calcant, itaque pedes inquinant, idcirco eos tantú deinde lauant. Nota Secundò, Christú per anagogen, hîc more suo à lotione corporali ad spiritualem affurgere.q.d. Qui lotus est spiritaliter per baptismú, quo ego vos, ô Apostoli, ablui, aut qui lotus est per contritionem & pœnitentiam, hic totus est mundus in anima, sed tamen indiget ut folos pedes lauet, id est, ut animi affectus, qui ex terrenarum rerum, in quibus versantur, contagio subinde maculantur, & leues fordes contrahunt, fæpè expurget per contritionem, castigationem corporis, & similes virtutes (quarum hæc lotio mea est symbolum) præsertim ante sacrm Synaxim & Sumptionem Eucharistiæ.[13]

In the footwashing text's commentaries in *Guxin shengjing*, a much simpler explanation is paraphrased in Chinese. The text reads:

> 五。這是比喻。如人身有垢。下水洗澡。洗淨出水。穿衣。腳臢了。又要洗。洗澡。比作去大罪。濯足比去小罪。你們雖無大罪。不用洗澡。但有小罪。該濯足。洗澡。指領洗。告解。濯足。指默禱誦祈。鞭身痛泣。等善工。消滅小罪。

> V. This is an analogy. As for people's body having filth, (they) enter into water and take a bath. (They) wash clean, get out of the water, (and) put on clothes. (But their) feet get dirty and need to wash again. Taking a bath is like to remove major sin; washing feet is like to remove minor sin. Even though you have no major

---

13. Lapide, *Commentarius in Evangelium S. Lucae et S. Ioannis*, 449.

sins, no need to take a bath, but (you) have minor sins, (then you) should wash feet. Taking a bath means to receive baptism and to confess. Washing feet means to do meditation, to recite prayers, to whip body, to cry hard, and so good work, (in order to) eliminate minor sins.[14]

The handful of explanatory notes in *Guxin shengjing* address none of the profound theological matters. Instead, the commentary provides a digest version of the author in a smooth or even superficial manner, limiting possibilities for potentially exploring the Bible verses. Poirot's commentary seems not into any biblical exegesis; on the contrary, Lapide's work adopts a critical approach to collocate different interpretations involving plenty of materials and Greek expressions. The expositions of Bible verses provided therein not only contain scholarly acumen but also commit to piteous devotion. None of these is spotted in *Guxin shengjing*.

Still, the commentary in *Guxin shengjing* may have been prepared after consulting the sources available in Lapide's compilation. Lapide's book already had encompassed massive expositional references, based on which Poirot could select, simplify, and continue to mold these or other references into a cohesive unit of his own commentary in his language.

At any rate, Poirot's efforts made it easy for his Chinese readers to understand and to communicate the Gospel verses. The principle of making expositions in *Guxin shengjing* was to safeguard the Bible verses with ready interpretations and to prevent any possible other understandings. It was meant to assist readers in reading the verses "correctly."[15] In doing so, Poirot used his own words to paraphrase his translation of the verses and to explain them in a literal sense. The commentary as such would eventually make Bible verses easily accessible for Chinese audiences, especially those with lower literacy levels. Even if readers obtained a shallow understanding, according to *Guxin shengjing*, this book would still help promote Christian Scriptures among audiences in the Chinese context.

Using the Book in Discrete Contexts

Poirot promoted colloquial Chinese, but *Guxin shengjing* was not an immediate text for oral preaching at the pulpit because its text neither communicated to audiences nor associated the verses with any daily routines.[16]

---

14. *CCT ZKW XB* vol. 33, 627.
15. *CCT ZKW XB* vol. 28, 7.
16. For the texts of sermons, homily, and orations, see chapter 10 of this book.

Rather, it should have been read as a book in the first place. Poirot constantly referred to reading books. He urged readers to focus on the meaning of words in this book and to read them with patience.[17] The reading could be done in private and in public. By "public," I mean that this book could appear in pastoral contexts.

One can imagine a scene of reading *Guxin shengjing* with the help of a testimony recorded in another Christian book, *Shengshi churao* 盛世芻 蕘 (ca. 1733). *Shengshi churao* was published around the same time and location in which Poirot was preparing *Guxin shengjing*. It portrayed a picture in which Chinese readers were reading a Christian book together. The testimony reads:

> 況窮鄉僻壤。安得人人而口授之。得此一編。各人自己批閱。即與聽講無異。若係不識字之人。或婦人女子。或衰老病軀。欲聞聖道而無人能講。只須一位識字之親友。看書朗誦。又與講道無異。正所謂書中有舌。如獲面談也。

> Let alone the remote backcountry, (therein) how could (missionary priests) reach out everybody and speak to them face to face? Having this book, everyone reads over it by themselves. That is not different from listening to (Christian) teachings. If concerning the illiterate, or women and girls, or the old and the sick, they desire to hear the holy teaching but have no one to speak with, what is only needed is one friend or relative who could read. (The person who can read) reads the book aloud with expression. That is again not different from preaching (Christian) teachings. It is just like there is a tongue in the book, as if (they) could have face-to-face conversations (with priests).[18]

Although this fragment does not say that those readers were reading *Guxin shengjing*, it sheds new light on how a book like *Guxin shengjing* could be shared in a small Christian community in remote areas in eighteenth-century China. In a likely scenario, relatives and friends nearby gathered in a village. Some of them had received education before, whereas the rest had only elementary literacy or simply were illiterate. They sat down with the Christian book, *Guxin shengjing*, or only a part of it. Those who had greater literacy led the group in reading certain verses from the book. He or she articulated what the verses were about; of course, the reader's understanding was augmented by the commentaries that accompanied the verses. Occasional words, passages, or stories may have stimulated discussions within the group, as what

---

17. *CCT ZKW XB* vol. 28, 9.
18. BnF Chinois 7052, f. 2a.

was written in that book pictured a fascinating world entirely different from the one in which they were living. This or more meetups may have been organized regularly. What is for certain is that with a series of meetings such as these, individuals in this group could gradually learn more about biblical stories, providing them with a light, especially when there were not enough priests to nurture their Christian religiosity.

The destiny of *Guxin shengjing*, in reality, fell short of Poirot's expectation because the book never received an endorsement from the authority of the Roman Church, unless it was secretly circulated. In 1803, the Secretary Mgr Domencio Coppola (?–?) proposed that *Guxin shengjing* should be approved under the decree of 1615 since the Holy Office had given permission to translate the Bible into the Chinese language of the literati.[19] Although the effort of Poirot was praised, *Guxin shengjing* was not allowed to be sent to press.[20]

As a book containing the most substantial amount of Bible verses in Chinese before the twentieth century, the value of *Guxin shengjing* was appreciated elsewhere. Most important of all, this book as a major reference had a long-term impact on later translations of the Bible. The first official Catholic Bible, *Sigao shengjing* 思高聖經, prepared during the years of 1964 and 1968, was based on the Bible verses in *Guxin shengjing*. Gabriele Allegra, FM (1907–1976), consulted a manuscript of this book in the former Beitang Library.[21] Fei Jinbiao 費金標 (?–?), who was a Chinese Catholic playwright based in Shanghai, also used *Guxin shengjing* for composing his biblical dramas in the early twentieth century.[22]

---

19. Bontinck, *La lutte autour de la liturgie chinoise*, 36–44.
20. Bontinck, *La lutte autour de la liturgie chinoise*, 383.
21. Song, "'Benyi' yu 'tuyu' zhijian," 35.
22. Malek, "The Bible at the Local Level," 155.

Part II

Varied Narratives Composed by Missionaries and Chinese Converts

THIS PART GATHERS THE Chinese footwashing narratives that vary from the biblical pericope in different narrative components. There is a very rich diversity that can be observed from these Chinese remodelings of the original story. In comparison to the deviant versions in the third part, these still are not that divergent from the prototype. These texts are found in nine Christian books that include *Yanxing jilüe* 言行紀略, *Chuxiang jingjie* 出像經解, *Shengti yaoli* 聖體要理, *Zhaoyong shenjing* 照永神鏡, *Moxiang shengong* 默想神功, *Tianzhu shengjiao kouduo* 天主聖教口鐸, *Zhounian zhanli kouduo* 週年瞻禮口鐸, *Kouduo richao* 口鐸日抄, *Tianjiao mingbian* 天教明辨.

Following chapter 3 in the previous part, chapter 7 collectively analyzes the footwashing narratives incorporated in these texts with the three-layer framework. Some of these books were prepared by the same author, and some were composed in the same form. The next chapters in this part adopt different ways to group them. Chapter 8 presents two closely connected books, *Yanxing jilüe* and *Chuxiang jingjie*. Chapter 9 introduces three missionary-authored books for practicing Christians to use. Chapter 10 displays four books compiled by Chinese Christians. Throughout, the contexts to prepare each book and their readerships still vary.

These books were indeed meant for specific readerships: some for Chinese converts and religious leaders, and some for circulation beyond the circle of inners. The distinction between insiders and outsiders is stressed in Part III of this volume; this part particularly identifies the preparation of each book. Production of Chinese Christian books is always a collaborative process due to interactions between missionaries and their indispensable Chinese co-workers. Sometimes, the role of Chinese correctors and revisers are recognized in the products, but not often; for instance, transcribers making multiple handwritten copies and engravers who eventually made prints are basically invisible. I hope to insert this perspective in our understanding of the biblical and parabiblical texts.

7

Diverged Versions Made for Chinese Readers

UNLIKE THE EXAMPLES SHOWN in the previous part, many Chinese versions are not equivalent to the biblical pericope. They present more footwashing narratives in various shapes. These versions are incorporated in the books composed by European missionaries such as *Yanxing jilüe, Chuxiang jingjie, Shengti yaoli, Zhaoyong shenjing,* and *Moxiang shengong,* as well as in books from the hands of Chinese Christians such as *Tianzhu shengjiao kouduo, Zhounian zhanli kouduo, Kouduo richao,* and *Tianjiao mingbian.*

This chapter shows how the prototype's principal narrative components were subject to change. A variety of changes can be demonstrated in the nine Chinese versions. In contrast to the examples discussed in Part I, these versions are a bit different from the prototype in distinct ways, but they are still not as indirect as the examples in Part III.

Fabula-Layer Elements

The fabula-layer elements of the footwashing prototype start with the Passover dinner. Except for this setting, its major plot consists of three sections: the preparatory actions of Jesus, the conversations between Jesus and Peter, and the final speech of Jesus. Throughout the Latin pericope, the protagonist Jesus and his disciples are present. Judas plays a part, as his name is mentioned, and Peter has lines while conversing with Jesus.

The Chinese alternations of these fabula-layer elements usually fall into three categories: 1) those that completely leave out a prototype's element; 2) those that adopt it precisely as in the original version; 3) those that reframe it with small yet significant changes (such as to reduce certain elements, to introduce connotations different from the prototype, to add extra elements from elsewhere). All of these adjustments can be found in the following Chinese versions that represent a broad spectrum.

Diverging from John 13:1–15, a particular fabula-layer element often appears in Chinese texts. Many Chinese versions put stress on the attitude and reaction of Peter toward Jesus and his footwashing offer. Exaggeration is involved, and sometimes the role of Peter is transferred to the entire group of apostles. The majority of versions analyzed in this chapter incorporate this element on their fabula layers.

Settings

In the Latin pericope, the footwashing event took place at the table of the Passover dinner. Verses John 13:1 and John 13:3 underscore that Jesus knew that the hour of his return was coming, and that he had loved the world to the end. Verse 2 inserts a reference to Judas and his later betrayal under the influence of the devil. The setting is placed in a farewell discourse.

However, the prototype's setting can be modified in varying ways. In many Chinese versions, the role of Judas is omitted. So is the entire fabula-layer setting. For instance, the version in *Moxiang shengong* leaves out the event's time and location. It merely introduces the footwashing event with Jesus knowing the time of the passion. The text of *Moxiang shengong* reads:

吾主耶穌。知受難之期已至。

Our Lord Jesus knew the time for suffering had come.[1]

The collocation "shounan" (受難) in Chinese means "accepting suffering or hardness."[2] It is the expression often seen in many Chinese versions to refer to the passion. As such, the footwashing story in the text of *Moxiang shengong* is linked to a discourse of the passion and the Eucharist.

The John verses place the footwashing event with the farewell discourse in a strict sense by revealing that Jesus was aware of the time of his leaving. Meanwhile, the original pericope also could entail different interpretations, as it alludes to the passion and the rite of the Eucharist. The reference to the passion is expressed in John 13:1–3, wherein Jesus is said to be mentally ready for what waited for him. The Eucharist is not mentioned in the footwashing pericope; nevertheless, the chronology of the Synoptic Gospels places the Eucharist as subsequent to the Passover dinner. In Chinese texts, the explicitly expressed farewell discourse and

---

1. *VZX CK* vol. 38, 652–56.

2. It was used to translate "passus" (suffered) in the Creed in the earliest editions in Matteo Ricci's *Shengjing yuelu* 聖經約錄; see *CCT ARSI* vol. 1, 98.

the implied discourses of the passion and Eucharist are usually remodeled with connotations different from the prototype.

The Chinese versions explore these interpretations, but they do so differently. To start with, the version in *Yanxing jilüe* simplifies the inner thought of Jesus by only pinpointing the farewell discourse. The text reads:

耶穌向愛其徒特甚。至將別。其愛愈篤。

Jesus has always loved his disciples very much, till the time to depart, his love being deeper.[3]

The undertone is restricted in the text of *Yanxing jilüe* without engaging with any other contexts. Many more Chinese versions underline both the passion and the Eucharist but avoid noting the departure of Jesus. The texts of *Shengti yaoli*, *Tianjiao mingbian*, and *Tianzhu shengjiao kouduo* adopt the same approach. For example, the text of *Shengti yaoli* reads:

蓋當其受難前夕。欲立聖體大禮。

It was about the eve for him to receive suffers, (he) desired to establish the grand rite of the Eucharist.[4]

The text of *Tianzhu shengjiao kouduo* avails more words to put stress on the passion and Eucharist. It reads:

今日吾主將受难。 . . . 乃忘了自己的难。立这圣体大礼。. . . 所以未立圣体之前。先教宗徒濯足。

Today our Lord was about to suffer . . . he chose to forget the suffering but to establish the rite of the Eucharist . . . Therefore, before the Eucharist had not yet been established, (Jesus) first taught the disciples washing their feet.[5]

In the version in *Kouduo richao*, the institution of the Eucharist is associated with the setting of the footwashing event as a related but independent theme. It places the footwashing story entirely in the context of Eucharist as if the event occurred particularly and only for the purpose of the Eucharist. When mentioning "this rite," the text of *Kouduo richao* refers to the rite of the Eucharist. It reads:

耶穌將立此禮。各濯宗徒之足。

3. *CCT ARSI* vol. 4, 277–78.
4. *CCT BnF* vol. 18, 271–76.
5. *CCT ZKW XB* vol. 20, 38–52.

> When Jesus established this rite, he washed the apostles' feet one by one.[6]

In addition, some versions add fabula-layer elements to manufacture different settings by drawing sources elsewhere. The extra description or narration can sometimes be identified with specific Bible verses. For instance, the text *Chuxiang jingjie* inserts a conversation between Jesus and Judas while setting up the footwashing narrative. The reply of Jesus alludes to the betrayal, and it echoes Matthew 26:25. It reads:

茹荅斯昧心曰是我乎。耶穌微醒之曰。爾自云矣。

> Judas dishonestly asked, "Is that me?" Jesus enlightened him in a subtle way by saying "tell yourself."[7]

The version in *Zhounian zhanli kouduo* has an even longer addition. It invents a line of Jesus and inserts it to the fabula-layer setting. In the text of *Zhounian zhanli kouduo*, Jesus said:

我久願同汝輩食罷斯卦于我受難之前。此後不同席矣。

> "I have for a long time desired to eat the Passover with you before I receive suffering. After this, (we) will not eat together."[8]

This line does not exist in the John pericope. However, the biblical reference of this line goes back to Luke 22:15–16. The Luke verses read:

> He said to them, "I have eagerly desired to eat this Passover with you before I suffer, for, I tell you, I shall not eat it (again) until there is fulfillment in the kingdom of God."[9]

The first sentence of the cited Chinese text above is a literal translation of Luke 22:15. The second one echoes Luke 22:16 but is a paraphrase of the Bible verse as it simplifies the original verse by leaving out the reference to the kingdom of God. The simplification would be friendly to Chinese readers of this text as the exegetical reference would be too complicated for them.

---

6. Zürcher, *Kouduo Richao*, 504. Zürcher's translation is adjusted here for emphasizing the nuances in the footwashing action.

7. BnF Chinois 6750.

8. *CCT BnF* vol. 9, 561–63.

9. Luke 22:15–16 (NAB).

Preparations

The first part of the prototype's plot is that Jesus prepared for washing his disciples' feet. The original pericope depicts a series of six movements: Jesus rose from the table, took off his coat, took a towel, girded it around his waist, poured water into a basin, and finally began to wash and to wipe the feet of his disciples.

The Chinese versions portray these movements differently. Some skip the preparations. For instance, the footwashing story in the text of *Tianzhu shengjiao kouduo* does not involve any action of Jesus. Some versions include all six moves fully, following the Latin prototype. The text of *Yanxing jilüe* does so. It reads:

> 因起離席。脫表衣。以素布繫腰。注水于盤。欲爲諸徒洗足。

> Hence (Jesus) rose from the dinner, took off his outer garment, with a white cloth to gird around his waist, poured water into a basin, intending to wash feet for the disciples.[10]

In many cases, the series of actions is reduced to only several moves, although the simplification still occurs in different ways. The version in *Chuxiang jingjie* includes most movements but skips the pouring water part. It reads:

> 耶穌離席脫表衣。以布繫腰。欲爲宗徒洗足。

> Jesus stepped away from the dinner, took off his outer garment, with a cloth to gird around his waist, intending to wash the feet for the disciples.[11]

The version in *Shengti yaoli*, on the contrary, only mentions that Jesus poured water into a basin, with no more movements of Jesus included. It reads:

> 先注水於盤。欲爲宗徒濯足。

> (Jesus) at first poured water into a basin, intending to wash the feet for his disciples.[12]

There is another nuance incorporated in the preparation of Jesus. In the Latin prototype, the last part of John 13:5 reads that Jesus "began

10. *CCT ARSI* vol. 4, 277–78.
11. BnF Chinois 6750.
12. *CCT BnF* vol. 18, 271–76.

to wash the disciples' feet and dry them with the towel around his waist." However, to "dry them with the towel" is omitted in most Chinese versions. Only a few texts speak of Jesus wiping the disciples' feet after washing them. The version in the text of *Zhounian zhanli kouduo* does so. It simplifies the entire sequence of movements of Jesus but emphasizes the wiping part. The text reads:

因起離席。持盆注水。濯拭徒足。

Hence (Jesus) rose from the dinner, took a basin and poured in water, washed and wiped the disciples' feet.[13]

The text of *Moxiang shengong* also includes this detail. It combines the wiping and washing together to describe what Jesus did. Moreover, the wiping cloth has exegetical significance herein. This text continues elaborating on the cloth and its symbolic meaning, which will be discussed later. The action of Jesus in this text is:

吾主既濯宗徒之足。以帨巾拭之。

Our Lord had washed the feet of the disciples, (then) with a cloth wiped them.[14]

Also, the preparation action of Jesus as a fabula-layer element can be remodeled. It is seen in many Chinese versions that when certain elements from the six movements are left out, new moves are added to the array at the same time. Generally speaking, three additional elements often appear as fabula-layer action in the Chinese versions: first, a scene in which Jesus commanded his disciples to sit down and to let him wash their feet; second, a mention of Jesus kneeling in front of his disciples for washing their feet; third, a statement that Jesus washed the disciples' feet one by one. Some Chinese versions creatively weave one of these three scenes into a unique fabula-layer plot, while selectively taking up the movements in the prototype.

Two texts that I examine in this chapter fall in this category: *Kouduo richao* and *Zhaoyong shenjing*. The version in *Kouduo richao* uses one character to succinctly point out that the washing of disciples' feet was done one by one. The Chinese character "ge" (各) means "individually." The text reads:

各濯宗徒之足。

---

13. *CCT BnF* vol. 9, 561–63.
14. *VZX CK* vol. 38, 652–56.

(He) washed the apostles' feet one by one.[15]

The version in *Zhaoyong shenjing* differs further from the prototype. It dramatizes the scene of washing by adding a melodramatic description to the actions of Jesus. It calls attention to Jesus, who was kneeling in front of Peter, and praises this mighty gesture with a long passage of flowery prose. Moreover, this version also claims that Jesus did the washing one by one but uses another Chinese phrase "zhuyi" (逐一). It reads:

跪於愚魯漁人之前。... 故而逐一洗濯徒足。

(Jesus was) kneeling in front of the foolish and rude fisherman. . . . Hence (he) washed the feet of his disciples one by one.[16]

Three Conversations

In the prototype, verses John 13:6–10 unfold three conversations between Peter and Jesus in the form of questions and replies. Peter first asked, "Master, are you going to wash my feet?" Jesus replied, "What I am doing, you do not understand now, but you will understand later." But Peter kept on refusing Jesus, and he said, "You will never wash my feet." Jesus still insisted. He said, "Unless I wash you, you will have no inheritance with me." When Peter reversed his attitude, he requested, "Master, then not only my feet, but my hands and head as well." However, Jesus said, "Whoever has bathed has no need except to have his feet washed, for he is clean all over; so you are clean, but not all." As far as the fabula-layer is concerned, the analysis here is only to identify in individual Chinese versions which part of these conversations is included or removed, which talking point is reframed or added to the content of the lines of Jesus or Peter.

All sorts of situations can be found in the Chinese texts. Some versions omit the dialogues between Peter and Jesus, like the ones in the texts of *Chuxiang jingjie* and *Zhounian zhanli kouduo*. In contrast, some versions, such as the one in the text *Yanxing jilüe*, keep the three conversations intact and consistent with the prototype.

In most versions, only one or two dialogues remain; moreover, it is usually the lines of Jesus that are retained. One interesting example is the version in *Kouduo richao*. This version does not even include the role of

---

15. Zürcher, *Kouduo Richao*, 504. Zürcher's translation is adjusted here for emphasizing the nuances in the footwashing action.

16. *CCT ZKW XB* vol. 19, 286–99.

Peter; hence, there is no fabula-layer conversation in this version. However, the last sentence of what Jesus replied to Peter in John 13:10 is taken up. The line of Jesus in the text of *Kouduo richao* is:

曰潔淨者但須濯足。

(Jesus) said, "whoever is clean only needs to wash his feet."[17]

The version in the text *Shengti yaoli*, which the version in *Tianjiao mingbian* follows, contains the conversation as part of its fabula-layer plot. But only the line of Jesus is included, and it corresponds to John 13:8 (*Respondit ei Jesus: Si non lavero te, non habebis partem mecum*). The text of *Shengti yaoli* reads:

吾主曰。倘我不濯爾足。爾輩將與我不相涉也。

Our Lord said, "if I do not wash your feet, you people will no longer relate to me."[18]

Interpretations of the phrase "*non habebis partem mecum*" (not having part of me) in John 13:8 can vary. Different approaches to expressing it in Chinese can be found in the Chinese versions as well. I will return to the linguistic issue for the text-layer analysis.

More complicated and innovative is that some versions insert extra contents to the prototype's fabula-layer conversations. When an insertion happens, it usually happens to the line of Peter. The additional lines to Peter express his gratitude and emotions by lowering the apostle himself and praising Jesus. Across different Chinese versions, these lines seem to work out the same effect, but again, they appear differently in different Chinese versions. For example, the added line to Peter in the text of *Moxiang shengong* reads:

聖伯多祿當茲時云。爾爲造物大主。其高無比。其尊無匹。其廣大無際。乃天堂之榮光。神聖之暢豫。眾人之安慰。萬類之歸向。萬福之真原。我爲至卑至賤。至小至醜惡。何敢當此。

Saint Peter at this moment said, "You, being the Creator Grand Lord, with incomparable highness, unsurpassable honor, and unlimited greatness, are the glorious glory of the Heaven, the unstrained image of the divine saints, the reassurance to the mass humans, the return direction of all kinds, the true origin

17. *CCT ARSI* vol. 7, 421–23.
18. *CCT BnF* vol. 18, 271–76.

of all blessings. I am the most lowly, the most despicable, the most ugly and the most vicious plebeian. How (do I) dare receive this?"[19]

Similarly, the text of *Zhaoyong shenjing* uses no fewer phrases for the eulogy. It adds expressions to Peter's lines, explaining that Peter rejected the washing of his feet in the first place because this gesture of Jesus was too much for him to receive. The melodrama is, in fact, meant for the audiences of *Zhaoyong shenjing*, designed to achieve a rhetorical effect to generate its Chinese audiences' compassion. The words used in this text will be discussed later.

Final Speeches

The last faula-layer element of the prototype's plot is the speech of Jesus in the end. In the Latin pericope, Jesus instructed his disciples, saying, "Do you realize what I have done for you? You call me 'teacher' and 'master,' and rightly so, for indeed I am. If I, therefore, the master and teacher, have washed your feet, you ought to wash one another's feet. I have given you a model to follow, so that as I have done for you, you should also do." These are the four verses of John 13:12–15. In the Chinese versions, the linguistic expressions of the same content of the instruction vary. The fabula-layer concern is only about the completeness of the final speech.

In some Chinese versions, the four sentences are taken up thoroughly, but the text of *Yanxing jilüe* is the only case among the texts examined in this part. Sometimes, the entire speech of Jesus is left out, as seen in the versions of *Chuxiang jingjie* and *Tianzhu shengjiao kouduo*. If a Chinese version contains part of the final instruction as its fabula-layer element very often, the first sentence corresponding to John 13:12 is missing; in contrast, the fourth (John 13:15) always remains.

The texts of *Shengti yaoli*, *Tianjiao mingbian*, and *Moxiang shengong* leave out only the first sentence, "Do you realize what I have done for you?" in John 13:12. The rest of the final speech is still included therein. The texts of *Kouduo richao* and *Zhounian zhanli kouduo* skip the first sentences but keep the last two sentences that correspond to John 13:14–15. In the text of *Zhaoyong shenjing*, the footwashing event is closed with just one line of Jesus, and that is equivalent to John 13:15.

Besides, it is very rare to see any Chinese text attributing a word to Jesus without biblical origin, as has been noted in the previous analysis of

19. *VZX CK* vol. 38, 652–56.

the conversations. I have not seen any case that adds extra content to the solo speech of Jesus either.

Disciples' Reactions in Chinese Versions

Except for the primary fabula-layer elements found in the prototype, a special element regarding the role of Peter is constantly featured in Chinese versions. As the main actor alongside the protagonist, Jesus, in the prototype Peter only emerges from his conversations with Jesus. However, some Chinese versions portray a series of active actions. Moreover, the portrayal of Peter often covers the entire group, which means that the lines of Peter and his changing attitude portrayed in the Latin pericope are attributed to the disciples in general in some Chinese versions.

The text of *Chuxiang jingjie* makes Peter represent the whole group. It conveys the sentiments and body movements of Peter at first, in line with the prototype. In the end, this version adds a depiction of the whole group as following Peter. The text reads:

> 伯鐸羅惶悚固辭。復恐見棄。乃全聽命。宗徒亦皆不勝感愧。

> Peter, being anxious and frightened, initially refused (his feet being washed by Jesus); later he was afraid of being abandoned and then fully obeyed the command (of Jesus). The disciples were all overwhelmed too by feelings of gratitude and shame.[20]

In some other texts, the role of Peter disappears but is replaced by the collective disciples. The version in the text *Shengti yaoli* delineates a conversation between Jesus and a disciple, but the disciple is represented in the plural, without pointing out a specific figure. The text reads:

> 宗徒惶愧。謝不敢。吾主曰。倘我不濯爾足。爾輩將與我不相涉也。宗徒聽命。

> The disciples, being anxious and ashamed, declined (the offer to washing), claiming that they did not dare. Our Lord said, "If I do not wash your feet, you people will no longer relate to me." The disciples obeyed the order.[21]

The Chinese word "zongtu" (宗徒), meaning "a disciple or disciples," could be either singular or plural. However, the reply of Jesus refers to a

---

20. BnF Chinois 6750.
21. *CCT BnF* vol. 18, 271–76.

collective "you" in a Chinese collocation "erbei" (爾輩). This word confirms that Jesus was addressing all the disciples. In this way, the particularity of Peter in the prototype is stripped off; but the image of Peter can be extended to disciples in general and later to followers. This rendering helps create a space through which readers could connect themselves to the story.

The text of *Zhaoyong shenjing* adds a very flowery description to depict Peter's reaction. It attributes words to Peter that do not appear in the prototype or any other Chinese versions. The text reads:

> 聖伯多祿。見主跪於己之足前。驚駭曰。主。爾洗我足乎。爾乃我之主。實乃天主之子。榮福聖父之光。普世至尊之帝。普天神聖之皇。威嚴無比之君。我乃受造泥土之器。窮困多罪。污穢不堪。愚魯下賤之僕。爾乃洗我至賤之足乎。憑爾如何強迫。萬不敢受此駭奇之禮。

> St. Peter, seeing that Jesus was kneeling in front of his feet, exclaimed, "Lord! Do you wash my feet? You are my Lord. (You) truly are the son of the Heavenly Lord, the light of the glorious and blessed Holy Father, the supreme ruler of highest honor in the universal world, the sacred and holy god of the whole universe, and the stately emperor without parallel. I am a created thing made of mud and dust, poor and sinful, extremely filthy and foul, a foolish, rude and unworthy servant. Are you going to wash my most worthless feet? No matter how you urge (me), (I) never dare receive this extraordinary rite."[22]

These lines are irrelevant to the footwashing narrative. They exemplify Peter's worship of Jesus, highlighting his connection to Jesus. The text of *Zhaoyong shenjing* imitates the tone of Peter to praise Jesus. The purpose is to humble receivers of the footwashing. These words could affect Chinese readers' reception of the footwashing story as they could generate readers' reflection through the role of Peter. These lines, as part of the footwashing narrative, were meant to become the words of Chinese audiences when they thought of their connections to Jesus.

Story-Layer Aspects

For making a unique storyline, fabula-layer elements should be organized by a story-layer narrator with certain techniques and decisions. The footwashing prototype's narrator, John, operates presentational modes and focalizations to comprise its story-layer aspects. Specific presentational manners and

22. *CCT ZKW XB* vol. 19, 286–99.

focalization principles are involved in the Latin pericope. They also entail diversities as the varying Chinese versions render the prototype's story-layer aspects in different ways. Some Chinese versions adopt the prototype's presentational mode but use alternative focalization methods; some employ opposite techniques. With the two story-layer aspects, I continue to show how the prototype's story line unfolds differently in the Chinese texts.

Presentational Modes

In the prototype, the narrator at first mentions what is to occur ahead of the footwashing event; for instance, Jesus would depart from his apostles in the near future, and he knew in advance about his departure. This mention is presented in prolepsis. From verse 4 to verse 10, the narrator directly records the progress of the preparation of Jesus and cites the conversations between Jesus and Peter with direct speech. At last, the narrator again outlines the movements of Jesus and directly quotes his final speech in verses 12–15. To sum up, two major techniques are involved: the way of presenting the setting is prolepsis, and the way of presenting the lines of Jesus and Peter is direct speech.

With prolepsis, or so-called flash-forward, the narrator in the John verses refers to moments in the future. Many of the Chinese texts also use prolepsis to introduce their footwashing story; some texts adopt the flashback or analepsis approach. The versions analyzed in this part, if they do contain the fabula-layer setting, bring in the footwashing event by inserting what would happen afterward. Still, different subsequent scenes after the Passover dinner are associated with the footwashing event in different versions. For instance, the text of *Yanxing jilüe* introduces the footwashing event like the prototype. It reads:

耶穌向愛其徒特甚。至將別。其愛愈篤。

Jesus has always loved his disciples very much, till the time to depart, his love being deeper.[23]

It uses the device of prolepsis to allude to the future moment of departure, and the departure relates the footwashing event to the farewell discourse. But, diverging from the prototype and the version in *Yanxing jilüe*, the version in the text of *Tianzhu shengjiao kouduo* flashes forward to the initiation of the Eucharist. The text states:

23. *CCT ARSI* vol. 4, 277–78.

今吾主受难。单单為我人。所以未立圣体之前。先教宗徒濯足。

On this day, our Lord received suffering, only and entirely for us. Therefore, before the Eucharist had not yet been established, (Jesus) first taught the disciples washing their feet. Our Lord desired to remove people's filth and foul matters.[24]

This version interprets the inner thought of Jesus and the meaning of washing feet by referring to the Eucharist. The initiation of the Eucharist should follow after the footwashing event, according to the four Gospels, but the text of *Tianzhu shengjiao kouduo* mentions it in advance. This rendering is also an application of the literary device prolepsis but diverges from the prototype.

Another major fabula-layer element that needs to be arranged on the story layer is the lines of characters. The prototype includes three conversations between Jesus and Peter and a final instruction of Jesus. A speech can be presented either directly or indirectly. In the prototype, all appear as direct speech. In other words, the characters Jesus and Peter spoke their own words as quoted by the narrator John.

It requires analysis to decode whether a word is directly cited or indirectly paraphrased in Chinese texts because writings before the modern time employ no quotation marks. Again, some Chinese versions use direct speech, whereas others use indirect speech. Except for the ones not containing the fabula-layer speech in the first place, the majority of the Chinese texts present the speeches of Jesus and Peter in a direct manner.

As for the versions analyzed in this chapter, they all include the fabula-layer speech, and they all use direct speeches at least when it comes to the speech of Jesus. Two examples are particularly interesting in this regard. The texts of *Zhounian zhanli kouduo* and *Tianzhu shengjiao kouduo* directly quote the lines of Jesus but meanwhile draw indirect speech into their narratives. The text of *Zhounian zhanli kouduo* provides a great example of using both—direct speech and indirect speech—the distinct forms to present the same line of the same character. In the version of *Zhounian zhanli kouduo*, the final instruction of Jesus is cited. The text reads:

謂諸徒曰。我為尔師且為尔主。猶濯尔足。尔輩宜互相濯相愛。以微爲吾徒也。

24. *CCT ZKW XB* vol. 20, 38–52.

(Jesus) spoke to the disciples, "I, being your Master and your Lord, still wash your feet. You people had better wash each other, and love each other, be my disciples by lowering (yourself)."[25]

This line of Jesus is immediately paraphrased and reworked into another expression. The version in *Zhounian zhanli kouduo* continues:

吾主 . . . 惟教吾人互相親爱。然後可為吾主之徒。

Our Lord . . . only taught us to care for and love each other. Then, (we) may become the disciples of our Lord.[26]

This sentence actually reports and interprets what Jesus meant in the above citation of his words. The paraphrase makes the words of Jesus more accessible for the target audiences of this text. In the text of *Zhounian zhanli kouduo*, the same content is formed in both direct and indirect speech because the text-layer author needs to explain the message of Jesus to his audiences. This rendering narrates the biblical story and facilitates the audiences' acceptance of the story at the same time. The other text, *Tianzhu shengjiao kouduo*, also uses both devices for the sake of the audience. More complex issues are involved therein, and I will further examine this text later.

Focalizations

Presentational modes determine how the narrator presents whatever he observes. At a deeper level, it is the lens with which the narrator can observe an event. Focalization of the lens directs how the narrator observes. The focalization of the footwashing prototype continually changes. In verses 1–3, the spotlight is simultaneously on Jesus and Judas. When the narrator refers to what would happen after the footwashing event, his lens moves with a temporal sequence. Verses 4–5 portray the successive actions of Jesus, indicating that the preparation is oriented toward washing the disciples' feet. The lens also moves in both time and space. In verses 6–10, the lens moves from one interlocutor to the other, capturing both Jesus and Peter in the focus. In verse 11, no spatial or temporal sequence is involved in the pause; the spotlight encompasses the whole group as the narrator alludes to the betrayer among the disciples. In verses 12–15, the focus is still on Jesus, but the vision is panoramic, for Jesus addresses his disciples in the plural form of "you" (*vos*). To sum up, the prototype's story-layer focalization entails

---

25. *CCT BnF* vol. 9, 561–63.
26. *CCT BnF* vol. 9, 561–63.

temporal and spatial changes, as the lens of the narrator John moves in time as well as in space. Both dimensions can be found in Chinese versions.

Regarding spatial focalization, two specifics can help to calibrate it: the spotlight and the narrator's vision. In the prototype, the focus always is on Jesus but sometimes on Peter and Judas too because John 13:2 and John 13:6–11 refer to the two disciples explicitly. The vision of the prototype is overall panoramic since Jesus addressed the disciples in plural pronouns that allude to the whole group. The Chinese versions analyzed in this part by and large follow the same pattern: Jesus as the protagonist always occupies the focus; meanwhile, the lens is set in a panoramic mode to include all the disciples. Individual cases prove to diverge from the prototype.

For instance, the version in the text *Shengti yaoli* throws the spotlight only on Jesus, neither Peter nor Judas being included; it still encompasses the group of disciples in an expanded vision. In some other versions, another particular element is featured, namely feet, which has indistinct singular and plural forms in Chinese. They give special mention to feet. The text of *Kouduo richao* spends half of its narration of the footwashing event to deal with the role of feet. In the beginning, the image of feet is already zoomed out through focalization. The version in *Kouduo richao* reads:

嗚呼。人之足。未有不欲居人上者。誰俯面承人之足哉。

Alas! People's feet! There is not a person who does not want to be above other people. Who would face upward to hold up other people's feet?[27]

This sentence is an exclamation of the text-layer author, but it is inserted in the footwashing storyline after stating that Jesus went to wash the disciples' feet. Continuously, the text of *Kouduo richao* elaborates on the unusual gesture of Jesus in contrast to how people would usually treat feet. It reads:

微論上而君公皆我頭上人。即或爲人下而實承人足者。亦莫不欲于群衆中。爭出一頭地。孰相下而相遜。孰相愛而相濯。乃俯面承人之足哉。

Barely talking about the highness and rulers who are all above us, even those who are beneath people and naturally holding up others' feet, none of them does not desire to stand out from the mass to strive for a place to have his head ahead. Who would lower themselves and humble themselves to others? Who would

27. *CCT ARSI* vol. 7, 421–23.

love and wash others? (Who) would face upward to hold up other people's feet?[28]

Moreover, it provides an exposition focusing on the feet. With the focalization still on the role of feet, the text of *Kouduo richao* continues:

耶穌之教人以謙也。躬承爾足。雖然。又有意焉。人之足日行于途。最易染塵。勿論身之微垢。悉宜刷淨。即至足上纖塵。亦當修剔勿遺。

Jesus, teaching people the lesson of humility, personally held up your feet. He had another message. People's feet walk on rod every day hence are the easiest to catch dust. No mention that tiny stains on body should all be brushed clean, even when it comes down to a little bit of dust on feet, (they) also should be trimmed and removed without missing (anything).[29]

With regard to temporal focalization, the narrator's lens moves not only from one spot to another but also from one moment to another. The movements in time sometimes engage with sequential arrangements, sometimes not. The prototype has a simple way to deal with temporal focalization by portraying different moments and streaming them with a sequence. Some Chinese versions also operate in this way, but some do not engage with any time change.

For example, the version in the text of *Yanxing jilüe* includes a series of movements of Jesus for preparing the washing. Smoothly, the lens in this narration moves and features what is captured through the lens with a temporal sequence. The texts of *Shengti yaoli*, *Tianjiao mingbian*, *Tianzhu shengjiao zhanli*, and *Zhounian zhanli kouduo* also arrange their fabula-layer elements chronologically.

In contrast, the version of *Zhaoyong shenjing* does not involve any time flow. The long and extravagant passages in the text dramatically describe Peter's reaction, but none of the consecutive orders is involved therein. The lack of turning points diminishes this version's temporality in storytelling. Also, the versions in the texts of *Kouduo richao*, *Chuxiang jingjie*, and *Moxiang shengong* feature the occurrence of the footwashing event without using sequential focalization. Their narration of the footwashing story is scenery because of their respective forms and genres, which will be demonstrated later.

---

28. *CCT ARSI* vol. 7, 421–23.
29. *CCT ARSI* vol. 7, 421–23.

Text-Layer Words and Messages

The text-layer author of a narrative plays an intermediate role between the story and its audience. The original footwashing pericope would be grasped by readers of the Latin Vulgate. Every Chinese version of the footwashing narrative was created for specific readerships in various contexts of textual practice, religious or not-religious, liturgical or not-liturgical. Thereby, in each Chinese version, the text-layer author's voice would be adjusted for respective audiences. If a Chinese text does not engage with another authorial voice, but only adheres to the voice of John that corresponds to the prototype's story-layer narrator John and the text-layer author John, it signals its attempt to imitate the Gospel of John to claim a potential authority for telling the biblical story in Chinese. If in a text there is no pretentious device to claim the author himself as the original narrator John, the text is merely delivering to its audiences the biblical story—it indicates that the text has a clear identification of its text-layer author whose voice is addressing his current audiences. This distinction relates to readers and contexts of writing and reading each Chinese text. I will discuss this in later chapters.

As far as the three-layer framework is concerned, the analysis of each Chinese version's text layer focuses on the messages it conveys and the words it uses to convey them. The Latin pericope entails messages that can open doors to multiple interpretations due to the inherent ambiguity of Bible verses. The equivocal meaning of Bible verses is usually spelled out in a new linguistic, historical, and social context, with nuances that may or may not be consistent with the original words. When the footwashing narrative is transformed into the Chinese language, so is its exegetical power. After examining the Chinese versions, I have put together four interpretations of the footwashing narrative: two symbolic meanings and two empirical ones, in spite of the prototype's potential for generating much more complicated exegesis.

The majority of Chinese versions convey several messages by combining some of the four meanings. The combination happens differently again in different versions. Among other versions analyzed in this chapter, the text of *Yanxing jilüe* stands closest to the prototype, as it fully conveys the four interpretations and inherits certain ambiguity from the original pericope.

To start with, the version in the text of *Yanxing jilüe* contains a symbolic meaning of separation. The text of *Yanxing jilüe* highlights the departure of Jesus from the disciples. It states:

耶穌向愛其徒特甚。至將別。其愛愈篤。

Jesus has always loved his disciples very much, till the time to depart, his love being deeper.[30]

The fabula-layer setting is expressed as "zhi jiangbie" (至將別) in Chinese. The Chinese phrase word by word underlies that for the washing of feet to take place, the time of Jesus to leave had come. The second symbolic meaning, however, is not spelled out in the text of *Yanxing jilüe*. It reads:

耶曰。倘我不濯爾足。爾亦與我不相涉矣。伯鐸羅恐見棄。

Jesus said, "If I do not wash your feet, you too will not involve with me." Peter was afraid of being abandoned.[31]

These sentences regard the change of Peter's attitude. In the Latin pericope, Jesus said, "Unless I wash you, you will have no inheritance with me." (*Si non lavero te, non habebis partem mecum*) The "*non habebis partem mecum*" part speaks of no inheritance or no part of Jesus. In the Chinese sentences in *Yanxing jilüe*, this message is interpreted as no relation, no involvement, no connection between Jesus and the disciple. This version successfully conveys a symbolic meaning involving Christology and salvation and has unclear connotations as well. When compared to the rendering of the same verse in the text of *Shengjing zhijie*, which uses "xiang" (享) to express "having part of me," the text of *Yanxing jilüe* loses a bit of richness and exactness.

Thirdly, the footwashing event is a manifestation of the virtue of humility and service, which is expressed through the final instruction of Jesus. Corresponding to the Latin pericope, the text of *Yanxing jilüe* uses the following sentences to write the lines of Jesus in Chinese:

爾知我所行乎。爾稱我爲師。爲主。是矣。我既爲師且主。猶濯爾足。正示爾宜相濯足。即相遜相愛。以徵爲我徒也。

"Do you know what I have done? You call me as Master, as Lord. Yes! I, now being Master and Lord, still wash your feet. (This) exactly show you that (you) had better wash feet for each other. That is, be humble to each other, and love each other, in order to certify (you) as my followers."[32]

---

30. *CCT ARSI* vol. 4, 277–78.

31. *CCT ARSI* vol. 4, 277–78.

32. *CCT ARSI* vol. 4, 277–78.

The fourth message of the footwashing narrative relates to the context of the Eucharist. In the text of *Yanxing jilüe*, it is done in a way similar to the original pericope that has the Passover dinner and the initiation of the Eucharist chronologically arranged in the Gospels. The footwashing text of *Yanxing jilüe* does not use a specific word to pinpoint the Eucharist, but it has a commentary to develop this point. It also has preceding and subsequent chapters in the book *Yanxing jilüe* to elaborate on the establishment of the Eucharist. My examination of the entire book later will explain more on this issue.

Other texts analyzed in this part usually convey two to three meanings of the footwashing account. The versions in the texts *Shengti yaoli*, *Tianjiao mingbian*, *Moxiang shengong*, and *Kouduo richao* link the washing feet with three meanings: its symbolic meaning as a symbol of the departure of Jesus, as an empirical activity to showcase that Jesus was very humble, and Jesus' demand that the disciples be cleansed. Each text uses different wording to deliver its messages.

For example, the text of *Shengti yaoli* firstly points out three virtues as prerequisite conditions for receiving the Eucharist, that is purity, humility, and benevolence. Only later does it start the footwashing narrative. The text requests:

> 遠備有三德。曰潔。曰謙。曰仁。三德備。而後大恩可受也。... 夫此三德。昔日吾主耶穌巳身行之。以示我矣。

> In the long term (one should) equip (themselves) with three virtues, namely purity, humility, and benevolence. (If) the three virtues are ready, and afterward, the great grace (of the Eucharist) can be received.... (Concerning) these three virtues, our Lord Jesus already conducted them in person, in order to show us.[33]

Following this beginning, the entire footwashing narrative in this text is narrated through the three virtues. For instance, the benevolence of Jesus is pointed out at the fabula-layer setting of the footwashing event, which implies the departure of Jesus from his disciples. At the end of this version in *Shengti yaoli*, it again highlights the three virtues to conclude its footwashing story. The text reads:

> 噫。吾主此爲。其示人以謙潔仁之德備矣。

> Yay! This deed of our Lord showed people (what it means to) equip the virtues of purity, humility, and benevolence.[34]

33. *CCT BnF* vol. 18, 271–76.
34. *CCT BnF* vol. 18, 271–76.

The second symbolic meaning, which is to view washing feet as part of the salvation of Christ, is relatively less common in Chinese versions. Only a few Chinese texts point out this soteriological-Christological significance, and one case is the version in *Zhounian zhanli kouduo*. In addition to communicating other meanings of washing feet, this version connects the footwashing story with eternal salvation. It opens the setting of the footwashing event with a detailed explanation of Passover, as Chinese audiences were unfamiliar with the custom. The text reads:

巴斯卦。譯言過去之日。似吾中國之除夕。而年[?]也。除夕者。除舊而生新也。天主降生救世。取肉身之性。而于是日成救世之功。贖世之罪。使人得有復生之日。亦除去其古教之禮。而行新教。

"Passover" (is) a translated word that speaks for a day in the past. (It is) alike our Chinese New Year Eve. Regarding the . . . the "New Year Eve" (means) to remove the old and to give birth the new. The Heavenly Lord was born (in Incarnation) to save the world, adopting the nature of a flesh body. Then (it is) at this day that (he) completed the achievement of saving the world and redeemed the sin of the world, in order to allow people to have of a chance to be reborn. (He) also abandoned the rite of his old teaching but implemented the new teaching.[35]

This "new teaching," in the words of the text *Zhounian zhanli kouduo*, is initiated by Jesus washing the disciples' feet. With the Passover as the fabula-layer setting and the attentive elaboration at the text layer, this version interprets the footwashing story as part of redemption and ultimate salvation.

Another overview of these versions conveying messages is that most of them emphasize the washing of feet as an experience associated with the virtue of humility and service. The theme of establishing and receiving the Eucharist is particularly stressed too, as the footwashing practice is considered a cleaning process. For instance, the version in the text of *Tianzhu shengjiao kouduo* exclusively elaborates one message, and that is to wash off sins before the Eucharist. It spells out this meaning in two places. While introducing the footwashing event at the beginning, the version of *Tianzhu shengjiao kouduo* starts with:

所以未立圣体之前。先教宗徒濯足。

---

35. *CCT BnF* vol. 9, 561–63.

Therefore, before the Eucharist had not yet been established, (Jesus) first taught the disciples washing their feet.[36]

Immediately following this narration, the text-layer author adds an explanation to address the audience directly. The text reads:

吾主欲去人之污穢也。

Our Lord desired to remove people's filth and foul matters.[37]

The "filth and foul matters" of people are dirt on feet in the literal sense and sins on souls in the figurative sense. Subsequent passages in this text of *Tianzhu shengjiao kouduo* are all about physical and spiritual cleansing. It points out that Jesus, while washing his disciples' feet, commanded cleaning and confession. More discussion on this and other texts' composition for target audiences can be found in later chapters.

36. *CCT ZKW XB* vol. 20, 38–52.
37. *CCT ZKW XB* vol. 20, 38–52.

8

Biography and Illustrations Integrated

This chapter centers on two interconnecting books attributed to the same author, Giulio Aleni, SJ (1582–1649). They are *Yanxing jilüe* in the form of biography, and *Chuxiang jingjie*, an illustrated Christian book. As one series, *Yanxing jilüe* and *Chuxiang jingjie* delivered the life and ministry of Jesus according to the Gospels to broad Chinese audiences who were lacking a Chinese Bible. Moreover, they were reprinted and reproduced many times in later years. Both have gained a classic status in the history of Christianity in China.

Yanxing jilüe: Abbreviated Records of Words and Deeds

Yanxing jilüe is a typical writing that reached out to readers beyond the Christian community. It is regarded as one of the most important sources for introducing Jesus and Christianity to Chinese audiences.[1] Because of its famous author, Giulio Aleni, who was one of the most active and prolific missionary writers in contact with Chinese scholars, *Yanxing jilüe* has attracted modern scholars' attention for decades. Existing scholarship has discussed whether and how the author translated a European book into *Yanxing jilüe*. I shift the focus to the composition of this book from an angle of the reading experience. The goal is to understand better how *Yanxing jilüe* connected to its target readers.

The copy that I examine is a facsimile reproduced in *CCT ARSI*. Its original print was published in 1635 in Fujian Province. The cover page bears a Chinese title, *Tianzhu jiangsheng jilu* (天主降生紀錄), but its paratexts and the body text show another title as *Tianzhu jiangsheng yanxing jilüe* (天主降生言行紀畧). It is common to see variant titles referring to the same book, especially when it comes to the massive Chinese Christian texts. As other

---

1. Criveller, *Preaching Christ in Late Ming China*; Standaert, "The Bible in Early Seventeenth-Century China"; Pan, "Shu er bu yi"; Song, "Cong jingdian dao tongsu."

copies of this book have their titles registered as *Tianzhu jiangsheng yanxing jilüe* (天主降生言行紀畧), I follow this convention.

The Footwashing Story in the Biography of Jesus

As the book title suggests, *Yanxing jilüe* renders the words and deeds of Jesus with each chapter focusing on one theme. The footwashing text previously analyzed is part of one chapter in the book *Yanxing jilüe*. The chapter has a headline, "zhuozu chuixun" (濯足垂訓), which means "washing feet to leave lessons." It is the second chapter in the seventh volume, following the chapter "performing the old rite before the passion" (受難前夕行古禮) and prior to the chapter "establishing the grand rite of the Eucharist" (立聖體大禮). Together with these accounts, the footwashing story is one instance documenting the life and ministry of Jesus in this book.

The entire book of *Yanxing jilüe* chronologically presents biblical accounts before and during the years of Jesus on earth, containing but not limited to the annunciation, the genealogy and birth of Jesus, his early childhood, his baptism, the temptation, the crucifixion, resurrection, ascension, and descent of the Holy Spirit. The footwashing event is thus included; other biblical miracles and parables from the Gospels (such as the story of the prodigal son and healing the man with leprosy) are recorded too. In successive chapters, this book synchronizes the life and ministry of Jesus into one coherent narration.

Due to its content, the book of *Yanxing jilüe* is considered as translated from the European work *Vita Christi* by Ludolphus de Saxonia (ca. 1300–1378). More specifically, the arrangement of the events in *Yanxing jilüe* suggests that an abbreviated version of *Vita Jesu Christi e quatuor Evangeliis et scriptoribus orthodoxis concinnata* is more likely to be its source.[2]

However, focusing on the composite features of *Vita Christi* and the Chinese book, one can notice that the European work may be used as an inspiration or reference but cannot be the reason for Aleni to make a Chinese edition out of it. *Vita Christi* was indeed very popular and had an impact on the Jesuit tradition of spiritual training; in spite of that, it encompasses the personal agenda of Ludolph, such as a vivid and detailed portrait of chivalric tales in the time of Ludolph. The Chinese book *Yanxing jilüe* does not involve such personal reflection, nor need it do so.[3] Also, *Vita Christi* was structured with "lectio," "meditatio," and "ratio." None of these sections is seen

---

2. Standaert, "The Bible in Early Seventeenth-Century China," 41; Pan, "Shu er bu yi," 143–60.

3. Shore, *The Vita Christi of Ludolph of Saxony*, 5–9.

in the Chinese book. Stimulating an imagined mental world to assist readers' meditation upon the scenes recorded therein was the agenda of *Vita Christi*. Reading *Yanxing jilüe* and *Chuxiang jingjie* together may bring about a similar effect, but not the book of *Yanxing jilüe* alone.

I think the issue is not whether or how Aleni translated Ludolph's *Vita Christi* into Chinese; rather, the question involves how Aleni employed the storytelling technique seen in *Vita Christi* to write the life and ministry of Jesus for Chinese readers of the time. The answer lies in the composition of *Yanxing jilüe*, which integrates European Gospel harmony and Chinese biography writing.

As a genre to chronologically recount the life of Jesus by combining accounts from different Gospels, Gospel harmonies have become more and more prevalent in Europe since the sixteenth century.[4] For instance, *Monotessaron* (1420) was a Gospel harmony written by Jean Gerson (1363–1429), consisting of chronological narratives based on the four Gospels.[5] Its structure even bears a resemblance to the selection and arrangement of the events in *Yanxing jilüe*. Both start the life circle of Jesus with the conception of John, which resonates a harmony genre centering on the Gospel of John. By way of selecting and rewriting major biblical scenes in this manner, the accounts in the four Gospels are synchronized in the book of *Yanxing jilüe*. As Aleni clarified in the preface, his intention was to provide readers with contents of the Gospels. He said:

今將四聖所編。會攢要略，粗達言義。言之無文。理可長思。令人心會身體。以資神益。雖不至隕越經旨。然未敢云譯經也。

For the time being (I), from what the Four Saints (Evangelists) had compiled, take and assemble the essential and summary parts, to roughly deliver the meaning of the words (in the Four Gospels). (Although my) writing does not have literary merit, the ideas (that it expresses) can be thought through. (The intention of mine is) to make people understand (the Gospels) in mind and perceive (the Gospels) in practice. Even though (this book) does not lead to damaging or transgressing the purpose of the scriptures, still, (I) dare not to claim (it as) a translation of the scriptures.[6]

---

4. Cox and Easley, *Harmony of the Gospels*, 6–8.

5. For more references on *Monotessaron*, see Lang, "Gospel Synopses from the 16th to the 18th Centuries"; Lang, "Jean Gerson's Harmony of the Gospels (1420)."

6. *CCT ARSI* vol. 4, 28–29.

The idea of making a Gospel harmony in Chinese would suit Aleni, especially when he could pattern it after Chinese biography writing, a genre that could promise the popularity of this book among broad audiences of the time. The Chinese predilection for biography is manifested in its long-lasting historiography. As a conventional form, biography writing can be traced back to ancient Chinese classics. In traditional dynastic histories, there is always a section of biographies for legendary figures, like emperors, generals, and respectable scholars of the time. Across different traditions, Confucius and Buddha all have more than a few biographies, sometimes with illustrations. This genre has evolved with a series of subgenres such as "xing" (行), "zhuang" (狀), "zhuan" (傳), and "ji" (記/紀) until the seventeenth century. The book of *Yanxing jilüe* is consistent with this literary line. To historicize Jesus and his mission in this writing form would be appealing to Chinese audiences who could easily find themselves familiar with *Yanxing jilüe*. It is not surprising to see that, in the eyes of traditional Chinese Christian scholars, *Yanxing jilüe* was a biography of Jesus.[7]

While providing a synchronized biblical portrayal of Jesus by integrating genres echoed in both European and Chinese traditions, this book utilizes other literary devices to assist its readers too. The body part, in addition to the main text, consists of two forms of notes: annotations and commentaries. Like the print design seen in other Chinese Christian books, the main writing and notes are printed differently in *Yanxing jilüe*, and symbols for highlighting Christian terms and names also are employed.

Specifically speaking, interlinear annotations explain terms and insert quotations from church fathers (such as Augustine), making the main text comprehensible. They appear smaller than characters of the main text, with two lines in one column. If Chinese characters are there to mimic the sound of a Latin word, those characters are marked with, for example, squares for names of countries and places, and underlines for names of persons (figure 14).

---

7. Xu, *MingQingjian yesuhuishi yizhu tiyao*, 38.

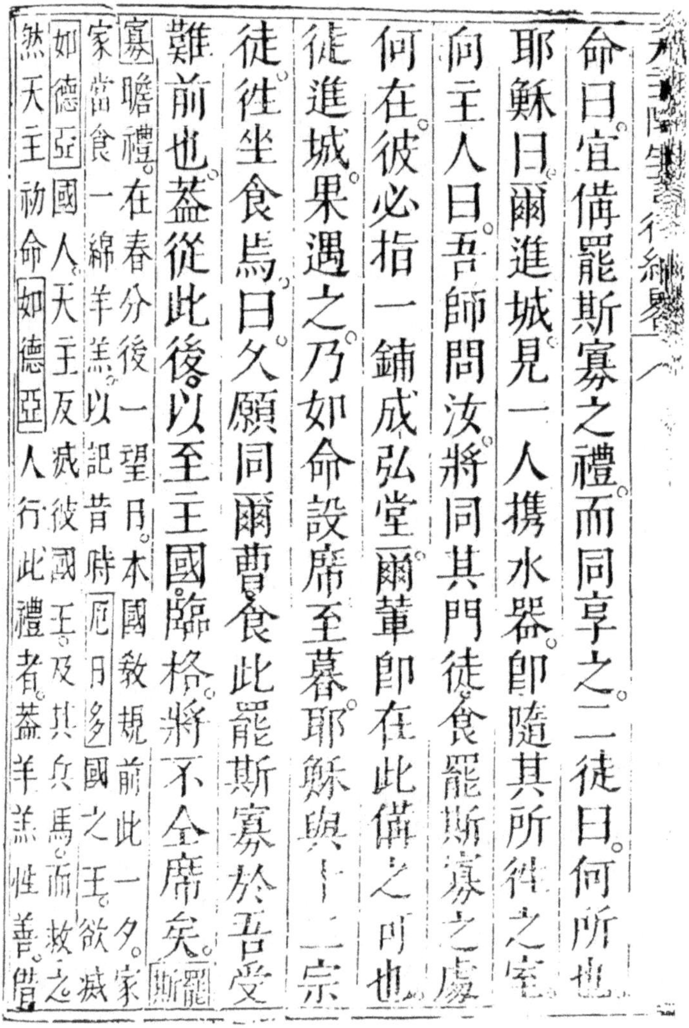

命曰宜備罷斯寡之禮而同享之二徒曰何所也
耶穌曰爾進城見一人攜水器卽隨其所往之室
向主人曰吾師問汝將同其門徒食罷斯寡之處
何在彼必指一鋪成弘堂爾輩卽在此備之可也
徒進城果遇之乃如命設席至暮耶穌與十二宗
徒徒坐食焉曰久願同爾曹食此罷斯寡於吾受
難前也葢從此後以至王國臨格將不全席矣 [斯罷]
[寡]瞻禮在春分後一望月木國敎規前此一夕家
家當食一綿羊羔以記昔厄日多國之王欲滅家
如德亞國人天主反戒彼國王及其人馬而救之
然天主勑命如德亞人行此禮者葢羊羔性善僭

Figure 14

Long commentaries occasionally appear at the end of chapters. The chapter on the footwashing theme does not have a commentary, whereas its subsequent chapter on the establishment of the Eucharist does.

Broad Distribution as Witnessed

In addition to its genre, narrativity, and storytelling manner, up-to-date editorial techniques and the fame of its author also add weight to the popularity of *Yanxing jiüe*. Since its first publication in 1635, numerous reprints have been made, and different editions of this book have emerged, widely circulated, and ended up in many library catalogs. Registrations of this book even appear inconsistent sometimes because different catalog entries are based on different editions of *Yanxing jiüe*.[8]

In terms of introducing Christianity to China, this is one of the most prevalent Chinese Christian books. Readers from high-ranking literati to members of the broader public have appreciated it. This book was so well received that it was translated into Korean too.[9] Two abridged versions of this book also were in circulation, namely *Tianzhu yesu shengji* 天主耶穌聖蹟 (ca. 1640–1840) and *Yesu yanxing jilüe* 耶穌言行紀略 (ca. 1650–1800).[10] Together with another three texts produced in the seventeenth century (*Wanwu zhenyuan* 萬物真原, *Tianzhu jiangsheng yinyi* 天主降生引義, and *Zongtu liezhuan* 宗徒列傳), *Yanxing jilüe* was reprinted again in the anthology *Daoyuan jingcui* 道原精萃 (1887) two centuries later.[11]

Other Chinese Christian texts also testify to the broad reception of *Yanxing jilüe*. At least in the circle of literate Chinese Christians, *Yanxing jilüe* gained classic status. For instance, Chinese Christian scholar Zhang Xingyao 張星曜 (1633–1715?) in his book, *Tianru tongyi kao* 天儒同異考 (1702–1715), recognized *Yanxing jilüe* in the array with *Shengjing zhijie* as two important works for the transmission of the Scriptures.[12] Chinese clergy Zhou Zhi 周志 (?–?) wrote *Shenxin siyao* 身心四要 (c. 1649) based on his studying and reading experience of many Christian texts. Whenever coming across important theological matters such as the incarnation, passion, ascension, and salvation, he directly referred to *Yanxing jilüe*.[13]

Yanxing jilüe was constantly recommended to general audiences of Western learning. Li Jiugong 李九功 (?–1681) once suggested a "minimum reading program" for scholars who were interested in overall Western thought or "Heavenly Studies," which was indistinctively coined in the Chinese term "tianxue" (天學). This program included some scholastic texts

8. See CCT Database.
9. Baker, "A Note of Jesuit Works in Chinese," 33.
10. See CCT Database.
11. A copy is available at the Ricci Institute Library at the University of San Francisco.
12. *CCT BnF* vol. 8, 558.
13. *CCT ZKW XB* vol. 18, 66.

of philosophy and technical texts, and *Yanxing jilüe* was listed as literature delivering the meaning of salvation and redemption.[14]

As a major text introducing and defending Christianity, *Yanxing jilüe* also was mentioned for confronting opponents. Yang Tingyun 楊廷筠 (1562–1627), one of the three pillars of the Christian mission in late Ming China, had a special section for presenting *Yanxing jilüe* in his book, *Tianshi mingbian* 天釋明辨 (1645). Yang drew an analogy between the account of Jesus and that of the earliest Chinese King Tang in the time of remote antiquity. He argued that King Tang's legend was never questioned, and thus, the account of Jesus should not be challenged. He regarded *Yanxing jilüe* as a reliable source that documented the life of Jesus, the same as the Chinese records of King Tang's legend. He even criticized Buddhism as untrustworthy because there was no comparable Buddhist book like *Yanxing jilüe* to trace the incarnation of Buddha.[15]

The influence of *Yanxing jilüe* went even further, beyond the learned ones. During the ban on Christianity, this book still was found in households of less-educated village men.[16] Perhaps educated laity could orally retell what was written in this book, allowing the ones who could not read to learn of the stories of Jesus and salvation history.

There is another book that can shed light on reading *Yanxing jilüe*, and it is *Chuxiang jingjie*. It contains illustrations that visualize the biblical narration provided in *Yanxing jilüe*. The two works together make an illustrated biography of Jesus with representative biblical scenes from the Gospels. Reading both books together resembles a reading experience of Bartolomeo Ricci's *Vita D. N. Jesu Christi et verbis Evangeliorum in ipsismet concinnata*, which is designed with a folio of illustration and a folio of verbal text side by side. The link between the two is not visible in the book of *Yanxing jilüe* but is noted on every page of *Chuxiang jingjie*.

Chuxiang jingjie: Explanation of Illustrated Classic

Chuxiang jingjie is also attributed to Giulio Aleni. It has been studied by modern Chinese and European scholars across fields. The existing literature has identified that the source of *Chuxiang jingjie* is *Evangelicae Historiae Imagines ex Ordine Evangeliorum, Quae Toto Anno in Missae Sacrificio Recitantur*, a European book containing illustrations of Gospel stories by

14. Zürcher, *Kouduo Richao*, 112.

15. *WXXB*, 340–41.

16. *Qing zhongqianqi xiyang tianzhujiao zaihua huodong dang'an shiliao*, vol. 3, 1267.

Jerónimo Nadal, SJ (1507–1580).[17] Taking into account the technical and iconographical aspects, my examination of this book focuses on the foot-washing case and emphasizes its role among other Christian books in terms of delivering biblical accounts to Chinese audiences.

The illustrated book *Chuxiang jingjie* was first published in 1637 and reprinted many times, each time with a few changes. Therefore, the prints preserved until today often appear different from one another.[18] The copy that I examine is a large in-octavo from the National Library of France. It is a woodblock print made in Fujian Province. Its cover page is missing, and thus, this copy bears no title itself; nevertheless, it contains a complete set of paratexts.[19] It has a text written by Aleni titled "Tianzhu jiangsheng chuxiang jingjie yin" (天主降生出像經解引), as an introduction to this book. According to Aleni,

> 吾西土 . . . 復有銅板細鏤吾 主降生聖蹟之圖數百餘幅 . . . 余不敏嘗敬譯降生事理於言行紀中 . . . 茲復倣西刻經像圖繪其要端 . . . 而茲數端又不過依中匠刻法所及翻刻西經中十分之一也 . . .

> We in the Western land . . . still have hundreds of copperplates engraving the holy scenes of the Incarnation of Our Lord . . . I, the unintelligent one, once translated ministry and teaching of the Incarnation in *Yanxing ji* (referring to the book *Yanxing jilüe*) . . . Hereby (I/we) again imitate the Westerners-carved classics ("jing," in the original word of Aleni), portraits, and images, and outline the essential ones . . . Yet, these are just done by Chinese craftsmen' carving, (what they have achieved) is one tenth of duplicates the Western classic.[20]

Despite the lack of specific information, from what Aleni wrote, one can learn that at first, this book was composed after the words and deeds of Jesus written in the book of *Yanxing jilüe*. One of the many editions *of Chuxiang jingjie* has a variant title, *Tianzhu jiangsheng yanxing jixiang* (天主降生言行紀像), which has "*Yanxing jixiang*" patterned after "*Yanxing jilüe*." According to Aleni, this illustrated *Chuxiang jingjie* was made to imitate European illustrations but in Chinese craftsmen's hands, which was

---

17. *The New Hollstein Dutch and Flemish Etchings, Engravings and Woodcuts*, vol. 2, 9–10.

18. Dehergne, "Une vie illustrée de Notre-Seigneur au temps des Ming," 103–15; Sun, "Cultural Translatability and the Presentation of Christ as Portrayed in Visual Images from Ricci to Aleni," 477.

19. The copy of BnF Chinois 6751 bears the title *Tianzhu jiangsheng shengxiang* (天主降生聖像); the facsimile in *CCT ARSI* vol. 3 has a variant title: *Tianzhu jiangsheng yanxing jixiang* (天主降生言行紀像).

20. BnF Chinois 6750.

106 PART II: VARIED NARRATIVES COMPOSED BY MISSIONARIES AND CHINESE CONVERTS

woodblock carving. More features of this book can be uncovered through the footwashing page included therein.

The Footwashing Story in Interactive Image and Text

In this copy, there are fifty-five illustrated pages, and one of them is on the theme of washing feet (figure 15).

Figure 15

BIOGRAPHY AND ILLUSTRATIONS INTEGRATED   107

The entire page consists of text and image. The footwashing story that has been analyzed earlier from the text of *Chuxiang jingjie* is only the linguistic text as part of this page's full presentation. In addition to the previous narrative analysis, I revisit the footwashing theme by examining both the Chinese woodblock printing and the corresponding copperplate engraving from the European source *Evangelicae Historiae Imagines* (figure 16). Both illustrated pages adopt interactive arrangements for icons in the image and words in the text, guiding readers to obtain a lively reading experience.

Figure 16

The page layout of the Chinese footwashing page has three sections: the title above, the central image, and the annotations below. Each has corresponding areas in the European plate. Nevertheless, modifications were made to all of these in order to serve Chinese audiences.

To start with the Chinese page, its caption title at the top reads, "zhuo-zu chuixun" (濯足垂訓), which means "washing feet and leaving lessons." Interestingly, this title is precisely the same as the footwashing chapter's title in *Yanxing jilüe*. Meanwhile, the title panel includes none of the references of the footwashing theme to its original pericope in the Gospels or the feast day when it should be used in meditation, all of which are indicated in the European plate in *Evangelicae Historiae Imagines*. The simplicity could serve better Chinese audiences, who had little prerequisite knowledge on the learning or practice of Christianity. They could still appreciate *Chuxiang jingjie* without being distracted by unfamiliar information.

Below the title is an image with a series of tags pointing out individual icons and scenes, which are described and explained in annotations at the bottom. On the Chinese page, five sequential numbers mark five spots in the image, with Chinese Stem-Branch called "ganzhi" (干支) system, "jia" 甲, "yi" 乙, "bing" 丙, "ding" 丁, and "wu" 戊, that respectively equal A, B, C, D, and E. All of the five numbers link to annotations beneath the image; the corresponding texts one by one narrate what is happening at the tagged areas. Each is a focal point to read and to meditate upon. If looking closer at this page and its corresponding European plate, one can find that the tagging methods in the two images differ. There are five tagged areas on the Chinese page but six in the European model. Also, the Chinese annotation explaining the five tags is a paraphrase rather than a translation of the Latin words. The writing made the footwashing narrative more accessible to Chinese audiences. It took into account that they had not much prior knowledge regarding the biblical account.

Moreover, the footwashing image in the Chinese book includes additional elements beyond its European model. To start with, it adds details to the backdrop. The plain wall at the back in the European image is replaced by a standing screen filled with a typical Chinese scenery painting, which creates a spatial sense to put the main theme into perspective. The floors and walls in the Chinese *Chuxiang jingjie* are represented with parallel lines forming shapes of rhombus and square, the method of which can be commonly seen in market-oriented illustrated fictions of that time. The water vase, basin, and the small wooden bench are decorated in imitation of contemporaneous Chinese households so that they would look familiar to Chinese viewers and add more details to make the dining hall look splendid. All of these elements add up to an indoor view that could help

Chinese audiences mentally picture a vivid image of the locale where the footwashing event took place.

By the end of the footwashing page, which is to the left of the text's frame, there is a short note in Chinese. It states:

見行紀七卷二

See the second in the seventh volume of *xing ji*[21]

The abbreviation "*xing ji*" is a reference to another book of Aleni, which is the *Yanxing ji* previously mentioned in the introduction writing as well as the *Yanxing jilüe*. This note links the footwashing page in *Chuxiang jingjie* to the footwashing chapter in *Yanxing jilüe*, suggesting that one can read the two books side by side. This sort of note runs on every page throughout *Chuxiang jingjie* to provide a reference external to this book itself. Apparently, the European work neither refers to Aleni's Chinese book nor has any similar note.

On the footwashing theme, the European plate and the Chinese page both integrate image and text, but each would work for its own readers. Nadal's *Evangelicae Historiae Imagines* was meant to provide annotations and assist in meditation upon the Gospels; the Chinese book *Chuxiang jingjie* could serve the same purpose, but more important was for its Chinese readers to obtain first-hand experience of the visualized footwashing story. The Chinese carving was designed to help readers generate familiarity and compassion as if they could "see" the footwashing event themselves. The rest of this book follows the same pattern after the footwashing example so that readers could experience another fifty-four narratives in the life and ministry of Jesus.

Converting Nadal's Masterpiece for Chinese Audiences

Nadal's *Evangelicae Historiae Imagines* was a great facilitator for spiritual exercises; so could be the Chinese book *Chuxiang jingjie*. Moreover, *Chuxiang jingjie* could be accessible for audiences in a broader circle that included outsiders. The entire book of *Chuxiang jingjie* was produced not only for Christians and their meditation practice but also for people who could become acquainted with the life and ministry of Jesus and Christianity. The reader-oriented production of *Chuxiang jingjie* can be noted from its creative adaptation from the European model.

---

21. BnF Chinois 6750.

Except for the background outlines and icons, as seen in the footwashing page, there are other features purposefully designed for serving Chinese audiences. For instance, only around one-third of the plates in *Evangelicae Historiae Imagines* were selected to make the Chinese book *Chuxiang jingjie*. Moreover, among the fifty-five illustrated Chinese pages, only forty-eight can find their equivalents in Nadal's work; but the other seven are results of combining another sixteen plates from the *Evangelicae Historiae Imagines* because every two or three images were merged to become one individual page in *Chuxiang jingjie*.

From *Evangelicae Historiae Imagines* to *Chuxiang jingjie*, European illustrations were selected, arranged, and reworked to forge a new coherent visualization of the life circle and ministry of Jesus. The illustrated Chinese book was structured with select motifs in which the Chinese audiences at the time were most interested. They were ordered chronologically and sometimes different from the European work. Starting from the conception of John before the annunciation, which was the very first theme in the *Evangelicae Historiae Imagines*, the Chinese book *Chuxiang jingjie* contained a series of major events in a person's life (such as birth, circumcision, death); and moreover, it included scenes of miracles during the ministry of Jesus, the teachings of Jesus regarding worldly matters, and afterlife imagery from heaven, hell, and the resurrection. The footwashing narrative was contained as part of the entire presentation.

Even for each of the forty-eight Chinese pages that corresponded to forty-eight plates in *Evangelicae Historiae Imagine*, as the footwashing example has shown, the formation was newly made. The footwashing narrative in *Chuxiang jingjie* was formed differently from that in *Evangelicae Historiae Imagines*. With tags and annotations particularly prepared for Chinese audiences who lacked systematic knowledge of biblical themes, the Chinese book diverged from its European model.

In addition to the selection of themes and arrangements of illustrations, there is always an external link to the Chinese Christian book *Yanxing jilüe* appearing on every page in the book of *Chuxiang jingjie*. References of a similar kind did not exist in the European work so that Chinese readers would have more sources to continue looking into those biblical scenes illustrated therein.

Another feature that sheds more light on the readership of the illustrated Chinese Christian work is that Chinese figures were projected within the image. One particular instance in this regard is the theme of coronation. This page in the Chinese book *Chuxiang jingjie* (figure 17) has its exact source in the European work, *Evangelicae Historiae Imagines* (figure 18).

Figure 17

112 PART II: VARIED NARRATIVES COMPOSED BY MISSIONARIES AND CHINESE CONVERTS

Figure 18

Distinctions can be spotted in many features, and the portrayal of its audience in each stands out. The Chinese book depicts crowds in the lower part of the image. This area is marked by a third tag, "bing" 丙 (equal to C in sequential alphabets), for which the corresponding annotation explains that the people looking up to the coronation are from all over the world. The text reads:

諸國帝王士民祈望聖母為萬世主保恩母

Emperors, kings, members of the gentry, and commoners from all countries are praying to the Holy mother who is the merciful lady who blesses the world forever.[22]

A closer look into the image can reveal that on the left side is a group of people dressing in traditional Chinese garments. This group consists of children, common workers, women, and literati and officials from different times as they wear high caps fashioned in different dynasties. The rest of the picture represents people from other lands with a different style of clothing. The whole section as such highlights an idea of the universal Catholic Church with generations of Chinese included. Projecting audiences on paper has theological significance since it speaks of the universal evangelization of Catholicism; moreover, their inclusion could stimulate readers' and viewers' compassion. Having been portrayed inside the image, Chinese audiences of that time may have considered themselves receivers of the Gospels and equals to Europeans in a united church. In comparison, the image in *Evangelicae Historiae Imagines* does not involve this concern.

Power of Illustrated Pages

Reading the book of *Chuxiang jingjie* could bring about different experiences and effects, all due to the power of visualization. The title of this book "chuxiang" (出像) means "selecting or transmitting images," especially the imagery of a person "xiang" (像).[23] While providing Chinese audiences with vivid images, *Chuxiang jingjie* had a wide circulation. At any rate, the first publication of *Chuxiang jingjie* was followed by a large number of reprints and editions.[24] They reached Chinese audiences of different types, including both insiders and outsiders of Christian communities.

To practicing Christians, seeing is believing. *Chuxiang jingjie* could help them to imagine the place and time in which Jesus had lived. During meditation, images could assist mnemonics and guide meditative contemplation. Moreover, images of Jesus and other biblical figures are not only objects for

---

22. BnF Chinois 6750.
23. For the Chinese character "xiang" and its undertone in the context of meditation and spiritual exercises, see Standaert, *An Illustrated Life of Christ Presented to the Chinese Emperor*, 78; Standaert, "The Composition of Place."
24. See CCT Database.

meditation but also are sacred subjects that can cause an effect. As stated in the preface to this book, Aleni intended readers or viewers to look at these illustrations as if they could see what Jesus did and hear what Jesus said face-to-face. He urged readers to explore the immaterial god by tracing material images, to see the invisible world through visible pages, and to grasp the spirit of the Creator and to incorporate that in themselves, especially when meditating on what was portrayed in the book.[25]

To outsiders, non-Christian readers in a broader circle, *Chuxiang jingjie* could introduce them to the world of Christianity through visualized biblical narration. Images are always useful in delivering messages and more powerful and appealing than verbal texts to less-educated individuals.[26] The ones contained in illustrated books like *Chuxiang jingjie* could especially help Chinese audiences who had little background knowledge of Jesus or the Roman Empire. Visualizing biographies of heroic individuals or sages, such as pictorial biographies of Confucius, as well as that of Buddha and Daoist deities, carried out the current trend of illustrated Chinese books in late imperial China.[27] In this context, *Chuxiang jingjie* was a prevalent Christian book comparable to this genre in other traditions. At least the illustrations contained therein were in high demand. They were still collected and reprinted in the nineteenth century, from which another Christian book, *Daoyuan jingcui* 衛原精萃 (1887), benefited.[28]

25. BnF Chinois 6750, preface.
26. D'Elia, *Le origini dell'arte cristiana cinese (1583–1640)*, 691–93.
27. Murray, "Illustrations of the Life of Confucius"; Murray, *Mirror of Morality*.
28. Sun, "Cultural Translatability and the Presentation of Christ," 484.

9

Works Prepared by Missionaries

THE BOOKS INTRODUCED IN this chapter were made primarily by missionaries to meet pastoral needs. They were meant to be used by readers within the discourse of Christianity, such as religious leaders in local communities and laypeople. Each can represent one type of Christian books: *Shengti yaoli* provides catechesis on the Eucharist, *Moxiang shengong* is a guidebook for assisting readers in meditating, *Zhaoyong shenjing* collects pieces in one anthology for Chinese Christians to improve their doctrinal religiosity.

Shengti yaoli: Instruction on the Eucharist

Shengti yaoli focuses on the sacrament of Eucharist. Its title is close to the Chinese expression "jiaoli" (教理), which means "teachings of the religion" in modern mandarin Chinese. Through the seventeenth and eighteenth centuries, a series of Christian books titled with this or other expressions like "jiaoyao" (教要) or "yaoli" (要理), meaning "essential teachings," were all educational texts but not always written in a question-and-answer form as with modern catechisms. The earliest catechesis in Chinese was derived from *Doctrina Christiana*, when Matteo Ricci composed *Tianzhu jiaoyao* 天主教要 (1605) to present an overall account of Christian doctrine for catechumens and believers. Later works following this line were more diversified and detailed in terms of instructing converts and Christians-to-be.[1] *Shengti yaoli* was one of them, providing full instruction on the Eucharist primarily for insiders to learn doctrine and teachings regarding this sacrament.

A twentieth-century Chinese Christian historian and bibliographer, Xu Zongze 徐宗澤 (1886–1947), once commented on *Shengti yaoli*. He said, "This book is about catechesis. Regarding how to receive the Eucharist and how to express gratitude in a good manner, it slightly differs from

---

1. For the differences between catechism and doctrina Christiana, see Criveller, *Preaching Christ in Late Ming China*, 40; Ricci, *Fonti Ricciane*, 2:289–93.

Verbiest's explanation of the Eucharist."[2] Ferdinand Verbiest, SJ (1623–1688), in 1675 wrote a catechism on the Eucharist titled *Shengti dayi* 聖體答疑 for answering questions in that regard. The difference is that Aleni's *Shengti yaoli* provided more accounts on the ritual of receiving the Eucharist that would be useful for Chinese converts not only to comprehend but also to practice the sacrament.

The book of *Shengti yaoli* was first printed in 1644 in Fujian Province, and the copy that I consult is a facsimile in *CCT BnF*. This copy has two volumes, respectively explaining what the Eucharist is and prescribing how to receive it. The first volume accounts Christian doctrine and teachings regarding the Eucharist. It includes the meaning of the Eucharist, its imagery in the Old Testament, the grace of the Eucharist, its mystery, and the salvation coming from it. The second volume is about the rite of the Eucharist and individuals' experience. It meticulously elaborates on the prerequisites for one to receive the Eucharist, the rules of receiving it, and the prayers to recite before and after receiving the Eucharist.

Reading the Footwashing Text before the Eucharist

The footwashing story contained in *Shengti yaoli* analyzed earlier is found in a section on conditions and exercises before receiving the Eucharist, which is headlined in the Chinese "ling shengti yiqian gongfu" (領聖體以前功夫).[3] As has been analyzed, the footwashing narrative is meant to convey messages on the Eucharist in this book. By reading the footwashing text, taking into account how it is brought up in this book, one can better grasp the author's voice.

Before the footwashing narrative, the author introduces three virtues—humility, cleaning, and benevolence. It is said that these three are essential for one to be eligible to receive the Eucharist. The author's words read:

> 遠備有三德。曰潔。曰謙。曰仁。三德備。而後大恩可受也。... 夫此三德。昔日吾主耶穌已身行之。以示我矣。

> In the long term (one should) equip (themselves) with three virtues, namely purity, humility, and benevolence. (If) the three virtues are ready, and afterward, the great grace (of the Eucharist)

---

2. Xu, *MingQingjian yesuhuishi yizhu tiyao*, 179.
3. *CCT BnF* vol. 18, 271.

can be received. . . . (Concerning) these three virtues, our Lord Jesus already conducted them in person, in order to show us.[4]

Following this general introduction is the narration of the footwashing story, which is taken as a manifestation of the three virtues. All the narrative components are interwoven so that the preparation of Jesus for washing the disciples' feet is described, the speech of Jesus directly is quoted, and the disciple's reactions are portrayed. The author concludes that Jesus had established an example of how his followers should cultivate themselves to acquire the three virtues before receiving the Eucharist. The author again directly addresses his readers by saying:

噫。吾主此爲。其示人以謙潔仁之德備矣。

Yay! This deed of our Lord showed people (what it means to) equip the virtues of purity, humility, and benevolence.[5]

The author's role plays back and forth between speaking of the footwashing narration and speaking of his readers. There is no pretense in telling the footwashing story as a third-party author rather than a witness. The text continues speaking to readers:

所以泰西教宗及司教者。每年於吾主立聖體大禮之晨。必集貧人十二。親爲濯足。皆以效耶穌之至德也。夫以吾主至尊。猶必行謙潔仁以示表。人而無此三德。將何以領受大恩哉。

Therefore, the Pope and priests in the West, every year in the morning of the rite of the Initiation of the Eucharist of our Lord, surely collect the poor twelve (and) wash their feet in person. All is for imitating of the ultimate virtue of Jesus. Well, given the immensely venerated (status) of our Lord, (he) still must practice the humility, the cleaning and the benevolence, in order to show an example. People yet without these three virtues, how will (you) receive the great grace?[6]

In this passage, the author speaks of the ritual tradition in the church. It has been explained previously that the Roman Missal of 1570 prescribed the footwashing ceremony be performed in the morning of the feast day of the establishment of the Eucharist. The author of *Shengti yaoli* then explains to his Chinese readers the situation in the church, imparting to them what Jesus

---

4. *CCT BnF* vol. 18, 271–76.
5. *CCT BnF* vol. 18, 271–76.
6. *CCT BnF* vol. 18, 271–76.

did at the footwashing event, what the church inherited from it, and what his Chinese readers should do before receiving the Eucharist.

Useful Catechesis

The book of *Shengti yaoli* is known to modern scholars due to the fame of its author Giulio Aleni, which also facilitated the popularity of this book. There are indeed countless records of this book as its title appears in all sorts of traditional catalogs made by missionaries. These are shreds of evidence witnessing its wide circulation and a large number of reprints. After two hundred years, *Shengti yaoli* was still being revised and produced, at least in the year of 1881.[7]

To Chinese readers, some editorial and printing features of this book could be useful. For instance, it lists relevant titles on specific subjects for further reading, and the suggested titles are printed in smaller characters functioning like today's footnotes. One page extracted from *Shengti yaoli* contains a note at the end of a passage (figure 19).

---

7. Pfister, *Notices biographiques et bibliographiques (1552–1773)*, 134.

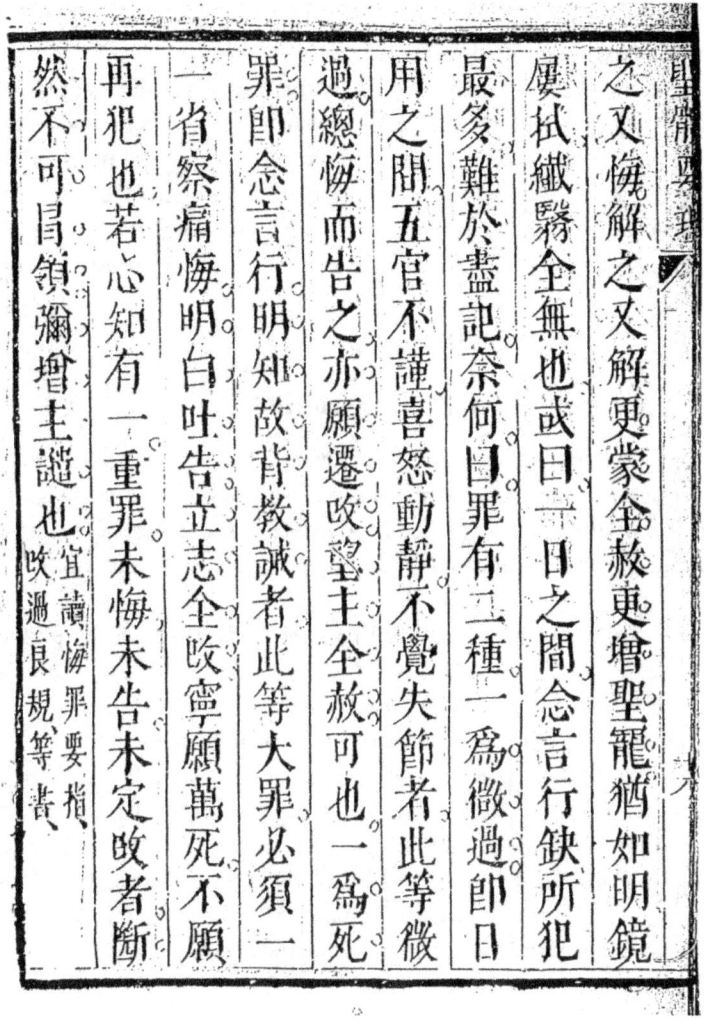

Figure 19

It reads:

宜讀悔罪要指。改過良規。等書。

(One) ought to read books such as *Huizui yaozhi* and *Gaiguo lianggui*.[8]

Two books on the subjects of confession and redemption are recommended here. The first is *Huizui yaozhi* 悔罪要指 (ca. 1630s), another book

8. *CCT BnF* vol. 18, 270.

of Aleni, co-authored by Lazzaro Cattaneo, SJ (1560–1640). The second is already missing from bibliographies.

Readers did treat *Shengti yaoli* seriously. A Christian scholar named Zhang Xingyao must have studied this book carefully, as he quoted significantly from Aleni's work, digested and compiled material into parts of his own book, *Tianjiao mingbian*. In this study, I have involved footwashing texts from both Aleni's *Shengti yaoli* and Zhang Xingyao's *Tianjiao mingbian*; the latter is, in fact, based on the former. I will continue with this case in the next chapter.

Moxiang shengong: Marvelous Meditation

The book of *Moxiang shengong* also covers a full range of knowledge and practice as a handbook on meditation. The book was prepared by the Mexican missionary, Pedro de la Piñuela OFM (1650–1704), around 1695 by adapting from *Tratado de la oración y meditación* of Pedro de Alcántara (1499–1562).

The author explained this title *Moxiang shengong* in his preface. By rendering the two Chinese words—"moxiang" (默想), which means "meditation" and "shengong" (神功), which means "spiritual power or divine achievements"—he argued that cultivating spiritual efficacy was to worship God, and meditating was the way to gain that power. He also actively responded to potential challenges, given that meditative traditions had existed in other religions in China. In the preface, he put stress on Christian connotations of the Chinese words to distinguish Christian meditation from the rest. He stated that what characterized the practice of Christian meditation is the words of Christian doctrine that one should think, recite, and contemplate upon. His words in *Moxiang shengong* read:

> 然想則想矣。何必信經四末之是貫哉。曰。此正天教之所以別異端也。釋家之想在于空。老子之想在于無。無空何物。而可以混超天國也。聖教慕人上見。

But meditating is just thinking, why is that the Creed, the Four Ends and so forth (are needed to) go through (the thinking)? I say, this (is) exactly why the Heavenly Teaching can be differentiated from the heterodox ones. Buddhist meditation is about emptiness. Laozi's meditation is about nothingness. What is the emptiness or the nothingness so that they could confuse or surpass the Heavenly Kingdom? Admirers of the Holy Teaching should have high opinions.⁹

This book was at first printed before late 1696. Afterward, it circulated widely, as witnessed in multiple entries in traditional bibliographies and in various copies available today. The copy that I consult is now preserved in Biblioteca Apostolica Vaticana and collected in *VZX CK*. Its body text comprises two volumes. Similar to the arrangement seen in the previously presented *Shengti yaoli*, the two volumes respectively explain what meditation is and guide readers in how to meditate. The first volume contains four chapters to demonstrate the utility of meditation, its necessity, general regulation, and particular rules for meditating upon the passion. These are what one should understand while stepping into the zone of meditation. The second volume has six chapters on what one should make use of during meditation practice. They provide readers with ready texts: six items to focus on before and after the meditation, prayers for the divine love of God, three spiritual approaches for meditation, a range of systematical prayers to prepare for meditation, seven observations to know for meditation, and finally, considerations to repel temptations.

Meditating upon the Footwashing Scene

The footwashing story is found in the fourth chapter contained in the first volume of this copy. It appears as a scene for meditating on the second feast day relating to the initiation of the Eucharist and the passion. What is more important is that it does not form a storyline of the biblical account but instead guides readers through meditation practice. The footwashing text extracted from the book of *Moxiang shengong* is a result of integrating the biblical prototype and the author's own interpretation into one narration. For instance, included are details on Jesus wiping and washing the apostles' feet. The text reads:

吾主既濯宗徒之足。以帨巾拭之。

Our Lord had washed the feet of the disciples, (then) with a cloth wiped them.¹⁰

This sentence highlights the specific fabula-layer element that Jesus used a cloth to wipe after the washing. And, the cloth serves as a starting point for the author to continue elaboration. Immediately after this

---

9. *VZX CK*, vol. 38, 598.
10. *VZX CK* vol. 38, 652–56.

sentence, a long passage follows to interpret the symbolic meaning of the cloth. The interpretation unfolds:

未濯未拭之前。足污濁而帨潔净。旣濯旣拭之後。足潔净而帨污濁。蓋我等靈魂。其污濁由于罪惡。吾主爲至美之宗。至净之原。

Before being washed and wiped, the feet (were) dirty, but the cloth (was) clean. After being washed and wiped, the feet (became) clean but the cloth (became) dirty. As for our spirit and soul, their filth (is) due to sin and evil. Our Lord is the genesis of the most beautiful, the origin of the cleanest.[11]

These sentences bear no resemblance to the biblical prototype as they depart from the moment of the footwashing event but speak to readers directly. During the course, the author's words refer to himself and readers in "wodeng" (我等), meaning "our" herein. The shift in tone highlights the lesson on cleansing souls as can be delivered from the footwashing story to readers of *Moxiang shengong*.

Welcomed by Different Groups

Readers of *Moxiang shengong* did follow the text carefully. At least in this copy, many traces can be found. There is an example page full of handwritten notes and circles to show that marks were made to underscore some words after the book had been printed (figure 20). These were responses from readers of this book.

11. *VZX CK* vol. 38, 652–56.

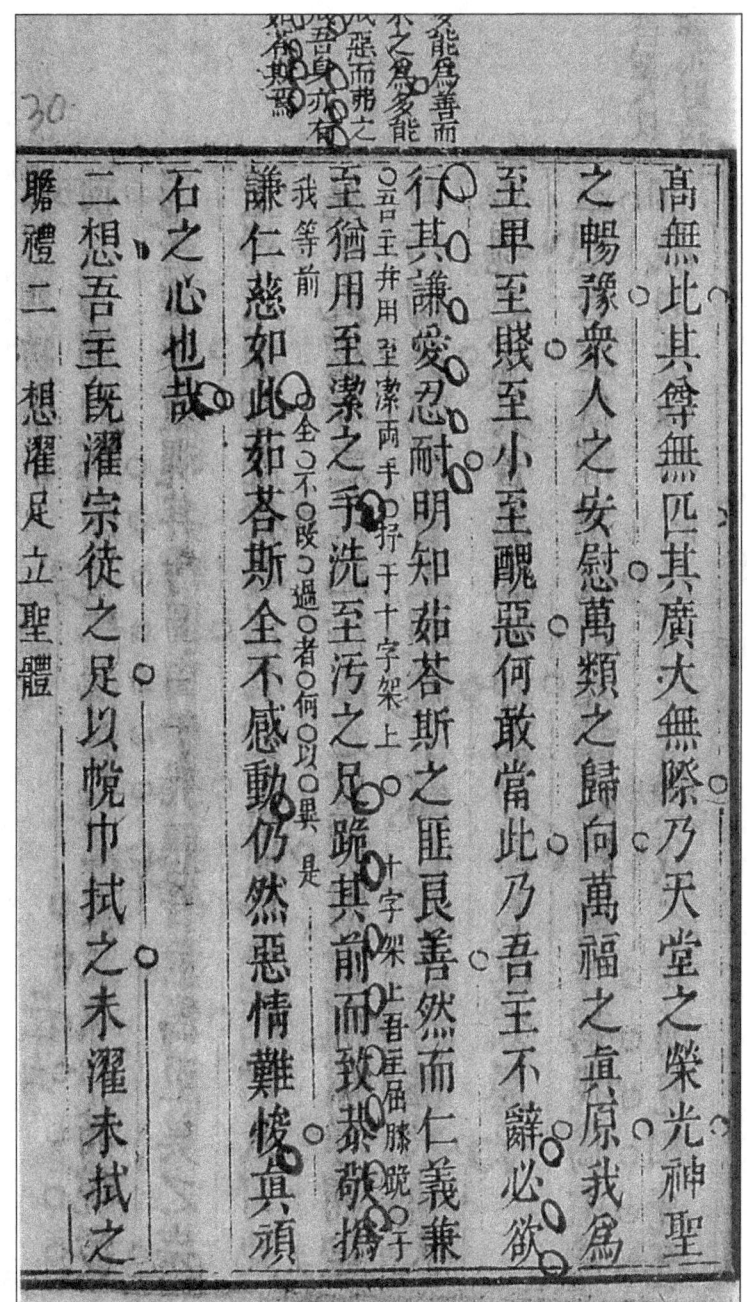

Figure 20

More evidence regarding the reception of this book can be seen in the document *Summarium Nouorum Autenticorum Testimoniorum* (1703), which investigated the Chinese Rites Controversy. When defending their use of Chinese terms "tian" (天), "shangdi" (上帝), and "jingtian" (敬天), the Jesuits and some Chinese Christians mentioned *Moxiang shengong*, a book composed by the Franciscan Pedro de la Piñuela.[12] Apparently, both Chinese characters "zhu" (主), meaning "Lord" and "shen" (神), meaning "God" were used in this book to represent the Trinity. *Moxiang shengong* was prepared at the dawn of the Chinese Rites Controversy. Such dealing with Chinese terms for God was particularly a strategic move to avoid or to reconcile disputes between different camps. And the Jesuits' mention of this book was strong proof that *Moxiang shengong* was welcomed among missionaries of different orders.

Zhaoyong shenjing: Divine Mirror Illuminating Eternity

Zhaoyong shenjing is an anthology collecting Christian lectures prepared by João de Seixas, SJ (1710–1785). The book title in Chinese means "a divine mirror that could illuminate eternity." It would be peculiar even to Chinese readers. In one preface to this book, Chinese convert Wu Dani 吳達尼 (?–?), who was probably a collaborator or assistant of João de Seixas, provided an answer to this inquiry. According to Wu, European scientists used two pieces of glass to make a telescope look at things thousands of miles away. All things from afar would look as if they were just in your hands. The achievement of astronomers formed an analogy of what this book could achieve. He explained:

> 今吾泰西德瑤林公。不但窮格物理。製器觀天。而且窮神達化。用本超二性之理。配合而為神鏡。能將永遠無窮之事。置於簡編。亦如舉手可握。舉目了然者。... 總在使暫世之人。先明永遠之事。故名照永神鏡。亦可謂之常生路引云耳。

> Now our Western teacher Lin (João de Seixas) not only knows the best principle of physics and manufactures objects for astronomic observation, but also knows the best the arrival and transformation of divine deity. (He) applies the principle of the two qualities, namely innate characteristics and supernatural property, and matches and combines (the two qualities) to make a divine mirror. (His crafts) can place the infinite and endless

---

12. Standaert, *Chinese Voices in the Rites Controversy*, 65.

issues into the uncomplicated book, also as if you can grasp them just by taking up hands or clearly look into them just by using eyes . . . Overall, (this book) makes people of the temporary world be enlightened with the eternal things in advance. Therefore, (this book) is entitled Divine Mirror Illuminating Eternity, or to be called an introductory cloud that leads one toward the way of long-living.[13]

As Wu observed and commented, this book was written in, natural and supernatural, two qualities, as of using two pieces of glass to make a telescope. With the two perspectives combined, this book, like a divine mirror, would allow readers to look into their qualities and to find answers for their final destiny beyond the world. Such a slogan of devotional literature would sound appealing to Chinese readers then. The popularity of *Zhaoyong shenjing* did bring about a unique textual history, and the aftermath of its wide distribution resulted in numerous copies of this book. Among all the available editions, I consult a reprinted facsimile in *CCT ZKW XB*.

Learning Gratitude by Reading the Footwashing Story

The body text of *Zhaoyong shenjing* develops sixteen kinds of subject matter systematically in four volumes. Each volume includes four chapters, and each chapter focuses on one subject to expound on it. The footwashing text analyzed earlier is found in the first volume, in the fourth chapter regarding the Eucharist. There are three sections of this chapter, namely the marvelous trace of the Eucharist, the reason for one to do something worthy of grace, and stories of saints receiving the Eucharist. The footwashing story is placed there to illustrate what one could do in order to be worthy of the grace of the Eucharist and why one should do it.

As the narrative analysis has pointed out, the version in *Zhaoyong shenjing* invents a special and extra fabula-element that involves Peter responding to Jesus. The portrayal of Peter beyond the biblical prototype is meant to recall readers' compassion, as they could find themselves in Peter. The text of *Zhaoyong shenjing* reads:

> 聖伯多祿。見主跪於己之足前。驚駭曰。主。爾洗我足乎。爾乃我之主。實乃天主之子。榮福聖父之光。普世至尊之帝。普天神聖之皇。威嚴無比之君。我乃受造泥土之器。窮困多罪。污穢不堪。愚魯下賤之僕。爾乃洗我至賤之足乎。憑爾如何強迫。萬不敢受此駭奇之禮。

---

13. *CCT ZKW XB* vol. 19, 11–13.

St. Peter, seeing that Jesus was kneeling in front of his feet, exclaimed, "Lord! Do you wash my feet? You are my Lord. (You) truly are the son of the Heavenly Lord, the light of the glorious and blessed Holy Father, the supreme ruler of highest honor in the universal world, the sacred and holy god of the whole universe, and the stately emperor without parallel. I am a created thing made of mud and dust, poor and sinful, extremely filthy and foul, a foolish, rude and unworthy servant. Are you going to wash my most worthless feet? No matter how you urge (me), (I) never dare receive this extraordinary rite."[14]

This long passage spices up the footwashing story with extravagant lines of Peter. Immediately following Peter's words to Jesus, the author directly addresses readers. In the author's voice, the text turns to readers and speaks to them:

此時聖伯多祿。深知自己之卑。固辭不受。

At this moment, Peter deeply knew his lowliness, he stubbornly refused (the offer of Jesus to wash his feet).[15]

The text reads as if the author suddenly turns toward his audience to speak to them. This sentence is not part of the prototype or any other versions; it is the author's interpolation in this book. The author's explanation is interwoven back and forth with the narration of the biblical story, which happens very often. The involvement of the author directly addressing readers could help them to comprehend the story and to remember it.

Broad and Enduring Readership

Then, who were readers of this book? The author João de Seixas stated clearly in his preface written in 1769. He said:

聖教典籍。前輩著作已多。．．．但前人所作之書。道理淵深。意旨奧妙。可備雅士之觀覽。難為庸流之翻閱。．．．余繼前人之志。而作是書。不顧語言之粗淺。只求道理之顯明。不但文人學士達其意。及販夫豎子。亦可以明其理。爾也知之。我也知之。互相講論。豈不成一快事哉。余故不揣。纂此一十六篇。以備八日避靜之用。

14. *CCT ZKW XB* vol. 19, 286–99.
15. *CCT ZKW XB* vol. 19, 286–99.

Books of the holy teaching, there have already been many composed by (our) forefathers.... But the books written by the precursors, with profound theory and marvelous ideas, that can be ready for scholars to read can hardly let commoners to browse.... I as a continuation of the forerunners' will hence write this book. Regardless the shallow and unrefined language, (I) only wish the holy teaching to be clear and illuminating. (I hope that) not only literary people and scholars get its meaning, also street traders and young chaps are able to see its principle. You too know it, I too know it, (so that) we discuss it and speak to each other, isn't it such a pleasure? I therefore not measuring myself (to recognize my limited ability), compile these sixteenth chapters, in order to prepare (readers) for the eight-day retreat.[16]

According to João de Seixas, he prepared *Zhaoyong shenjing* for ordinary people that, in his mind, did not exclude lettermen. He took full consideration of the needs of larger audiences with limited literacy. This book was expected to deliver Christian teachings not only to educated minds but also to people on the street such as salesmen, servants, and those of younger generations. One can imagine that with *Zhaoyong shenjing*, those readers would converse about the footwashing story, and more semi-literate or illiterate audiences could hear this unusual story and join in the discussions. Still, the majority of readers of this book would be within the circle of Christian discourse, and this book could be of use during an eight-day retreat for converts, not for outsiders.

Not every book intended for a large readership could reach out to its audiences, but *Zhaoyong shenjing* did. This book gained popularity during the next hundred years after it was composed, as can be told by its own complicated textual history. After 1769, when the book was first composed by its original author João de Seixas and translator Inácio Francisco, SJ (1725–1792), Louis-Gabriel Delaplace, CM (1820–1884) led another revision and finally published the current edition in 1878. Before the first printing of *Zhaoyong shenjing* was out, this book had already been in circulation in forms of manuscripts and handwritten copies.

According to Louis-Gabriel Delaplace, João de Seixas wrote this book during a year of the Emperor Qianlong (1711–1799, reign 1735–1796), which actually was 1769, but it was not heard further in the first place. During the years of Emperor Xianfeng (1831–1861, reign 1850–1861), a priest whose Chinese surname was Lü discovered one copy of this book in Hebei Province around the capital in the northern region. Scholars in the capital city Beijing started making copies of this book and distributed them. Readers

16. *CCT ZKW XB* vol. 19, 15–17.

keen on Christianity welcomed this book, and it was readers who passionately produced handwritten copies and spread the words. However, errors were inevitably made and accumulated from one copy to another.

When Louis-Gabriel Delaplace was aware of this book, he recognized that it could benefit people who were to follow Christian teaching. Hence, he decided to correct the copies that he saw and publish the book for a wider readership.[17] This edition was then printed in 1878 with three prefaces respectively written by Louis-Gabriel Delaplace who eventually made the publication happen, João de Seixas who originally composed this text, and a Chinese convert named Wu Dani who might have been an assistant to João de Seixas. From then on, the printed form was continuously reproduced many times.[18]

---

17. *CCT ZKW XB* vol. 19, 8–9.
18. See CCT Database.

10

Works of Chinese Clergies and Laity

THIS CHAPTER COLLECTS WRITINGS composed by Chinese authors. Some are texts of oral admonitions prepared by Chinese clergies for giving sermons daily through a liturgical year. Some are notes jotted down by Chinese Christians after listening to sermons and having conversations with missionaries. Some are reading digests and personal writings. Initially, sermons on paper were meant for religious leaders in local communities to use. Later circulation of these texts took place not only among insiders but also beyond.

Oral Admonitions in Chinese "Kouduo"

The word "kouduo" (口鐸) consists of the first character meaning "mouth" and the second character meaning "bell." It is no longer a frequent expression in modern Mandarin Chinese; it is not even a frequent phrase in traditional dictionaries. However, it appears as part of titles of more than several Christian books produced since the sixteenth century. These works together make up a subgenre of Chinese Christian texts.

As was explained in the Christian discourse, "kouduo" texts were oral admonitions or orations. They contained words that represented "the reverberating sounds [of the warning bell] by which the two masters Ai [missionary Aleni] and Lu [missionary Rudamina] awaken the world while propagating the Heavenly Studies [Christian doctrines and teachings]."[1] The sound of the warning bell could be heard by audiences, and so would the admonitions be recounted and proclaimed day by day. It can be understood that "kouduo" texts provide Christian homilies, sermons, and so on. The words of "kouduo" texts would be primarily communicated among priests, clergy members, and audiences within Christian communities and then preached to a broader public at informal gatherings.

1. Zürcher, *Kouduo Richao*, 183.

I have found the footwashing narrative in three texts of this kind: *Tianzhu shengjiao kouduo*, *Zhounian zhanli kouduo*, and *Kouduo richao*. The first two are books containing sermons on paper, but *Kouduo richao* involves another level of receiving sermons in Chinese Christians' everyday lives.

Tianzhu shengjiao kouduo: Orations of the Heavenly Lord's Holy Teaching

Tianzhu shengjiao kouduo contains sermons on the main feast days of a year (ca. 1650) before 1656. Its author was a Chinese clergy, but someone unnamed. Due to limited bibliographical information, current scholarship has not yet paid attention to this text. In this study, I consult a handwritten copy facsimiled in *CCT ZKW XB*.

The overall structure of this book follows dates in a circle of the Chinese lunar year instead of an ecclesiastical year.[2] Sermons start on the feast of the Apostle Andreas (November 30, during the early Advent period). In *Tianzhu shengjiao kouduo*, the footwashing story is located in the homily on the feast day of the Initiation of the Eucharist. The headline for this day is "jianding shengti dali zhanli" (建定圣体大礼占礼), written in simplified Chinese characters that indicate the less scholarly tradition of its author, copy transcribers, and readers.

On that day, the author opens the footwashing text by directly speaking to audiences about the passion. The footwashing story is interpreted as a demonstration of the sacrifice that Jesus made for people, including audience members of this lecture. The text starts:

> 今日吾主將受难。非不知难之將至。乃忘了自己的难。立这圣体大礼。. . . 今吾主受难。单单為我人。所以未立圣体之前。先教宗徒濯足。吾主欲去人之污穢也。

> Today our Lord was about to suffer. (It was) not (that he) did not know the suffering was coming along, he chose to forget the suffering but to establish the rite of the Eucharist. . . . On this day, our Lord received suffering, only and entirely for us. Therefore, before the Eucharist had not yet been established, (Jesus) first taught the disciples washing their feet. Our Lord desired to remove people's filth and foul matters.[3]

---

2. See CCT Database.
3. *CCT ZKW XB* vol. 20, 38–52.

As seen in the previous narrative analysis of the footwashing story in *Tianzhu shengjiao kouduo*, its fabula-layer elements and story-layer aspects diverge from the prototype and other Chinese versions. It is because they are totally subject to the text-layer author's control. The author's power is exerted to make the footwashing story different from the Gospel pericope but more friendly to Chinese audiences. For instance, the reaction of Peter is expressed directly in his verbal response to Jesus in the Gospel of John but paraphrased and reported in the version of *Tianzhu shengjiao kouduo*. The mind of Peter is explained through the author's intervention. The text reads:

伯多禄以至尊至貴之主。來洗其足。伯多禄不敢当。不肯受主之洗。

Peter considered that the mightiest and most honorable Lord came to wash his feet. Peter dared not to accept it, not willing to receive the washing (offered by) the Lord.[4]

The above narration clearly shows that Peter rejected the offer of Jesus to wash his feet. When showing the willingness of Peter in receiving the washing, the text reads:

伯多禄始則不肯洗。既則求吾主。連頭与身子。多多洗了一遍。

Peter initially was not willing to wash. Since then (when Jesus explained him the cleaning issue), (he) begged our Lord, including his head and body, all to wash once.[5]

It is in reporting speech that the reaction of Peter is described, and the exact word used to recount what Peter did is a Chinese character "qiu" (求), meaning "begging." Also, the author takes liberty to specify that Peter requested his head and body be washed while the prototype has only "hands and head" in John 13:9. Moreover, the request of Peter is expressed in "duo-duo xile yibian" (多多洗了一遍), a habitual way of speaking in colloquial Chinese. Elementary wording is used; it is the language style that the author and audiences of this book would be familiar with.

The language use of *Tianzhu shengjiao kouduo* is, in general, straightforward. Even the words of Jesus follow the same style. However unique, this footwashing text in *Tianzhu shengjiao kouduo* assigns extra lines to Jesus, which are seldom seen in any other Chinese versions. The text reads:

---

4. *CCT ZKW XB* vol. 20, 38–52.
5. *CCT ZKW XB* vol. 20, 38–52.

吾主告以為人一身至齷齪。不潔者。莫如足。如人之大罪一般。若頭面身体之污垢。如人之小罪一般。今洗足。要汝輩先去大罪。永久不犯也。又曰。大罪果不可犯。小罪亦不宜犯。

Jesus told (him), letting him know, "People's whole body is extremely filthy. The uncleaned is even not like feet. (Feet), are the same as people's major sins. Supposing the dirt and stain on the head, face and body, (they) are the same as people's minor sins. Today washing (your) feet, I (want) you all first to remove major sins, never committing forever." He said again, "Major sins indeed cannot be committed; minor sins should not be committed either."[6]

These lines of Jesus do not appear in the original biblical pericope; they are crafted by the author in the text of *Tianzhu shengjiao kouduo*. The author invents the words of Jesus and interweaves them into conversations with his audiences. At this point, the message of washing feet is spelled out, condensed, focused, and made accessible to audiences; it emphasizes cleansing issues. The author draws an analogy between cleaning feet and cleaning souls. Feet are very dirty, like critical sins; washing feet is done to remove dirt, and so is spiritual cleaning is done to redeem ones' mistakes. This parallel is not to complicate the footwashing story, but to relate it to the importance of confession and reception of the Eucharist, which would help Chinese audiences to comprehend the biblical narrative through a daily habit of washing feet. Following this text, the audiences who washed their feet every day could understand the biblical footwashing easily.

Beyond the footwashing text, the book of *Tianzhu shengjiao kouduo* contains sermons on each feast day developed through other biblical accounts. This book could be used by clergies and leaders in local communities for delivering a homily to audiences. There is little information uncovered to tell the use and reception of this book. But for sure, it must have been actually looked into, as traces of text revisions left on the paper can be spotted (figure 21). Texts of the same kind are often seen in traditional Chinese bibliographies of Christian books.[7]

---

6. *CCT ZKW XB* vol. 20, 38–52.
7. Xu, *MingQingjian yesuhuishi yizhu tiyao*, 93.

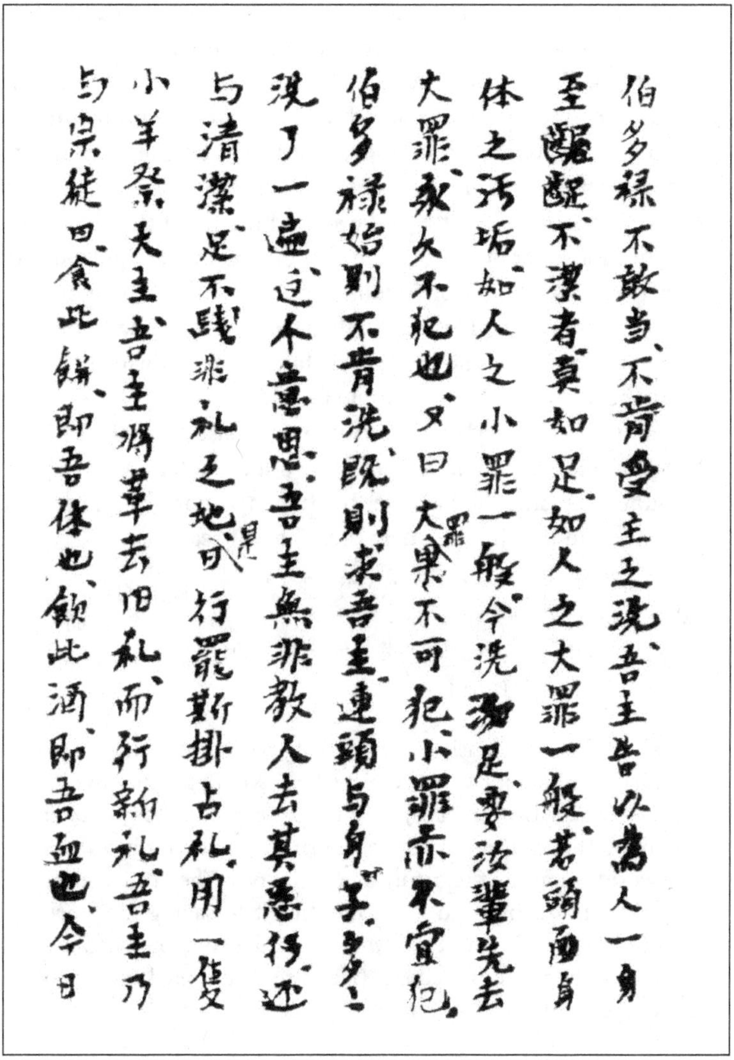

伯多禄不敢当、不肯受主之洗、吾主告以為人一身
至醜醒不潔者莫如足、如人之大罪一般、若頭而身
体之汚垢如人之小罪一般、今洗却足、要汝輩先去
大罪、永久不犯也、又曰大罪不可犯、小罪亦不宜犯、
伯多祿始則不肯洗、既則求吾主連頭與身、洗多之
洗了一遍、這不是吾主無非教人去其惡後還
与清潔足不踐非礼之地、或行罷斯掛古礼用一隻
小羊祭天主吾主將羊去旧礼而行新礼吾主乃
与宗徒囘食此餅、即吾体也、領此酒、即吾血也、今日

Figure 21

Zhounian zhanli kouduo: Orations on Feast Days in a Liturgical Year

Zhounian zhanli kouduo is of the same kind. Its author is unknown but is probably Lu Xiyan 陸希言 (1630–1704), a Chinese Jesuit and catechist. This book contains short daily sermons for 374 successive days in an ecclesiastical year, from January 1690 until January 1691.[8] What I consult is a handwritten copy consisting of eight volumes facsimiled in *CCT BnF*.

In this book, the footwashing text is found in the third volume that covers a period from January 18 in 1690, which was a Wednesday before Sunday Septuagesima, until March 25 in 1690, which was an Easter Sunday. It is marked in the Chinese lunar calendar that the sermon text was to be given on March 11 in 1690, the twelfth in the second month of the lunar calendar in the twenty-ninth year of Kangxi Emperor (1654–1722, reign 1661–1722). That was a Thursday, the day of establishing the Eucharist. Imagine a group of Chinese Christians in a village in Southern China listening to their priest, or a local leader if there was no priest available to them. During the course of the sermon, the footwashing story would be told.

As examined earlier with the narrative analysis, the footwashing story in the text of *Zhounian zhanli kouduo* is introduced after a very long opening. The author explains the Passover by drawing upon the Chinese Lunar New Year's Eve and the shift to a new rite. The text reads:

> 巴斯卦。譯言過去之日。似吾中國之除夕。而年[?]也。除夕者。除舊而生新也。天主降生救世。取肉身之性。而于是日成救世之功。贖世之罪。使人得有復生之日。亦除去其古教之禮。而行新教。

> "Passover" (is) a translated word that speaks for a day in the past. (It is) alike our Chinese New Year Eve. Regarding the . . . the "New Year Eve" (means) to remove the old and to give birth the new. The Heavenly Lord was born (in Incarnation) to save the world, adopting the nature of a flesh body. Then (it is) at this day that (he) completed the achievement of saving the world and redeemed the sin of the world, in order to allow people to have of a chance to be reborn. (He) also abandoned the rite of his old teaching but implemented the new teaching.[9]

The entire narration starts with this opening and proceeds with a focus on redemption and ultimate salvation. A particular feature of this piece is that the author's voice is so overwhelming that the story is absorbed as part of his own speech. To put it in another way, the footwashing narrative in *Zhounian zhanli kouduo* is constantly cut into segments because of the author's interpolation. For instance, there is an extra line added for Jesus that is not included in the prototype, which has been analyzed earlier. The words of Jesus are:

8. See CCT Database.
9. *CCT BnF* vol. 9, 561–63.

> 我久願同汝輩食罷斯卦于我受難之前。此後不同席矣。

"I have for a long time desired to eat the Passover with you before I receive suffering. After this, (we) will no eat together."[10]

This line has its reference to Luke 22:15–16. Subsequent to it, an inference follows. The author adds a long interpretation of the preparation of the Passover dinner. The stress is still on salvation and redemption. The text continues:

> 命徒設席。件件俱若預先安定者。則知吾主之受苦難死之日。亦是預定者。非人所能為。非人所敢亂也。吾主預定此日。以成救贖之功。

(Jesus) commanded the apostles to set up the feast, everything (was) all (prepared) as had been arranged and settled in advance. (From this scene) then (we) know that the date of our Lord to receive the suffering to death had also been destined beforehand. That is not what human could do, that is not what human could intervene. Our Lord preserved this day, in order to complete the achievement of salvation.[11]

Just after the final speech that closes the footwashing narrative, the author again explores the words of Jesus. In order to make those words reach the ears and the hearts of listeners, the author recaps the footwashing episode with a lesson given to his audiences. The text reads:

> 吾主降生為人受難死。死後復活升天去矣。吾主人之性不能復接吾人。吾人不能復見吾主之聲容。故臨終猶特愛。惟教吾人互相親愛。然後可為吾主之徒。吾人欲師吾主。則當效法吾主。聽從吾主之訓。

Our Lord was born and suffered to death for people. After the death, (he) resurrected, raised up to sky/heaven, and left. The human quality of our Lord cannot connect us anymore. We cannot again see the sound and face of our Lord. Therefore, (he) particularly love (us) very much before the end, (he) so taught us to care and love each other, and after (that we) can be followers of our Lord. We want to call our Lord teacher, then (we) should imitate our Lord, obey the lecture of our Lord.[12]

10. *CCT BnF* vol. 9, 561–63.
11. *CCT BnF* vol. 9, 561–63.
12. *CCT BnF* vol. 9, 561–63.

What is next in this book is still the author's preaching and educative talk. The narration that resonates the footwashing prototype or resembles other Chinese versions is only a small portion; the rest of this text belongs to the author articulating and elaborating on the story. The effort as such facilitates the communication of the footwashing story and salvation message to audiences.

In the book of *Zhounian zhanli kouduo*, sermons on other days in the ecclesiastical year also were written in this way. The general instruction was coherent and accessible to commoners, and the language style was fluent without losing elegance. The actual use and circulation of this book are not well known yet, except that this text was constantly revised and rearranged.[13] Xu Zongze, the church historian and bibliographer, once referred to *Zhounian zhanli kouduo* as "jiangdao shu" (講道書), meaning "a book for preaching Christian teachings."[14] His observation was based on a copy of *Zhounian zhanli kouduo* made in 1822. In other words, this book was in circulation and actually consulted from 1690, when the first sermon was prepared, to the following one hundred years.

Kouduo richao: Oral Admonitions Collected in Written Journal

Kouduo richao collects a Chinese Christian's notes on European missionaries' preaching. It was compiled by Li Jiubiao 李九標 (?-1646?) in Fujian Province, and the missionaries recorded therein were four Jesuits, mainly Giulio Aleni, but also Andrius Rudamina, SJ (1596–1631), Bento de Matos, SJ (1600–1651), and Simão da Cunha, SJ (1589–1660). These records covered the years between March 1630 and July 1640. Moreover, questions posed by Chinese audiences and discussions between the missionaries and their friends also were included. According to the compiler Li Jiubiao, he regularly jotted down oral admonitions and communication that later became this book, *Kouduo richao*. He said, "Since the gengwu year (1630), after I had established close relations with the two masters, I spent all the time I had in frequent encounters. Sometimes we came together in church; sometimes we met at informal occasions; sometimes a master would address me [and start the conversation], or friends would stimulate me [to ask questions]. In the end my notes came to fill a book-wrapper."[15]

As a result, the book of *Kouduo richao* chronologically documents sermons and daily conversations. It is interesting to note that, along with

---

13. See CCT Database.
14. Xu, *MingQingjian yesuhuishi yizhu tiyao*, 93.
15. Zürcher, *Kouduo Richao*, 11.

"kouduo" texts to be used by clergies to prepare sermons (such as the ones like *Tianzhu shengjiao kouduo* and *Zhounian zhanli kouduo*), *Kouduo richao* seems to be a Chinese audience's strong testimony to interactions between the missionaries and their audiences in local Christian communities. The author's note-taking methods can lead us to a better understanding of how the sermons of missionaries were transferred to the Chinese Christian's journal. The footwashing text allows access for us to probe further.

The footwashing story is found as part of the note on the Maundy Thursday March 20, 1636, the feast day of Jesus establishing the Eucharist. Different from sermons on paper, this note starts by describing and citing from his priest. The text begins:

十四日。耶穌定[　]聖體瞻禮。先生曰。欲領聖體。先宜謙。宜潔。宜彼此相愛。昔[　]耶穌將立此禮。各濯宗徒之足。

On the fourteenth, the day of Jesus establishing the rite of the Eucharist. Teacher says, "In order to receive the Eucharist, (one) had better firstly be humble, be clean, be caring and loving each other. Anciently when Jesus established this rite, he washed the apostles' feet one by one."[16]

The missionary, whom Li Jiubiao called teacher, recounted the footwashing story, and Li noted down the missionary's words. Hence, the footwashing story ended up in the journal of Li on that day. It was not just a diary for Li Jiubiao himself to study; rather, he intended it to be distributed among more people who were willing to learn of Christianity. Through this piece, the footwashing story could be heard beyond small gatherings of missionaries and their immediate audiences.

Gradually taking shape day by day, *Kouduo richao* built a channel to send words of missionaries to people who were not present at sermons. To readers in the broader public, it was a medium to gain access to the inner circle of Christian communities. The target readership of *Kouduo richao* was "tonghao zhe" (同好者) which, in Chinese, means "minds that think alike." Those minds encompassed potential allies such as friends and future colleagues that the compiler Li Jiubiao met in provincial and capital cities when attending the civil service examination. After reading *Kouduo richao*, they may become interested in engagements with Christianity and become "fellows" of Li in the sense of religious faith.

In one of the prefaces to *Kouduo richao*, another Chinese Christian scholar and contributor to the compilation of this book, Lin Yijun 林一儁

16. *CCT ARSI* vol. 7, 421–23.

(?–?), advocated, "What is this Richao ("Diary")? They are the notes made by my friend Li Qixiang (= Li Jiubiao) for the benefit of fellow-believers while he constantly was waiting upon the two masters."[17] The "fellow-believers" or "fellow-sympathizers" were fellows to the Christian, Li Jiubiao, consisting of Chinese catechumen, classmates, relatives—all of whom had converted but had less opportunity to meet priests in person. Li Jiubiao and contributors like Lin Yijun documented the journals in this book to spread the word and pass on Christian messages to the broader circle.

Collecting "kouduo" was only part of this book's composition; "richao" was the part that facilitated circulation of oral admonitions and conversations. This "richao," meaning "daily copying and writing," was a traditional composition and literary exercise of Chinese lettermen. Repeatedly copying words from Scriptures and masters was especially regarded as an essential devotional practice. Having sermons documented in the form of "richao" was a devotional practice of these Chinese Christian scholars.

Erik Zürcher once translated "richao" into "diary" and regarded it as a kind of protocol to record sermons and dialogues because only a mere fraction of words spoken have been preserved in writing.[18] This view can be expanded through two more nuanced observations. First, "richao" was a study habit of Chinese students. It made its debut in the Song Dynasty (906–1279); for example, *Huangshi richao* 黃氏日抄 collected excerpts from Confucian classics and commented upon them with exegetical notes. This sort of books gained increasing popularity during the Ming and Qing; Chinese degree holders in the dominant literary culture then must be very familiar with them and the traditional exercise. Second, well-educated readers must enjoy reading and writing books in the form of "richao" because it was practiced in composing later Chinese Christian texts too. Another Chinese Christian scholar, Wu Li 吳歷 (1632–1718), wrote *Xu kouduo richao* 續口鐸日抄 (ca. 1698), which was also widely circulated and welcomed as a continuation of the legacy of *Kouduo richao*.

Tianjiao mingbian: Distinguished Heavenly Teaching

The book of *Tianjiao mingbian* is another kind of personal composition by the aforementioned Chinese Christian scholar Zhang Xingyao. Current studies about this book gradually bring it into view, yet more research is needed.[19] My focus is on its compilation—in particular, its intertextual

---

17. Zürcher, *Kouduo Richao*, 183.
18. Zürcher, *Kouduo Richao*, 11.
19. Mungello, *The Forgotten Christians of Hangzhou*, 70–91; Xiao, "'Qiutong' yu

relations to other Christian texts. The copy that I consult is a manuscript facsimiled in *CCT ZKW XB*.

If *Kouduo richao* can be described as a compilation of five hundred notes "about everything," in comparison, *Tianjiao mingbian* is about more.[20] *Tianjiao mingbian* elaborates on theological matters of Christianity, ranging from aspects regarding Catholic teachings, doctrines to rituals, and even subjects on metaphysics. The writing is based on Zhang Xingyao studying Chinese Christian texts prior to it. Generally speaking, Zhang studied Christian subjects by reading earlier Christian books prepared by missionaries; he then cited, paraphrased, and synthesized some parts of those books into this one; moreover, Zhang included his digest and reflections upon certain passages and noted down his exchanges with other Chinese Christian scholars.

Same Story by Two Authors for Different Readerships

The footwashing text found in *Tianjiao mingbian* also has a source text. As the earlier three-layer analysis has presented, the version of the footwashing story in *Tianjiao mingbian* stands alongside the version extracted from the text of *Shengti yaoli* at every fabula-layer element. They differ slightly from each other at the story-layer and the text-layer matters. Such a similarity suggests a one-on-one textual relation between the two versions, and there is one. The footwashing text in *Tianjiao mingbian* (figure 22) is patterned after the footwashing text in *Shengti yaoli* (figure 23).

'bianyi'"; Yang, "Tianxue zai Qingchu de chuanbo."

20. Zürcher, *Kouduo Richao*, 7.

天主之心故聖若望有言曰人自謂愛慕天主而不
能与弟兄互相親愛者非真能愛天主者也何也現前
兄弟共居共處習見習聞尚且如是豈未見未親之天
主猶能愛慕乎故能愛天主者未有不愛人也夫此二德
昔日吾主耶穌已親身行之以示我矣蓋当其受難前夕
欲立聖體大礼先脫衣一盤欲為宗徒濯足宗徒惶愧謝
不敢吾主曰倘我不濯尔足尔不相涉也宗
徒聽命濯畢又曰尔輩非以我為師為主者乎然我且濯
尔足尔輩亦相当互相濯足相下相愛以徵為我徒也歟
十三

Figure 23

Reading both pieces together and focusing on their respective authors' words can shed light on our understanding of the Chinese Christian scholar's composition.

At first glance, it seems as if the footwashing text in *Tianjiao mingbian* is simply copied from *Shengti yaoli*. However, a few changes are made, and the small yet significant changes show variances of the two pieces in terms of expressions, phrases, and formats, all of which would impact readers differently. I explain the different reading experiences using four examples.

First, whenever referring to a person of Jesus Christ in Trinity, the text in *Tianjiao mingbian* particularly adds a one-character space prior to those references. There always is a space before "wuzhu" (吾主), meaning "our Lord"; "dazhu" (大主), meaning "grand Lord"; "tianzhu" (天主), meaning "Heavenly Lord"; and "yesu" (耶穌), meaning "Jesus." It is significant to see that the handwritten copy of *Tianjiao mingbian* has such a formatting system while the print of *Shengti yaoli* does not, because the blank space characterizes a special role of those references to Jesus Christ. Reserving space in a traditional Chinese book is a convention used to underscore the importance of whatever follows the space, presumably to capture readers' attention. Usually, when an emperor or king is referred to in official documents, this formatting applies. Similar customs appear in earlier Chinese Christian texts too but are more obvious and consistent in later ones. Adding this feature to the book of *Tianjiao mingbian* suggests that the names of the Christian Trinity's three persons were divine or supreme in Zhang's eyes, no less than how the kings or emperors should be respected in books.

Second, a brief narration of Abraham washing the feet of visitors is added in *Tianjiao mingbian* to back up the story of Jesus washing his disciples' feet. This is not the case of the version in *Shengti yaoli*. The *Tianjiao mingbian* text reads:

> 又教規有旅遠來者。哀矜舍之。亦代為濯足。
>
> Another rule of the teaching, (if) there are travelers coming from afar, (one should) offer them supplies with empathy and also wash feet for them.[21]

This anecdote has its biblical reference in Genesis 18:1–8, and Zhang Xingyao may have learned about the Old Testament story from other books. It is drawn to add another positive layer to make the footwashing story less foreign as the hospitality demonstrated in Abraham's washing is welcomed in the Chinese society and very familiar to general readers. It helps to make a good impression of the biblical narrative on people outside of the Christian community. The same story in *Tianjiao mingbian* immediately becomes easier to accept for a broadened readership than in *Shengti yaoli*, which is an instruction for practicing Christians and catechumen.

Third, some phrases and sentences are rewritten in the text of *Tianjiao mingbian* to suit its readership, which is beyond that of *Shengti yaoli*. In *Shengti yaoli*, the footwashing story is for readers to learn about receiving the Eucharist. But *Tianjiao mingbian* has an alternative frame. Just after narrating the footwashing event, both texts explain the the rite as a church tradition. In the text of *Tianjiao mingbian*, the pope is explanatorily referred to as "xiguo jiaowang" (西国教王), which means "king of the teaching in Western

---

21. *CCT ZKW XB* vol. 10, 490–97.

countries"; in the text of *Shengti yaoli*, the same role is "taixi jiaozong" (泰西教宗), which is a coined Chinese term to present the pope in the institutional church openly. The author's intervention makes the text of *Tianjiao mingbian* more accessible for the public outside the Christian community.

Fourth, there are still minor alternations, all of which cannot be meticulously listed. For instance, the text of *Tianjiao mingbian* uses simplified variants to replace some characters of complicated strokes (such as using "尔" instead of "爾"). Some expressions are remodeled in *Tianjiao mingbian* too (such as "ciwei" 此為 instead of "ciju" 此舉). Tiny changes such as these accumulate; together, they make the text of *Tianjiao mingbian* easier and more inviting to readers, especially more friendly to audiences with basic literacy.

A Book to Uphold One's Christian Conversion

The footwashing text, with its connection to the sourcebook *Shengti yaoli*, shows an example. The entire writing of *Tianjiao mingbian* involves as references many Chinese Christian books attributed to European missionaries. As the book itself indicates, these references include *Shengjing zhijie*, *Yanxing jilüe*, *Kaitian baoshi* 開天寶匙, *Dake wen* 答客問 (ca. 1643), *Buru wengao* 補儒文告 (1664), and many more. There are still other sources without clear references; some can be identified, but not all. Zhang Xingyao stated that he took earlier books of the Heavenly Teaching, omitting the complex and adapting the simple, as in his own words, "qu tianjiao zhishu shanfan jiujian."[22] (取天教之書刪繁就簡)

Responding to earlier books is a traditional way of learning and writing for Chinese students. The same still holds true for Chinese Christian scholars. Chloë Starr rightly states that Chinese theology is "a theology that does not just draw from the church and reflect back church thinking but asks readers to comment on and add to the debates as the texts are written and circulated."[23] *Tianjiao mingbian* is exemplary in this regard. It is a result of Zhang Xingyao's personal writing on the basis of reading and reflecting upon passages from existing Christian books. To put it in another way, the book of *Tianjiao mingbian* is Chinese Christian scholar Zhang Xingyao in dialogue with earlier Christian texts.

Through selecting, editing, and rewriting the referenced sources, Zhang collected a rich and comprehensive overview of Christian subjects and expressed his thinking. He achieved a major step in composing *Tianjiao*

---

22. *CCT ZKW XB* vol. 6, 8.
23. Starr, *Chinese Theology*, 3.

mingbian; that is, to reshape missionaries' teaching and guidance into words independently written by Chinese laity. When Christianity, a religion that was rooted in another culture, was conveyed entirely from a Chinese letterman's perspective, the arrival of Christianity in China was completed.

Moreover, as a book of a Chinese scholar, *Tianjiao mingbian* would be welcomed by larger audiences. Educated minds in traditional Chinese society appreciated this kind of compilation. Readers would be more inclined to welcome this book than those authored by missionaries—let alone readers who had no direct contacts with European missionaries. In addition, Zhang spoke of his personal experience in learning Christianity, which was a major selling point of *Tianjiao mingbian*. Especially to outsiders, it would be very intriguing to see how Zhang called out other religions in China as distinctive from Christianity.

Its author, Zhang Xingyao, had several goals in writing this book. First, he desired to announce his conversion in public and to defend this choice. Considering himself a truth seeker, Zhang argued that he seized the opportunity to know the true God in learning Christianity. Zhang challenged the "foolish Confucians," in his words, who considered themselves Confucians yet behaved as Mohists and Buddhists. He argued that his conversion was an imitation of Confucius because he followed what Confucius said: "If a man in the morning hears the right way, he may die in the evening without regret." To Zhang Xingyao, the "right way" in his time could be found only in Christianity.[24]

Also, he wanted to use this book as a tool to fight against other traditions. Zhang believed that Christianity was the true Confucianism, and Christian rituals could supplement what Confucianism lacked. He reasoned that his fellow countrymen followed Buddhists and Daoists only because of their ignorance of Christianity.

More ambitious is that he intended *Tianjiao mingbian* to persuade peer scholars and officials to come along with him. He wanted this book "to let readers know the grace of redemption by 'tianzhu shangdi' (天主上帝) that means Heavenly Lord God, the hardships and determination for scholars from the far West [European missionaries] to come to save souls, and perhaps to allow them [readers] to live through their life and die peacefully." Zhang Xingyao believed that with the Christian teaching presented in *Tianjiao mingbian*, they could arrive in the land he dreamt of as "a society wherein people live in harmony, which was to restore the ruling of Tang and Yu in today's world."[25]

24. *CCT ZKW XB* vol. 6, 6–8.

25. *CCT ZKW XB* vol. 6, 8. Tang and Yu are believed to have been the earliest and

When he was still preparing the manuscript, *Tianjiao mingbian* was already circulated locally among friends and colleagues in his social network, some of whom also contributed to the compilation. But the aftermath of this book may not have satisfied the author's expectation. Zhang Xingyao mentioned a plan to print his manuscript; yet, no printed version of *Tianjiao mingbian* has been spotted so far; rather, several handwritten copies are preserved even today.[26] It is hence not clear yet how those copies were distributed, how the printing plan was executed or abandoned.

Documents on the reception of this book are still needed. In spite of that, *Tianjiao mingbian* should have engaged in deep conversation and developed intercultural hermeneutics. As the Chinese church historian Xu Zongze witnessed, this book did effectively promote Christianity against other religions because it concisely contained a large range of Christian theological topics to rebut the falsehoods of Buddhism and Daoism. He commented that *Tianjiao mingbian* was a thesis to study "dao" (道), which means "the way" and figuratively means "the truth."[27]

---

best kings in Chinese history.

26. Known copies are preserved in the Zikawei Library in Shanghai and the National Library in Beijing.

27. Xu, *MingQingjian yesuhuishi yizhu tiyao*, 121–22.

Part III

Divergent Narratives in Versatile Texts

THIS PART CLUSTERS CHINESE footwashing texts that are less complicated than the previous examples, as they contain fewer narrative components to make more straightforward deliveries. These versions diverge further from the prototype, and they are incorporated in disparate compositions that are lined up with the Chinese literature and book culture of the time. There are fourteen books in the array: *Pangzi yiquan* 龐子遺詮, *Tizheng bian* 提正編, *Jincheng shuxiang* 進呈書像, *Shengjiao yuanliu* 聖教源流, *Wanwu shiyuan* 萬物始元, *Yesu shengti daowen* 耶穌聖體禱文, *Moxiang gongfu* 默想工夫, *Jinshan lu* 進善錄, *Sizi jingwen* 四字經文, *Tianxue mengyin* 天學蒙引, *Song nianzhu moxiang guitiao* 誦念珠默想規條, *Sizheng enyan* 思正恩言, *Chaoxing liyin* 超性俚吟, and *Qike zhenxun* 七克真訓.

Chapter 11 is patterned after chapters 3 and 7. It shows fourteen renditions of the prototype, although these versions are not as diversified as seen in the previous parts. The other three chapters group the fourteen Chinese Christian books according to their compositions. Chapter 12 introduces books open to outsiders. Chapter 13 presents books serving insiders to foster their religiosity in terms of doctrinal learning and imagistic exercise. Six particular texts are introduced in chapter 14, as it focuses on their creatively distinct composite features shaped in the Chinese literary tradition.

The footwashing stories collected in this part deviate from the prototype, very often some texts losing major narrative components. In addition, another special profile of these texts can be observed, in that texts of similar genres and readerships are conveying more or less the same messages. For example, books for outsiders usually avoid associating washing feet with the Eucharist; on the contrary, texts for insiders' religiosity often put stress on the Eucharist, if not only the Eucharist. While incorporating all the biblical texts, the books presented in this part are especially fascinating. Their composite forms and styles manifest their target readerships. The readerships include learned readers as well as those with a basic education or even the uneducated.

11

Reinvented Versions in Differing Compositions

This chapter shows fourteen Chinese footwashing narratives. Some texts are found in books available to outsiders, including *Jincheng shuxiang*, *Pangzi yiquan*, and *Tizheng bian*. Some are contained in books primarily for insiders to foster their different modes of Christian religiosity, such as catechetical books *Wanwu shiyuan* and *Shengjiao yuanliu*, prayer books, and meditation manuals *Yesu shengti daowen*, *Song wuzhu yesu nianzhu guicheng*, *Moxiang gongfu*, and *Jinshan lu*. Some versions also are incorporated in books mainly for insiders, but their compositions stand out distinctively; that is the case with *Sizi jingwen*, *Tianxue mengyin*, *Sizheng enyan*, *Chaoxing liyin*, and *Qike zhenxun*.

The numbers of footwashing fragments are more than the combination of the previous parts, but the ways to render the prototype's narrative components are not that diverse. In most versions, the footwashing story is streamlined with simplified fabula layers and story layers, and there are still different ways to simplify the original biblical prototype.

Fabula-Layer Elements

With the protagonist Jesus and actors Peter and Judas, the primary fabula-layer elements of the footwashing prototype include setting and plot. According to John 13:1–15, the setting is the Passover dinner, and the plot consists of three sections, namely, Jesus preparing the washing of the apostles' feet, Jesus conversing with Peter, and Jesus leaving a lesson in the end.

These principal fabula-layer elements of the Latin pericope become varied in different Chinese versions. There are basically three ways to make changes: to leave out an element, to retain an element as it is in the prototype, and to reframe an element with certain twists. In the versions soon to be introduced in this chapter, fabula-layer elements are often lost and simplified.

Other kinds of changes still can be spotted in the sorted collection of these versions, all of which generally deviate from the prototype.

Settings

The original setting lies in verses 1–3. The backdrop for the footwashing event takes place at the dining table when the Passover dinner was finished. More specifically, the Latin pericope describes the situation as that Jesus knew about his return hour, and he loved the world to the end. These verses highlight a discourse of farewell. Other themes (such as the Eucharist and the passion) are implied as well in the Gospel.

This fabula-layer element is put differently in these Chinese versions. None of them has a setting that resonates with the prototype. The version in the text of *Sizi jingwen* has a fabula-layer setting that encompasses the original details the most. However, its narration is composed in a distinct form of Chinese verses, not even comparable with the biblical pericope. The text reads:

知期已到　　自願受難
難未到時　　預言來事
受難前夕　　巴斯卦禮
濯足宗徒　　定聖體儀

(He) knew the time had come, willingly (prepared to) receive sufferings.

The suffering had not yet arrived, (he) foretold things in the future.

Before the passion, it was the rite of Passover.

(He) washed the feet of the apostles and established the ritual of the Eucharist.[1]

In other versions, the prototype's setting is simply missing. It is completely omitted in the footwashing texts in prayer books *Yesu shengti daowen* and *Song nianzhu moxiang guitiao* and in other compositions like *Chaoxing liyin* and *Qike zhenxun*. The story in these versions is not introduced or situated but simply appears. For instance, the footwashing narrative in both texts of *Yesu shengti daowen* and *Song wuzhu yesu nianzhu moxiang guitiao* is a one-sentence prayer. The text of *Yesu shengti daowen* reads:

---

1. *CCT ARSI* vol. 2, 340–41.

爲爾至謙之德。濯爾門弟足者。　　主救我等

For your greatest virtue of humility in washing your disciples' feet.　　Lord, save us.²

The text of *Song wuzhu yesu nianzhu moxiang guitiao* frames the same story with different wording but still in one-sentence length. It reads:

十九想　　　　　　吾[ ]主親濯宗徒之足。

The nineteenth thought　　Our Lord in person washed the apostles' feet.³

Short or poetic sentences as such also possess narrativity that "makes artifacts narrative, grabs and holds the attention," as Mieke Bal argues.⁴ The narrative analysis describes specific segments of non-narrative texts and the narrative aspects of any text. T. S. Eliot's poems can be an object of analysis, so can the prayers that deliver the biblical story, although they contain only a few narrative components.

A series of texts reframe the prototype's fabula-layer setting by underscoring certain discourses. When John 13:1 and John 13:3 speak for the inner thought of Jesus on his returning hour, the footwashing event is placed in a farewell discourse. However, none of the Chinese versions collected in this part stresses the moment of separation. On the contrary, some versions emphasize other discourses.

In the text of *Tizheng bian*, the key word "Eucharist" is firstly proposed in a question, and then, the footwashing story also is brought up as part of the question. Its answer sets off to elaborate on the meaning of washing the apostles' feet. It is the question that raises the topic on the Eucharist to situate the story. The text of *Tizheng bian* reads:

或問　　耶穌定立聖體前。親濯宗徒之足。何意。

Someone asks, "Before establishing the Eucharist, Jesus in person washed the feet of the apostles. What does this mean?"⁵

Also adopting the question-and-answer form, another Chinese text, *Shengjiao yuanliu*, places the footwashing story entirely in an answer. It reads:

---

2. *CCT BnF* vol. 18, 295.
3. BnF Chinois 7349, f. 4b.
4. Bal, *Narratology*, 10.
5. BnF Chinois 6942, vol. 6, f. 30.

曰。解明耶穌將要建定聖體大禮。先脫上衣。親手拿水盆。下跪宗徒面前。一個一個洗他的腳。

(One) answers, "(In order to) clearly explain that he was going to establish the grand rite of the Eucharist, (Jesus) at first took off his top garment, with his own hands took a water basin, kneeled in front of the apostle, washed his feet one by one."[6]

The version in *Jinshan lu* highlights both the Eucharist and the passion without touching upon the departure discourse, as seen in the Latin pericope. The text of *Jinshan lu* reads:

吾主耶穌建定聖體大禮　　耶穌將受難之前一夕。先與宗徒濯足。

Our Lord Jesus established the grand rite of the Eucharist. Just one night before he was going to receive the suffering, Jesus at first washed feet for the apostles.[7]

As explained previously, the passion is expressed in Chinese as "shou-nan" (受難), a collocation that means "receiving sufferings." It is used in the text of *Jinshan lu*, and the text of *Jincheng shuxiang* uses the same phrasing. The version in the text of *Jincheng shuxiang* succinctly starts:

耶穌將受難。固命宗徒聽其濯足。

When Jesus was about to endure suffering, therefore, he ordered his disciples to allow him to wash their feet.[8]

The text *Sizheng enyan* poetically pictures the sadness of Jesus and subtly refers to one kind of suffering, but with another wording that does not immediately reflect upon the passion. The text reads:

主值離憂更欿然

Lord, when suffering from worries, filled with a sadness deeper and deeper.[9]

---

6. *CCT BnF* vol. 23, 105–6.
7. *CCT BnF* vol. 25, 101–3.
8. Standaert, *An Illustrated Life of Christ Presented to the Chinese Emperor*, 244. The translation is adjusted to emphasize the Chinese conjunction "gu."
9. *CCT BnF* vol. 22, 597.

The text of *Moxiang gongfu* underlines the presence of Judas at the event, which diverges from the prototype's mention of Judas and is not seen in any other Chinese versions. Focusing on Judas, the text reads:

且吾主被难之先。夜會宗徒於堂。茹荅斯亦在其內。吾主明識其賣己于願己死之敵人。而犹以聖手洗濯其足。並與之得領主之聖體。

Moreover, our Lord, before he (had to) accept the suffering, met the disciples at night in a hall, and Judas was among them. Our Lord clearly knew that Judas had sold him into the hands of the rivals who wanted him to die. Nevertheless, (Jesus) still washed the feet of Judas with his holy hands and allowed him to receive the Lord's holy body.[10]

This version even confirms that Jesus washed the feet of Judas, who was also allowed to receive the Eucharist. Another Chinese version calls special attention to Judas too, but in a distinct manner. The text of *Pangzi yiquan* expands the footwashing prototype's fabula-layer setting with a long narration. It reads:

耶穌所言死期既至。嘗以預告十二徒。曰。我自訂受難而死。今其時矣。受難先一日。耶穌與其徒行罷斯卦之禮。...而同食羊羔。因謂其徒曰。爾輩中有一謀負我者。眾皆惕然。問耶穌曰。吾師。或是我乎。耶穌答曰。與我同納手於盤者是也。惜乎彼負我。不如未生矣。茹答斯乃曰。我師。是我乎哉。耶穌曰。爾自証矣。禮畢。

The time of death had arrived as Jesus had spoken of. Once (he) prognosticated (it) to the twelve apostles, saying, "I have planned by myself to receive sufferings to die. Now is the time." The day before the passion. Jesus with his apostles conducted the rite of the Passover. . . . (Jesus and the apostles) were eating the lamb together, then (he) said to his disciples, "Among you there is one plotting to abandon me." They were all alerted and asked Jesus, "Our teacher, maybe is that me?" Jesus replied, "Whose hand is taken together with mine in the plate is it. How shameful! The one who will betray me, it is less good as if he has never been born." Judas then said, "My teacher, is that me?" Jesus said, "You prove yourself." The (Passover) rite finished.[11]

---

10. *CCT BnF* vol. 22, 384–86.
11. *CCT ARSI* vol. 2, 63–65.

This passage at first introduces the time frame just before the footwashing event. Its sketch includes the Synoptic Gospels' account of conversations occurring at the Passover dinner, whereas other versions' settings only mention the dinner. The narration summarizes Mark 14:12–21, Luke 22:7–17, and Matthew 26:17–25. These accounts are integrated into the fabula-layer setting of this version. When matching these Chinese sentences with the Bible verses, one can find that the beginning corresponds to Luke 22:14, "When the hour came, he took his place at the table with the apostles." Continuously, the text of *Pangzi yiquan* inserts conversations between Jesus and Judas that resonate with Matthew 26:21–25. The Bible verses read:

> And while they were eating, he said, "Amen, I say to you, one of you will betray me." Deeply distressed at this, they began to say to him one after another, "Surely it is not I, Lord?" He said in reply, "He who dipped his hand into the dish with me is the one who will betray me. The Son of Man indeed goes, as it is written of him, but woe to that man by whom the Son of Man is betrayed. It would be better for that man if he had never been born." Then Judas, his betrayer, said in reply, "Surely it is not I, Rabbi?" He answered, "You have said so."[12]

There are still another two versions' settings to show in this chapter. The text of *Wanwu shiyuan* and the text of *Tianxue mengyin* both add extra descriptions to the backdrop of the footwashing event, but each has sources drawn from different materials, and each remodels the prototype's fabula-layer setting uniquely.

The version in *Wanwu shiyuan* explains what a Passover dinner is at the beginning. The narration is a synthesis of the accounts on the preparation of the Last Supper in the Synoptic Gospels. The explanation provides succinct background information that would serve audiences who had not enough prior knowledge about the Passover tradition. The text reads:

> 巴斯卦時。耶穌遣使徒俗庭而後親到之。依古禮偕徒食羊羔。此所謂主晚飡也。

> While the Passover (drew upon), Jesus dispatched the apostles to prepare the (dining) hall and then afterward, he arrived himself. According to the old rite, (he) ate the lamb together with the disciples. This is what is called the dinner of the Lord.[13]

---

12. Matt 26: 21–25 (NAB).
13. *CCT BnF* vol. 13, 416–20.

The version in the text of *Tianxue mengyin* devotes extended words on this matter. It situates the footwashing event in a broad context that includes a series of narrations from the return of Jesus to the city of Jerusalem to Judas Iscariot in contact with the temple's priests for money. The Passover dinner also is presented in an extravagant manner. All is composed in Chinese verses similar to stanza. The footwashing text in *Tianxue mengyin* starts:

耶穌受難因期定
承期瞻禮入都城
羣民聞得耶穌至
通都歡擁折花迎
惡黨見得難輕舉
即在徒中誘一人
受得銀錢三十餅
對惡相商夜可擒
是日古來佳節氣
家家宴餉一羔羊
耶穌此日同徒宴
心痛今宵苦自傷

For Jesus to receive suffering by the time had been destined.

At the time for the feast day, he entered the capital city.

People crowd hearing about the arrival of Jesus,

They filled the entire city with happiness and picked flowers to welcome him.

The evil rivals saw the difficulty to take an action (to hurt Jesus) freely,

Then they seduced one among the disciples.

(Judas) obtained thirty pieces of silver money,

And conferred with the evil ones that they could capture Jesus in darkness.

This day was an auspicious festival since the ancient time,

Every family ate a feast of the lamb.

Jesus on this day dined with the disciples.

(He) felt heart-broken for this evening and himself bitterly saddened.[14]

Preparations

The Latin prototype's plot is carried out in three stages: the preparatory actions of Jesus, the conversations between Jesus and Peter, and the final speech of Jesus. As for the preparation, there are six successive movements expressed in verbs. It is recorded in the pericope that Jesus rose from supper and took off his outer garments, took a towel and tied it around his waist, poured water into a basin and began to wash the disciples' feet, and dried them with the towel around his waist.

The previous parts have demonstrated all sorts of Chinese versions that are similar to or different from the original portrayal of Jesus. As far as the versions in this chapter are concerned, none contains the sequential movements that are the same as the prototype. Most of them leave out this element, except for four texts.

The versions in both texts of *Sizheng enyan* and *Tianxue mengyin* sketch the actions of Jesus in a regulated verse form, although differently. The text of *Tianxue mengyin* mentions Jesus pouring water into a basin. Its lines read:

束腰注水于盆裡

濯足于徒顯誼長

(He) girdled the waist and poured water into the basin.

(He) (wanted to) wash feet for the disciples to manifest the friendship long.[15]

The text of *Sizheng enyan* has only one line to depict that Jesus loosened his clothes in preparation for the washing. The verse reads:

解衣手滌門生足

(Jesus) loosened clothes and washed the feet of his students with his own hands.[16]

---

14. BnF Chinois 7065, f. 8b.
15. BnF Chinois 7065, f. 8b.
16. *CCT BnF* vol. 22, 597.

The other two versions are respectively located in the texts of *Shengjiao yuanliu* and *Pangzi yiquan*, both in prose form. They seem to focus on the interactions between Jesus and the apostles. The text of *Shengjiao yuanliu* reads:

先脫上衣。親手拿水盆。下跪宗徒面前。一個一個洗他的腳。

(Jesus) at first took off his top garment, with his own hands took a water basin, kneeled in front of the apostle, washed his feet one by one.[17]

This narration specifies that Jesus kneeled before washing and that he washed both feet of Peter, with neither detail existing in the prototype. In the singular form of the word apostle "zongtu" (宗徒) in Chinese, this text states that Jesus "washed his feet one by one." The possessive pronoun "his" should allude to Peter's, but this statement is seldom seen in other Chinese versions.

The version in the text of *Pangzi yiquan* is an exception too. It at first numerates that Jesus gave a command to twelve apostles, and then it spells out that Jesus washed their feet one after another. The text reads:

耶穌命十二徒列坐。自解上衣。戽水於盤。而各濯其足。

Jesus ordered the twelve apostles to sit one by one. He loosened the top clothes by himself, baled water in a basin, then washed their feet one after another.[18]

Three Conversations

The second section of the prototype's plot consists of Jesus having conversations with Peter. In the Latin pericope, Peter asked, "Master, are you going to wash my feet?" Jesus answered, "What I am doing, you do not understand now, but you will understand later." Continuously, Peter kept saying, "You will never wash my feet." Jesus replied, "Unless I wash you, you will have no inheritance with me." Finally, Peter changed his attitude and said, "Master, then not only my feet, but my hands and head as well." Jesus responded, "Whoever has bathed has no need except to have his feet washed, for he is clean all over; so you are clean, but not all." These are three sets of conversations recorded in John 13:6–10.

17. *CCT BnF* vol. 23, 105–6.
18. *CCT ARSI* vol. 2, 63–65.

158　PART III: DIVERGENT NARRATIVES IN VERSATILE TEXTS

The Chinese versions in this chapter present a few possibilities to deal with the three conversations, because most of them completely drop this element. In some texts, the role of Peter even disappears. Only two versions incorporate the interactions between Jesus and Peter: the text of *Tianxue mengyin* and the text of *Qike zhenxun*.

In the version in *Tianxue mengyin*, part of what Jesus said in the prototype is encompassed, although the text itself is written in a short and regulated verse form. The original line of Peter is paraphrased. His role is actually transferred to the disciples as the text uses "jie" (皆) to refer to all the apostles. It reads:

門徒乍聽皆惶悚
誰敢相從褻至尊
耶穌謂爾今還昧
久後方知迥不群
似今不濯汝曹足
則必難云我後昆
門徒聞此方承命

Suddenly listening to (Jesus that he was about to wash their feet), the apostles were all frightened.

Who would dare to follow (that order, letting their feet to be washed by Jesus,) to insult the mightiest one?

Jesus told them, "You are still unaware,

(you) would finally know much later (that we shall) be separated, not being together.

It seems that if (I) do not wash your feet today,

then (you) must hardly claim as my descendants."

The disciples upon hearing this eventually received the command.[19]

The version in *Qike zhenxun* is the opposite. Peter is the main character in this piece. Not only does the role and speech of Peter in the prototype remain, but the original line of Peter also is rewritten dramatically. Instead, what is missing is what Jesus said in the Latin pericope. This version reshapes the footwashing story from a contrast between Jesus and Peter to a manifestation of the virtue of humility from both sides. The text reads:

---

19. BnF Chinois 7065, f. 8b.

主又要洗宗徒之足，聖伯多祿謙辭曰。你爲天地眞主。我乃至賤罪人。你洗我足。何敢當乎。

Lord also was going to wash the feet of the apostle. Saint Peter said in a modest speech, "You are the true lord in heaven and earth, (but) I am the most unworthy sinner. You to wash my feet, how dare I accept it?"[20]

Final Speeches

The last part of the footwashing prototype's plot is the final speech of Jesus portrayed in John 12–15. The Latin pericope presents the words of Jesus, "Do you realize what I have done for you? You call me 'teacher' and 'master,' and rightly so, for indeed I am. If I, therefore, the master and teacher, have washed your feet, you ought to wash one another's feet. I have given you a model to follow, so that as I have done for you, you should also do." In these four sentences, Jesus enlightened his disciples, and the pericope closes.

Not all of the four sentences are included in every Chinese version, but the majority of versions analyzed in the previous parts retain at least some of the speech of Jesus. As for the texts collected in this chapter, only three have this element, and they are the versions in the texts *Jinshan lu*, *Pangzi yiquan*, and *Tizheng bian*. Even so, none of them corresponds to the original pericope. Each version contains only a portion of what Jesus said in the prototype.

The texts of *Pangzi yiquan* and *Tizheng bian* have the words of Jesus that resonate with John 13:13–15; however, the lines are not equivalent to the Bible verses but have been rewritten. For instance, the last verse of the pericope reads, "I have given you a model to follow, so that as I have done for you, you should also do." However, the Chinese text requires a condition for the disciples to claim themselves as followers of Jesus that they should love each other and wash each other's feet as Jesus did. The text of *Pangzi yiquan* reads:

爾稱我爲師爲主。我實是也。我爲師且主。猶濯爾足。正示爾宜自相濯。即相遜相愛。若果能相愛。即此徵爲我徒也。

You call me as master, as lord. I indeed am. I, being master and lord, still wash your feet. (This) exactly shows you that yourself had better wash feet to each other. That is, be humble to each

---

20. The copy is available in the library at Hong Kong Baptist University, f. 52.

other, and love each other. If (you) truly can love each other, this immediately certifies that (you) are my followers.[21]

The same line of Jesus is rendered again but differently in the version in *Tizheng bian*. It adopts a rhetorical question to stress the role of Jesus himself as master and lord. In the text of *Tizheng bian*, Jesus said:

爾輩非以我爲師爲主者乎。然吾且濯爾足。爾輩亦當互相濯足相下。以徵爲我徒也。

"Don't you people consider me as master as lord? Nevertheless, I still wash your feet. You people also should wash feet to each other and lower yourself to each other, in order to certify (you) as my followers."[22]

The speech of Jesus is shortened in the text of *Jinshan lu*. Only the last two sentences in John 13:14–15 are encompassed. The words of Jesus therein are:

我既為師且主。猶濯尔足。正示尔宜互相洗滌。相遜相愛。以徵為我徒也。

"I, now being master and lord, still wash your feet. (This) exactly shows you that you had better wash each other, be humble to each other, and love each other, in order to certify (you) as my followers."[23]

Story-Layer Aspects

The story layer of the footwashing prototype consists of two matters, namely presentational models and focalization principles. Both are shaped by the narrator John's perspective based on the fabula-layer elements. Chinese versions also alter the two story-layer aspects. The texts shown in the previous parts have represented a great variety of the Chinese versions' story-layers. The ones in this chapter bring about some other renditions of the original footwashing storyline.

---

21. *CCT ARSI* vol. 2, 63–65.
22. BnF Chinois 6942, vol. 6, f. 30.
23. *CCT BnF* vol. 25, 101–3.

Presentational Modes

The prototype's presentational modes work on presenting two specific fabula-layer elements: one is the fabula-layer setting, and the other is the speech as part of the fabula-layer plot. For presenting each, a specific technique is involved. The prototype adopts prolepsis to situate the footwashing event by foretelling the forthcoming departure of Jesus from the world and from his disciples. And the lines of the actors during the footwashing event are given in direct speech.

In the original pericope, the narrator John refers to other events in the near future while reading the inner thought of Jesus. This storytelling method is called "prolepsis." Some of the Chinese versions follow the John verses, such as the ones in the texts of *Sizi jingwen*, *Jincheng shuxiang*, *Jinshan lu*, *Tizheng bian*, *Shengjiao yuanliu*, and *Sizheng enyan*. They introduce their footwashing stories by first putting what would happen later. For example, the text of *Jincheng shuxiang* opens its narration with a point of time in the future that Jesus was going to experience suffering. It uses a conjunction "gu" (固), meaning "therefore," to create an obvious linkage between the passion and the footwashing event. The text begins:

耶穌將受難。固命宗徒聽其濯足。

When Jesus was about to endure suffering, therefore, he ordered his disciples to allow him to wash their feet.[24]

Other versions that apply the prolepsis as the prototype do refer to the passion but in combination with either the departure of Jesus or the Eucharist. With this or that discourse to highlight, they all mention a future event in advance while presenting their fabula-layer settings.

Some versions use an opposite way of introducing their footwashing story, and that is called "analepsis." They usually play flashback and synchronize the Gospel accounts of the Last Supper. The version in the text of *Tianxue mengyin* is a typical case. The text reads:

耶穌受難因期定
承期瞻禮入都城
羣民聞得耶穌至
通都歡擁折花迎
惡黨見得難輕舉
即在徒中誘一人

---

24. Standaert, *An Illustrated Life of Christ Presented to the Chinese Emperor*, 244. The translation is adjusted to emphasize the Chinese conjunction "gu."

受得銀錢三十餅
對惡相商夜可擒
是日古來佳節氣
家家宴餉一羔羊
耶穌此日同徒宴
心痛今宵苦自傷

For Jesus to receive suffering by the time had been destined.

At the time for the feast day, he entered the capital city.

People crowd hearing about the arrival of Jesus,

They filled the entire city with happiness and picked flowers to welcome him.

The evil rivals saw the difficulty to take an action (to hurt Jesus) freely,

Then they seduced one among the disciples.

(Judas) obtained thirty pieces of silver money,

And conferred with the evil ones that they could capture Jesus in darkness.

This day was an auspicious festival since the ancient time,

Every family ate a feast of the lamb.

Jesus on this day dined with the disciples.

(He) felt heart-broken for this evening and himself bitterly saddened.[25]

    The above lines are all set just to introduce the background of the footwashing event. Such a long narration encompasses a series of narratives prior to the Passover dinner documented in the Synoptic Gospels, including the return of Jesus to Jerusalem and the deal Judas made with the temple priests. The flashback covers these scenes that had occurred before the Passover dinner; thereby, the text of *Tianxue mengyin* extends its time frame to a point before the footwashing event. In a similar but more straightforward manner, the versions in the texts of *Pangzi yiquan* and *Wanwu shiyuan* also use analepsis. Their settings cover only the preparation of the Passover dinner, which has been analyzed in the previous section.

---

25. BnF Chinois 7065, f. 8b.

Both prolepsis and analepsis are standard techniques to introduce an event in a narrative; however very often, neither is used in many Chinese texts grouped in this part. When a version leaves out its fabula-layer setting, naturally, it does not involve a presentational mode to present the non-existent setting. Their narration of the footwashing event should appear out of context, which is the case of the versions in the texts of *Yesu shengti daowen*, *Song wuzhu yesu nianzhu moxiang guitiao*, *Chaoxing liyin*, and *Qike zhenxun*. As the fabula-layer analysis shows, the one-sentence prayer respectively in *Yesu shengti daowen* and *Song wuzhu yesu nianzhu moxiang guitiao* stands alone as one narrative unit. The text of *Qike zhenxun* juxtaposes its footwashing narrative alongside another story without involving any context.

Regarding the mode for presenting speeches, the prototype directly shows the words of Jesus and Peter in the form of citation. Chinese versions do not always accord with the prototype. Some use direct speech, whereas some indirectly report the speeches. As for the versions collected in this chapter, only several incorporate this fabula-layer element. The texts of *Qike zhenxun*, *Tianxue mengyin*, *Jinshan lu*, *Tizheng bian*, and *Pangzi yiquan* adopt direct speech to present the lines of Jesus or Peter. Although the content of what the characters said in these versions do not exactly follow the prototype, their techniques are the same.

Unlike the versions examined in the previous two parts, the majority of the texts in this part leave out the characters' lines. It is interesting to note, in the texts of *Jincheng shuxiang* and *Wanwu shiyuan*, that what Jesus said in his final instruction in the Latin pericope is converted to the author's interpretation. The text of *Jincheng shuxiang* reads:

固命宗徒聽其濯足。示謙也。

Therefore, he ordered his disciples to allow him to wash their feet as a manifestation of humility.[26]

This is not a paraphrase of the words of Jesus; rather, the lesson of washing feet is inferred and subsumed as part of the narration. The same occurs in the version in *Wanwu shiyuan*, when the text reads:

洗諸徒之足。以設相事之法。而成其潔。

(Jesus) washed every apostle's feet, in order to set a rule on how to serve each other, and to help them to achieve their cleanliness.[27]

26. Standaert, *An Illustrated Life of Christ Presented to the Chinese Emperor*, 244. The translation is adjusted to emphasize the Chinese conjunction "gu."

27. *CCT BnF* vol. 13, 416–20.

In the prototype, the purpose of washing the apostles' feet is expressed in the speech of Jesus. However, in this version, the words of Jesus are omitted. The contents of the last verses in the original pericope become not even an indirect speech reported by the narrator but a message spelled out and inserted to conclude the story by the author.

Another two versions are exceptional at this matter. The texts of *Chaoxing liyin* and *Sizheng enyan* do incorporate what Jesus said in the Latin pericope but rewrite them entirely. It may not be proper to categorically label them as direct or indirect speech due to their writing forms. The text of *Sizheng enyan* reads:

解衣手滌門生足

入座聲明師傅權

千古愛情無限意

長留芳躅望年年

(Jesus) loosened clothes and washed the feet of his students with his own hands.

(He) returned to the seat and declared his authority as the master.

With forever love, care, and unlimited meanings,

(He) had left a virtuous example and expected others to follow year after year.[28]

In the above poem, the second line echoes the final speech of Jesus in John 13:13 wherein Jesus said, "You call me 'teacher' and 'master,' and rightly so, for indeed I am." This sentence is loosely paraphrased in the Chinese verse and transformed as part of the narration. The last two lines are sentimental. Rather than conveying the instruction of Jesus as in the prototype, they express compassion and devotion.

The text of *Chaoxing liyin* is a different case. In a similar composition, it reads:

親行濯足示謙光

提命諄諄黯自傷

幸喜我徒能継述

一宗萬派教無疆

---

28. *CCT BnF* vol. 22, 597.

(Jesus) personally performed the footwashing to show the honor of humility.

(He) exhorted (the apostles) earnestly and tirelessly but himself saddened inside.

"Fortunately, my followers could carry on (the lesson of washing feet).

The (Christian) teaching rooted in one origin with numerous branches (spreads) without borders."[29]

The second line of this poem portrays Jesus as lecturing the apostles but feeling gloomy himself. The seven characters sum up the original plot on Jesus giving the last speech. In the third line, the phrase "wotu" (我徒) means "my followers" or "my disciples"; the first-person possessive pronoun "my" indicates that what Jesus said are in direct quotations. Although representing the words of Jesus, the last two lines do not resonate with the verses in the original pericope or any other Chinese texts. They freely render what Jesus spoke to the disciples. The significance of this rendition is meant to call upon readers of this text to invoke their compassion.

Focalizations

Presentational modes modify how the narrator presents what he sees, but what he sees is determined by the narrator's lens. Some scenes are framed within the lens while some are not. As the narrator's lens moves, the focalization changes both in space and time. The moving lens from one spot to another and from one moment to another create two dimensions—spatial and temporal—to navigate the story layer of a narrative text.

Each footwashing text engages with certain focalizations in a spatial dimension. In the original footwashing pericope, the role of Jesus always occupies the focus as a protagonist. Meanwhile, the lens is generally in a panoramic mode to cover the whole group of disciples during the event.

All the Chinese versions that have been analyzed so far have a panoramic vision as they keep the disciples in the spotlight. Some even provide dramatic portraits to Peter or the group. However, not every text collected in this part develops this view. The disciples must appear since they are receivers of the footwashing action. But they do not necessarily appear in a panoramic vision. In many cases, they are out of the spot without being portrayed. As for the texts of *Sizi jingwen* and *Qike zhenxun*, the

29. *CCT ZKW XB* vol. 17, 48.

focal point is always and exclusively on Jesus, and no line or action of the disciples is highlighted.

The footwashing story in *Sizi jingwen* has a limited focalization with its spotlight on Jesus only. Jesus is the sole subject throughout this book. By way of avoiding endless repetition, the writing even omits the name or pronoun that can refer to Jesus. The text reads:

知期已到　自願受難
難未到時　預言來事
受難前夕　巴斯卦禮
濯足宗徒　定聖體儀

(He) knew the time had come, willingly (prepared to) receive sufferings.

The suffering had not yet arrived, (he) foretold things in the future.

Before the passion, it was the rite of Passover.

(He) washed the feet of the apostles and established the ritual of the Eucharist.[30]

Some versions do give a stage to other characters beyond Jesus, but still within a limited spatial focalization. The text of *Qike zhenxun* is an interesting example in this regard. It features both Peter and Jesus, but it makes a counterpoint by focusing its spotlight on Peter exclusively. The text reads:

主又要洗宗徒之足，聖伯多祿謙辭曰。你爲天地眞主。我乃至賤罪人。你洗我足。何敢當乎。

Lord also was going to wash the feet of the apostle. Saint Peter said in a modest speech, "You are the true lord in heaven and earth, (but) I am the most unworthy sinner. You to wash my feet, how dare I accept it?"[31]

Using a confined vision of a role other than Jesus is usually seen in the Chinese versions collected in this chapter. Very often, either Peter or Judas is included, not both. It is Peter in the text of *Qike zhenxun*; the version in *Moxiang gongfu* features Judas. The text of *Moxiang gongfu* gives Judas a special place but manifests the leniency and grace of Jesus. According to this

---

30. *CCT ARSI* vol. 2, 340–41.
31. The copy is available in the Library at Hong Kong Baptist University, f. 52.

version, Jesus used his hands to wash the feet of Judas. The unworthier Judas is, the more virtuous is Jesus. The text of *Moxiang gongfu* reads:

且吾主被难之先。夜會宗徒於堂。茹荅斯亦在其內。吾主明識其賣己于願己死之敵人。而犹以聖手洗濯其足。並與之得領主之聖體。

Moreover, our Lord, before he (had to) accept the suffering, met the disciples at night in a hall, and Judas was among them. Our Lord clearly knew that Judas had sold him into the hands of the rivals who wanted him to die. Nevertheless, (Jesus) still washed the feet of Judas with his holy hands and allowed him to receive the Lord's holy body.[32]

In addition to these, some versions zoom out another element with focalization, and that is the role of feet. There are several texts in the previous part developing the exegetical significance of feet. As for the ones in this chapter, only the version in *Jincheng shuxiang* pays extra attention to feet. Neither Peter nor Judas is in the spotlight, and the whole story is simplified in this text. It concentrates on the image of feet by drawing an analogy between feet and the feeling of the human heart. The text reads:

足比人心之情。身因足行。心因情行。其義正等。耶穌知其愛情之猶未純也。故濯其足。

Feet can be compared with the feelings of the human heart. A body walks because of its feet and the heart acts because of its feelings. The meaning is exactly the same. Jesus knew that their feeling of love was still not pure and therefore he cleansed their feet in order to teach them to keep their feelings pure and genuine.[33]

The other dimension of focalization is temporal. The moving lens can form a stream of storytelling with sequentially arranged moments; otherwise, a story does not involve changes in time but is a collection of scenes. In the footwashing prototype, what is used is sequential focalization, as the narrator John's lens shoots different moments with a sequence.

Some Chinese versions in this part do not involve time sequences, such as the texts of *Yesu shengti daowen*, *Song wuzhu yesu nianzhu moxiang guitiao*, *Sizi jingwen*, *Jincheng shuxiang*, *Qike zhenxun*, and *Chaoxing liyin*. Most of them are very short in making a narration. The one-sentence-long

---

32. *CCT BnF* vol. 22, 384–86.
33. Standaert, *An Illustrated Life of Christ Presented to the Chinese Emperor*, 244.

prayers are in this category. For instance, the prayer in the book of *Song wuzhu yesu nianzhu moxiang guitiao* is:

十九想　　　　　　　　吾[ ]主親濯宗徒之足。

The nineteenth thought　　Our Lord in person washed the apostles' feet.[34]

This one-sentence narrative omits any temporal points due to its brevity. However, it is only the inherent temporal complexity that it skips. The moments recorded in the prayers in this book follow a sequential order, and the footwashing event is just one instance within the circle. Before and after the footwashing prayer, which is the nineteenth, the eighteenth prayer is on Jesus and the disciples conducting the ancient rite of Passover, and the twentieth is on Jesus establishing the new rite of Eucharist. This arrangement gives the footwashing instance a sort of temporal sense externally.

Deriving from this prayer in the book of *Song wuzhu yesu nianzhu moxiang guitiao* are the footwashing texts in *Sizheng enyan* and that in *Chaoxing liyin*. Both are written in rhymed verse form. The version in *Sizheng enyan* features many moments with a temporal sequence; on the contrary, the version in *Chaoxing liyin* does not.

In the text of *Chaoxing liyin*, there is no obvious clue for the footwashing event to move forward in time. The whole story is situated in an expansive vision, especially when its last verse reads:

一宗萬派教無疆

The (Christian) teaching rooted in one origin with numerous branches (spreads) without borders.[35]

The focalization of this version thus lacks a timeline, and its storyline lacks temporal transition. In contrast, the version in the text of *Sizheng enyan* has both. The second line of *Sizheng enyan* underscores a moment when Jesus was worried. It sets a specific time for the footwashing storyline to unfold. The line reads:

主值離憂更欷然

Lord, when suffering from worries, filled with a sadness deeper and deeper.[36]

---

34. *BnF Chinois* 7349, f. 4b.
35. *CCT ZKW XB* vol. 17, 48.
36. *CCT BnF* vol. 22, 597.

From this moment onward, the subsequent narration flows. Not only the beginning, but the last two lines of this text also create a broadened vision, so that a long-term timeline runs through the entire poem. The lines read:

千古愛情無限意
長留芳躅望年年

With forever love, care, and unlimited meanings,

(He) had left a virtuous example and expected others to follow year after year.[37]

Other versions operating with time sequences show a great diversity of ways to indicate time flow. For instance, the text of *Wanwu shiyuan* uses adverbs such as "afterward," in Chinese "hou" (後), and prepositions such as "during," in Chinese "jian" (間), to clearly indicate temporal proceeding. The text reads:

巴斯卦時。耶穌遣使徒備庭而後親到之。依古禮偕徒食羊羔。此所謂主晚飱也。飱間。

While the Passover (drew upon), Jesus dispatched the apostles to prepare the (dining) hall and then afterward, he arrived himself. According to the old rite, (he) ate the lamb together with the disciples. This is what is called the dinner of the Lord. During the meal...[38]

The versions in the texts of *Tizheng bian* and *Pangzi yiquan* use the same word to signal time transition. The character "bi" (畢) means "the end" in Chinese. It is to mark that the washing had been done before Jesus instructed the apostles on the lesson. The text of *Tizheng bian* reads:

耶穌滌畢宗徒之足云。

Jesus completed washing the feet of the apostles and said.[39]

The text of *Pangzi yiquan* reads:

濯畢。謂之曰。

(Jesus) finished the washing, spoke to them.[40]

37. *CCT BnF* vol. 22, 597.
38. *CCT BnF* vol. 13, 416–20.
39. BnF Chinois 6942, vol. 6, f. 30.
40. *CCT ARSI* vol. 2, 63–65.

The text of *Shengjiao yuanliu* has an adverb "xian" (先), meaning "at first," in order to arrange the actions of Jesus for preparing the washing. It reads:

先脫上衣。親手拿水盆。

(Jesus) at first took off his top garment, with his own hands took a water basin.[41]

The footwashing story in the text of *Tianxue mengyin* employs a sequential focalization with more crafted words. Its narration encompasses different moments, scenes and events, all in the course of consecutive order. The storyline of what happened unfolds from the Passover dinner to the inner sadness of Jesus, to his preparation for washing the feet of the disciples, his words said to the group of apostles, the group's reaction and change of attitude, and then to the washing of the disciples' feet and Jesus changing his clothes and beginning to eat again. The text of *Tianxue mengyin* reads:

是日古來佳節氣
家家宴餉一羔羊
耶穌此日同徒宴
心痛今宵苦自傷
束腰注水于盆裡
濯足于徒顯誼長
門徒乍聽皆惶悚
誰敢相從褻至尊
耶穌謂爾今還昧
久後方知迥不群
似今不濯汝曹足
則必難云我後昆
門徒聞此方承命
濯後更衣進晚飱

This day was an auspicious festival since the ancient time,

Every family ate a feast of the lamb.

Jesus on this day dined with the disciples.

(He) felt heart-broken for this evening and himself bitterly saddened.

41. *CCT BnF* vol. 23, 105–6.

REINVENTED VERSIONS IN DIFFERING COMPOSITIONS 171

(He) girdled the waist and poured water into the basin.

(He) wanted to (wash) feet for the disciples to manifest the friendship long.

Suddenly listening to (Jesus that he was about to wash their feet), the apostles were all frightened.

Who would dare to follow (that order, letting their feet to be washed by Jesus,) to insult the mightiest one?

Jesus told them, "You are still unaware,

(you) would finally know much later (that we shall) be separated, not being together.

It seems that if (I) do not wash your feet today,

then (you) must hardly claim as my descendants."

The disciples upon hearing this eventually received the command.

(Jesus), after the washing, changed his clothes to have dinner.[42]

This text is written in the form of rhymed verses. It creates a succinct narration with crafted expressions to highlight every move in time. Therein, a complex time travel entails many points in a time that are represented by adverbial expressions including but not limited to: "shiri" (是日), meaning "this day"; "jinxiao" (今宵), meaning "this evening"; "jiuhou" (久後), meaning "finally much later in the future"; and "zhuohou" (濯後), meaning "after the washing feet action." These Chinese vocabularies collectively mark transitions between different times, recollecting the past, presenting the present, and alluding to the future. Along with these signals, the focalization of the footwashing story in this text moves. It departs from the feast day of the Passover dinner, then stops at the dinner in the evening. While putting Jesus and the disciples in the spotlight, the focalization captures the footwashing event and moments in the future.

Another two instances are adjusting their temporal focalizations. The books of *Jinshan lu* and *Moxiang gongfu* are both meditation manuals. Unlike the previously examined meditation texts, *Chuxiang jingjie* and *Moxiang shengong*, which chop their footwashing stories into discontinuous scenes to contemplate, these two texts put the footwashing story as one unit for readers to meditate upon. The versions in the texts of *Jinshan lu* and *Moxiang gongfu* also incorporate temporal turning points to unfold their storylines. For example, the text of *Jinshan lu* uses the adverb "xian" (先),

42. BnF Chinois 7065, f. 8b.

meaning "at first," to entail a time sequence. This character places the footwashing as the first main action of Jesus before the passion. The text reads:

耶穌將受難之前一夕。先與宗徒濯足。

Just one night before he was going to receive the suffering, Jesus at first washed feet for the apostles.[43]

Text-Layer Words and Messages

Fabula-layer elements and story-layer aspects are expressed in words, which already convey messages of a narrative. The question that remains as part of the three-layer analysis is what text-layer messages are delivered in each text, and how each text produces potential exegetical effects through linguistic arrangements. In the Latin pericope of John 13:1–15, the author's messages for readers of the Gospel of John are expressed with spoken and unspoken words that generate interpretations from multiple perspectives. As the previous two parts have shown, at least four discourses can be associated with the original footwashing narrative. It is a symbol of the separation of Jesus from his disciples and from the world; it is also a symbol of salvation because of what Jesus said to Peter. For those who wash others' feet, it promotes the virtue of being humble and serving others; for those who receive the washing, it is considered spiritual cleaning before receiving the Eucharist.

As of the four interpretations, every Chinese version has its own way to incorporate them, in part or full. Even for expressing the same meaning, many Chinese texts use different wording that indicate their respective readerships. When it comes to the versions collected in this part, it is interesting to note that they all relate their footwashing story to one empirical interpretation, which is to view washing of the feet as a manifestation of the virtues of modesty, service, and caring love to others. In different writing forms and styles, they all point out that Jesus washing his disciples' feet is a reversal of social convention and a moral lesson. I will not repetitively explain this matter in the following examination of each text.

Due to their various compositions, the texts in this part have disparate text layers. Their wordings are barely comparable; nevertheless, it is still plausible to gather messages of the footwashing narrative conveyed through each text. To start with, the text of *Pangzi yiquan* embodies a complete set of the four dimensions to interpret its footwashing story. It speaks

---

43. *CCT BnF* vol. 25, 101–3.

about the separation of Jesus from his apostles and the salvation at the very beginning. The text starts:

> 耶穌所言死期旣至。嘗以預告十二徒。曰。我自訂受難而死。今其時矣。受難先一日。耶穌與其徒行罷斯卦之禮。

> The time of death had arrived as Jesus had spoken of. Once (he) prognosticated (it) to the twelve apostles, saying, "I have planned by myself to receive sufferings to die. Now is the time." The day before the passion. Jesus with his apostles conducted the rite of the Passover.[44]

The above text from *Pangzi yiquan* introduces the Passover dinner, during which Jesus spoke of the death, the passion, his original plan and willingness to suffer. The narration of these scenes does not exist in the prototype. These extra words link the footwashing event to its soteriological-Christological significance as they spell out the sacrifice that Jesus made due to love. This beginning already suggests that the footwashing event is an indicator of separation and a sign of love and ultimate salvation. Following an opening like this, this version continues narrating the footwashing event. Another ethic-moral lesson is then expressed by directly presenting the final words of Jesus, as explained earlier.

In the version in the text of *Tianxue mengyin*, messages are also conveyed through the fabula-layer speech, more specifically, the words of Jesus. The text reads:

> 耶穌謂爾今還昧
> 久後方知迥不羣
> 似今不濯汝曹足
> 則必難云我後昆

> Jesus told them, "You are still unaware,
>
> (you) would finally know much later (that we shall) be separated, not being together.
>
> It seems that if (I) do not wash your feet today,
>
> then (you) must hardly claim as my descendants."[45]

In this version, the original line of Jesus to Peter is rendered in a unique way. Other Chinese versions usually adopt words such as "xiang" (享) or

---

44. *CCT ARSI* vol. 2, 63–65.
45. BnF Chinois 7065, f. 8b.

collocations like "xiangshe" (相涉) to express the prototype's "having part of me." The versions in *Shengjing zhijie* and *Yanxing jilüe* set an example in this regard, which has been explained previously. However, the text of *Tianxue mengyin* lays the stress on the symbolic meaning of the footwashing event as separation. In this version, Jesus said to the apostles that he would no more be with them after washing their feet.

The text of *Moxiang gongfu* also expresses this symbolic meaning. It situates the footwashing event in a context where Jesus was meeting the apostles before he was seized. The text reads:

且吾主被难之先。夜會宗徒於堂。

Moreover, our Lord, before he (had to) accept the suffering, met the disciples at night in a hall.[46]

In addition, this version in the text of *Moxiang gongfu* conveys the ethic-moral significance of washing feet by taking an interesting approach. It emphasizes that Jesus washed the feet of Judas, through which its footwashing story demonstrates moral lessons on service, humility, and forgiveness. The footwashing text is placed in a section in the book of *Moxiang gongfu*, and it has a headline that literally points out the virtue of lenience. The text reads:

耶穌甘忍茹苔斯奸徒謀害。尚以友呼之。

Jesus willingly tolerated the plot of the villainous disciple Judas, still calling him a friend.[47]

The moral value is exemplified by Jesus, the agent of washing feet. As an experience, the footwashing activity can be viewed from the perspectives of both sides: the agent shows the virtue of service and modesty; the receivers of the washing benefit from it as their feet become clean after the washing. Physical cleaning is easy to understand as linked to spiritual cleansing, which alludes to the making of confession before receiving the Eucharist. Some Chinese versions focus on the effect of having one's feet cleaned. In the texts of *Shengjiao yuanliu*, *Jinshan lu*, *Wanwu shiyuan*, and *Tizheng bian*, the footwashing story is interpreted as a prerequisite for one to receive the Eucharist.

In the version from the text of *Shengjiao yuanliu*, the messages of washing feet are spelled out in the text-layer author's words. The author

---

46. *CCT BnF* vol. 22, 384–86.
47. *CCT BnF* vol. 22, 384.

interprets the motivation of Jesus and speaks to audiences about it at the same time. The author states:

> 解明耶穌將要建定聖體大禮。. . . 立個衆人該學法謙遜相幫服事的樣子。另外教我們。凡要領聖體。必須先痛悔解洗諸罪。

> (In order to) clearly explain that he was going to establish the grand rite of the Eucharist . . . . This is to set an example that people should learn and model after on how people should be modest to each other, help and treat each other. In addition, (this is) to teach us that everyone to receive the Eucharist must at first do penance and confession to wash and resolve all sins.[48]

The omitted part narrates the occurrence of the footwashing event. In the words of this fragment, the virtue of humility and the effect of cleansing are jointly explained. The author of *Shengjiao yuanliu* reasons why Jesus washed his disciples' feet. At first, he elaborates on the virtue of humility as Jesus had set an example. In saying "lingwai jiao women" (另外教我們), which means "in addition, (this is) to teach us," the author instructs his audiences on another message of washing feet. He advises the audiences to wash away their sins before receiving the Eucharist.

In the text of *Jinshan lu*, the footwashing story is simple, in comparison to other Chinese versions. However, the author's interpretation reinforces two meanings of this version. The entire text of *Jinshan lu* consists of two passages, with one on the footwashing narrative and one on the author's interpretation. The entire text reads:

> 一想吾主耶穌建定聖體大禮　　耶穌將受難之前一夕。先與宗徒濯足。且諭之曰。我既為師且主。猶濯尔足。正示尔宜互相洗滌。相遜相愛。以徵為我徒也。

> 然先濯宗徒之足。而後賜之領聖體者。必也先潔其心。毫無罪垢。又謙下其志。以卑自處。及大發愛[ ]天主與愛人之真情者。方可領受斯恩。迎[ ]天主降臨吾心。以增諸恩德也。

> Our Lord Jesus established the grand rite of the Eucharist.
> Just one night before he was going to receive the suffering, Jesus at first washed feet for the apostles. And, (he) instructed them in saying, "I, now being master and lord, still wash your feet. (This) exactly shows you that you had better wash each other,

---

48. *CCT BnF* vol. 23, 105–6.

be humble to each other, and love each other, in order to certify (you) as my followers."

As such, (Jesus) firstly washed the feet of the apostles and then granted them to receive the Eucharist. That (sequence of firstly washing and secondly giving the Eucharist indicates that the apostles) must clean their heart at first, making them free from sins and foul matters, and then (they should) make their own wills humble, to place themselves in a lowly position. And (moreover), only the ones greatly express their genuine compassion for loving the Heavenly Lord and caring people can receive and accept this grace, welcome the Heavenly Lord to descend into my heart, in order to increase all of (His) blessings.[49]

The text of *Wanwu shiyuan* presents a similar case in terms of decoding messages of the footwashing story in the author's words. It uses linguistic signals to make the suggestion. Part of the author's narration reads:

... 以設相事之法。而成其潔。

... in order to set a rule on how to serve each other, and to help them to achieve their cleanliness.[50]

In the above excerpt, the word "yi" (以) means "in order to" or "as a means to." It shows the logic that Jesus performed the footwashing for the purpose of cleansing his disciples. The text of *Wanwu shiyuan* seems subtle if comparing it to the wording of the text of *Tizheng bian*.

The version in *Tizheng bian* not only speaks of the biblical story but also addresses the audiences of the book. The text reads:

或問　　耶穌定立聖體前。親濯宗徒之足。何意。曰。約有二義。一示吾人領聖體前。身心罪汚。洗滌宜盡。一示吾人效法謙遜毋輒自矜。

Someone asks, "Before establishing the Eucharist, Jesus in person washed the feet of the apostles. What does this mean?" (One) says, "(There are) about two meanings. One is to show us that before receiving the Eucharist, sins, and filth on the body and in heart should all be cleaned thoroughly. The other is to show us that (we should) imitate the humility but not always praise ourselves."[51]

49. *CCT BnF* vol. 25, 101–3.
50. *CCT BnF* vol. 13, 416–20.
51. BnF Chinois 6942, vol. 6, f. 30.

This text invents a set of questions and answers between two interlocutors. The question is raised at first to bring in the footwashing account and its implication. In response, the answer to the meaning of washing feet naturally flows. According to *Tizheng bian*, Jesus left lessons on modesty and cleaning through the footwashing event, and the lesson was not only for the disciples but also for the current readers, as included in the Chinese word "wuren" (吾人), meaning "us."

The message on cleansing in relation to the liturgical sense of washing feet is sometimes left out in some versions. The books open to non-Christian readers may have done so on purpose. After all, the liturgical significance of the footwashing story is associated with the establishment of the Eucharist. To those outside the Christian circle, this message can hardly go through. The version in the book of *Jincheng shuxiang* is a great example in this regard. It does not mention anything about the Eucharist because the book was prepared specifically for a non-Christian emperor. The author's interpretation adds to the story a spiritual meaning that is vastly appreciated by Chinese.

The composition is delicately done in the text of *Jincheng shuxiang*. After briefly narrating the footwashing story, it draws an analogy between the feet and feelings of the heart, as I have mentioned in the previous section. The text reads:

足比人心之情。身因足行。心因情行。其義正等。耶穌知其愛情之猶未純也。故濯其足。

Feet can be compared with the feelings of the human heart. A body walks because of its feet and the heart acts because of its feelings. The meaning is exactly the same. Jesus knew that their feeling of love was still not pure and therefore he cleansed their feet in order to teach them to keep their feelings pure and genuine.[52]

In this text, cleansing feet is somehow explained as if purifying one's heart. Without invoking Christian confession and liturgical needs for receiving the Eucharist, this version still manages to portray the footwashing story as an experience of spiritual cleansing. More important is that righteousness, sincerity, and feelings are notions prevalent in Chinese culture. In terms of delivering the biblical story to its target audiences, the footwashing text of *Jincheng shuxiang* achieves a great success.

As I mentioned earlier, the moral value of the footwashing story is embodied in almost all the texts collected in this part. Partly, it is also

---

52. Standaert, *An Illustrated Life of Christ Presented to the Chinese Emperor*, 244.

because of the virtue of modesty, lenience, service, and loving care that are easily acceptable and respected in Chinese society, which is the only message conveyed in some versions. The text of *Qike zhenxun* communicates no other message to readers but the virtue of humility. The texts of *Yesu shengti daowen*, *Chaoxing liyin*, and *Sizheng enyan*, only highlight the virtue of humility too, although for an alternative reason. In the book of *Yesu shengti daowen*, the prayer following the footwashing text is on the rite of the Eucharist; so are the poems following their footwashing texts in the two books *Chaoxing liyin* and *Sizheng enyan*. Hence in these cases, it is not necessary to repeat the linkage between washing feet and the Eucharist in the process of telling the footwashing story.

By comparison, the versions collected in this part convey fewer meanings of the footwashing story than do the ones in the previous parts. Many Chinese texts convey several messages through one footwashing story by combining some of the four interpretations. But, in this part, there is not much complex integration, though the simplicity serves the genres and readerships of these books. For instance, the footwashing story is a straightforward one-line sentence in the texts of *Sizi jingwen* and *Song nianzhu moxiang guitiao*. There is no specific meaning assigned to that sentence. However, the simple narrative in the two books should facilitate readers' comprehension, memorization, and meditation. Readers were expected to digest and to recite that footwashing sentence. They would generate understanding and compassion in the context of using the two books. In this case, receiving messages of the footwashing story depended on readers and their reading practice. Some other texts gathered in this part have a similar situation, which I will explain later. The following chapters will demonstrate features of the compositions and functions of these books that bridge their footwashing stories and readerships.

12

Writings and Images for Outsiders to Learn of Christianity

THE WORKS INTRODUCED IN this chapter are three: an illustrated Christian book, *Jincheng shuxiang*, a compilation of argumentative treatises, *Pangzi yiquan*, and an apologetic work, *Tizheng bian*. They were initially prepared to promote Christian teachings among non-Christian audiences. By way of using imagery and scholarly writing, their compositions were in line with the literary currents and book culture of the time.

Jincheng shuxiang: Presenting an Illustrated Book to His Majesty

Jincheng shuxiang was a famous work presented to the Chongzhen Emperor (1611–1644, reign 1628–1644) in 1640 by Johann Adam Schall von Bell, SJ (1592–1666). The copy that I examine is preserved in the National Library of France. For reference, there is a critical modern edition available with an English translation of the text.[1]

Producing Illustrated Narratives for the Chinese Emperor

Jincheng shuxiang was initially produced as a Chinese substitute to a colored parchment booklet, *Life of Christ*, containing miniature paintings. The latter was compiled in 1617. It was a gift of the Duke of Bavaria Maximilian I (reign 1597–1651) to the Chinese emperor. In order to make it understandable and appreciable to the emperor, Johann Adam Schall supervised the project to make a Chinese equivalent. The original Latin words were translated and adjusted into Chinese, and the original Dutch and Flemish prints were reproduced by woodcut printing. Then there came the Chinese book, *Jincheng shuxiang*, illustrating the life of Jesus. It is interesting to note that the four

---

1. Standaert, *An Illustrated Life of Christ Presented to the Chinese Emperor*.

180   PART III: DIVERGENT NARRATIVES IN VERSATILE TEXTS

Chinese characters in the title says that it is a book of images to present to the emperor, but the theme on the life of Jesus is missing there.

What comes first inside the book is an image of the four evangelists (figure 24).

Figure 24

It is titled in Chinese "zong ti tu" (總題圖), meaning "an image of the overall theme." At the center of the image, it states that the Chinese words are all delivering the meaning of the Western language, which means

Latin. This front piece bridges *Jincheng shuxiang* and the European miniature booklet, explaining the gist of this illustrated Christian book and reminding its Chinese readers of the gift from Europe. An introduction accompanies it to sketch a timeline from the birth of Jesus until the late sixteenth century when missionaries arrived in China. Still, there are a series of other elements in the front matter: a preface by the author Schall, a short thesis to promote Christianity as the true teaching of the Lord of Heaven, a narrative piece on the tribute made by the three kings and that of the four evangelists, and a note to readers on how to read European books from left to right, which is different from the right-to-left vertical layout of traditional Chinese books. These paratexts that precede the body part of *Jincheng shuxiang* help readers understand this book better.

This book encompasses forty-six themes in the life circle of Jesus from the annunciation to the ascension, including the footwashing episode. Every theme throughout the book is demonstrated with two pages: one image in a page on the right, and one short explanatory text on the left page. The footwashing narrative that has been previously analyzed is just the explanatory text on that theme. There is another image to accompany the text. Together, the illustration and the text complete the presentation of the footwashing theme (figure 25).

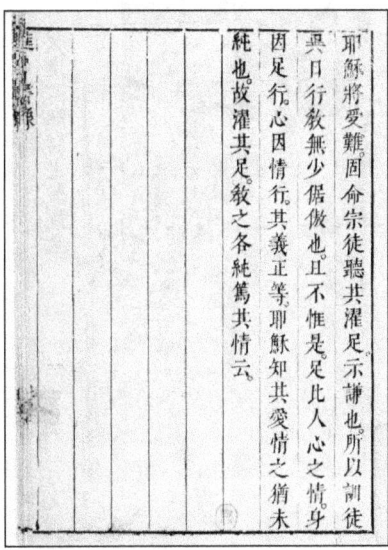 

Figure 25

In the book of *Jincheng shuxiang*, this image of Jesus washing the feet of the disciples is modeled upon *The Last Supper: The Washing of Feet* by

Theodore / Philippe Galle after Joannes Stradanus (Jan van der Straat; figure 26).[2] Although the Dutch print and the Chinese carving were executed in different materials with different techniques, the image on the Chinese page mirrors its European source almost in every detail.

29. Theodore Galle / Philippe Galle, after Joannes Stradanus (Jan van der Straat), *The Last Supper: The Washing of Feet*, in *Passio, mors, et ressvrrectio Dn. Nostri Iesv Christi*, Antwerpen, ca. 1575, no. 1, engraving, 196x152 mm.; Museum Plantin-Moretus / Stedelijk Prentenkabinet Antwerpen.

Figure 26

2. Standaert, *An Illustrated Life of Christ Presented to the Chinese Emperor*, 243.

What were rearranged at first are the frame and the way to deploy text and image on paper. While the European print has both image and text on the same page, the Chinese book renders its image and text respectively on two pages. The European page is framed with a sentence above the image and a description in the section below. In the Chinese book, the same image is given a title at its right side. To its left side, a piece of text is placed on a separate page to provide descriptions of the image. The rearrangement as such was made for Chinese readers, as placing text and image separately on two pages was a trending form of illustrated books at that time.

In addition, the Latin caption in the original image was not translated into Chinese. On the European page, the top section is about the account of Abraham offering to wash the three travelers' feet in the Old Testament. It reads:

> Et dixit Abraham—Afferam pauxillum aquæ, et laventur pedes vestri. Gen 18.[3]

This sentence can be traced back to what Abraham said in the first part of the Genesis 18:4. However, the Chinese title on this page in *Jincheng shuxiang* is irrelevant to the Latin reference. Pointing out the theme of the footwashing done by Jesus, the Chinese title is:

天主耶穌濯足垂訓像

Image of the Heavenly Lord Jesus washing feet to leave lessons[4]

The exact wording "zhuozu chuixun" (濯足垂訓), meaning "washing feet and leaving lessons," is the same as what is used in other Chinese Christian books. I have mentioned previously, the chapter that develops the footwashing narrative in Aleni's *Yanxing jilüe* uses the same wording; so does the title caption of the illustrated page in *Chuxiang jingjie*. If it were too reckless to assume Schall and Aleni had communicated regarding how to put this account into Chinese words, it is not hasty to recognize that a linguistic convention of telling the footwashing story or more biblical narratives was gradually taking shape, at least in Chinese Christian writings.

Moreover, the Latin text under the footwashing image does not relate to the Chinese piece as a source text. The Latin description is from the Vulgate Bible. It reads:

> surgit a cœna, & ponit vestimenta sua: et cum accepisset linteum, præcinxit se. Deinde misit aquam in pelvim, et cœpit lavare

---

3. Standaert, *An Illustrated Life of Christ Presented to the Chinese Emperor*, 243.
4. BnF Chinois 6757, vol. 2, ff. 32b-33a.

pedes discipulorum, et extergere linteo quo erat præcinctus. Iohan 13.[5]

This fragment depicts Jesus preparing washing the disciples' feet, as recorded in John 13:4–5. On the next page that follows the footwashing image, the Chinese text, which has been read through narrative analysis, bears no resemblance to the Latin words. The full Chinese text in *Jincheng shuxiang* is:

> 耶穌將受難。固命宗徒聽其濯足。示謙也。所以訓徒異日行教無少倨傲也。且不惟是。足比人心之情。身因足行。心因情行。其義正等。耶穌知其愛情之猶未純也。故濯其足。教之各純篤其情云。

> When Jesus was about to endure suffering, therefore, he ordered his disciples to allow him to wash their feet as a manifestation of humility. Herewith he instructed his disciples that another day when they would be teaching there should not be the slightest arrogance. But it is not only this. Feet can be compared with the feelings of the human heart. A body walks because of its feet and the heart acts because of its feelings. The meaning is exactly the same. Jesus knew that their feeling of love was still not pure and therefore he cleansed their feet in order to teach them to keep their feelings pure and genuine.[6]

This piece starts the footwashing narrative with a plain statement that Jesus would endure suffering by using the Chinese collocation "shounan" (受難), which literally means "Jesus accepting hardness" but usually refers to the passion in other Chinese Christian texts. In spite of that, the writing basically eliminates any other word to avoid any Christian discourses. The biblical story itself is only briefly accounted too. The whole piece has its weight on the second half that develops the author's interpretation of washing feet, in which feet are considered a symbol of the human heart, and washing feet is understood as keeping one's love and feelings in heart pure and deep. The author's words spell out messages of the footwashing narrative by underscoring the virtues and sentiments respected in Chinese society, such as humility, good deeds, merits, sincerity, purity, and innocence. To put it another way, Schall grasped what the Chinese emperor and general readers would readily accept and appreciate, with which he presented the biblical account as appealing as he could. Then, this version of the footwashing story is the result.

---

5. Standaert, *An Illustrated Life of Christ Presented to the Chinese Emperor*, 243.
6. Standaert, *An Illustrated Life of Christ Presented to the Chinese Emperor*, 244.

Circulation Reaching Out to Large Audiences

In the first place, *Jincheng shuxiang* was intended for the emperor; its circulation reached officials and large audiences at last. This book was at least a reference for Yang Guangxian 楊光先 (1507–1669) to learn about Jesus and his life. Yang was a Chinese Muslim scientist at the Bureau of Astronomy, also an opponent of the missionaries at the Qing court. When accusing the Jesuits of evil ambition, Yang quoted accounts regarding the ministry of Jesus. He initiated an attack on the Jesuits and confronted them, claiming that his knowledge was from the book of *Jincheng shuxiang*. The whole debate was recorded in another Chinese Christian book, *Budeyi bian* 不得已辨 (1665), a book compiled by Lodovico Buglio, SJ (1660–1682), to defend the standing point of the missionaries in China. According to this book, Buglio asked Yang for the source of his information. It reads:

今試問光先：" 惡黨以謀反之罪罪耶穌，從何知之？" 答曰："由《進呈書像》。"

Now may I ask (Yang) Guangxian, "(you say that) the evil ones alleged Jesus of plotting a rebellion, how do you know it?" Guangxian answers, "From *Jincheng shuxiang*."[7]

When reviewing the debate between Western missionaries and Muslim scholars in later years, this book was reviewed by more Chinese scholars. It is seen that in an apologetic work, *Chongzheng bibian* 崇正必辯 (1672), the Chinese Christian literati spoke highly of *Jincheng shuxiang* and considered it an honest presentation of a complete circle of the life of Jesus.[8]

As far as the reception of Chinese Christian books is concerned, this sort of evidence shows that *Jincheng shxuiang* was read by officials, including Yang Guangxian, and distributed among a broader circle of audiences. As a recommended Christian book at court, its circulation could go only further and broader. The popularity of *Jincheng shuxiang* was also due to the illustrations therein. Visualization is more useful and attractive than verbal texts, especially to less educated folks. This is also the case of illustrated Christian texts.[9]

---

7. *WX*, 284–86. The modern punctuation for book titles are added to the extract.
8. BnF Chinois 5002, vol. xia, ff. 2b–4a.
9. D'Elia, *Le origini dell'arte cristiana cinese (1583–1640)*.

Pangzi yiquan: Expositions Left by Master Pang

Pangzi yiquan was prepared by Diego de Pantoja, SJ (1571–1618). It was probably composed in 1610, as the last treatise inserted in this book indicates this year, and posthumous editing might be involved as well. The book was not published until 1617, the forty-fifth year of the Wanli Emperor (1563–1620, reign 1572–1620), according to historians and bibliographers Albert Chan, SJ (1915–2005) and Xu Zongze, who observed an edition published in Beijing. Chan quoted Xu, "Judging from the format and the paper used it can be well a Wan-Li edition."[10] There are multiple copies from different printing houses, and the one I consult is Hangzhou print facsimiled in *CCT ARSI*.

Explanations of Twelve Articles of the Creed

This copy has no paratexts, but the body part of *Pangzi yiquan* is quite extensive. It has four volumes in total. Each volume at its beginning has a subtitle of three characters, "xing bo lu" (性薄錄), a Chinese translation of "symbolum" or "simbolo." The task of this book is to explain the Twelve Articles of the Creed minutely. It is regarded as fine scholarly writing.[11] Two separate treatises are added at the end of the book.[12] Respectively focusing on angels and soul, they provide an account of the fall of man as the early history according to the Old Testament.[13]

The footwashing narrative is found under the exposition of the passion. It is part of the biblical account of Jesus being seized, tortured, crucified, and buried. As the three-layer analysis shows earlier, this version integrates pieces from the Synoptic Gospels into the text of *Pangzi yiquan* by synthesizing scenes regarding the Last Supper.

Providing integrated biblical accounts and comprehensible explanations is the function of this book. In terms of composition, expositions therein are organized in a typological manner, following a Chinese literary form of exegesis called "quan" (詮). Adopting the elite writing form seems to be a strategy to attract its target audiences that are learned Chinese.

---

10. Chan, *Chinese Books and Documents in the Jesuit Archives in Rome*, 133.

11. Standaert, "The Bible in Early Seventeenth-Century China," 48; D'Elia, "La passione di Gesù Cristo in un'opera cinese del 1608–1610," 276–307.

12. Pfister, *Notices biographiques et bibliographiques sur les jésuites (1552–1773)*, 72.

13. Wylie, *Notes on Chinese Literature*, 139.

A Useful Reference for Later Missionaries and Chinese

The book of *Pangzi yiquan* was written in the early stage of the China mission and then printed by printing houses and circulated later across the country. This facsimile copy that I examine is preserved in the Jesuit Archive in Rome (Jap.Sin. I, 82) today but was originally sent in July 1627 from Hangzhou in Zhejiang Province.[14] There are other copies made in Zhangzhou in Fujian Province.[15] Enough copies of *Pangzi yiquan* were indeed ready for readers.

For instance, *Pangzi yiquan* was mentioned more than several times in *Kouduo richao*, the previously examined book recording sermons and conversations between missionaries and Chinese. Very often, it was the missionaries who suggested this book for audiences to study the meaning of incarnation.[16] On another occasion in 1634, a Chinese interlocutor referred to *Pangzi yiquan* for asking questions about the Last Judgment. He said:

向讀龐子遺詮云將審判時人民病疫 ...

[I] recently read *Pangzi yiquan* that says, shortly before the Last Judgment, people are hit by the plague ... [17]

At least in *Kouduo richao*, it seems that *Pangzi yiquan* was a book that missionaries, Chinese Christians, people who were relatively new to Christianity—both outsiders and insiders—often spoke of in public. The reception of *Pangzi yiquan* also is evidenced in other Chinese Christian texts. In the previously mentioned *Budeyi bian* 不得已辨 (1665) that reviewed the debates between European missionaries and their opponents at court, the Jesuits also recommended *Pangzi yiquan* for larger audiences to read. It is regarded as one of the good references explaining Christian salvation history and accounts of Jesus.[18] *Wenda huichao* 問答彙抄 (ca. 1670s), a compilation of Chinese Christians, contains numerous excerpts from it.[19]

Given its comprehensive contents, some parts of *Pangzi yiquan* became a new Chinese Christian book too. For instance, a particular section on the passion developed therein was made into another independent text titled *Tianzhu yesu shounan shimo* 天主耶穌受難始末. It is instructions primarily for educating and assisting catechumen in saying prayers. Later on, it

---

14. Dudink, "The Japonica-Sinica Collections I-IV in the Roman Archives of the Society of Jesus," 494.

15. See CCT Database.

16. Zürcher, *Kouduo Richao*, 229–32.

17. Zürcher, *Kouduo Richao*, 465.

18. *WX*, 284–86.

19. *CCT ARSI* vol. 8, 235–604.

was included in a euchology book, *Shengjiao rike* 聖教日課, which collects prayer books and litanies for practicing Christians to use.[20] The part of this text that chronologically narrates the life circle of Jesus was still translated by Pasquale D'Elia, SJ (1890–1963), in twentieth-century China.[21] Through such a textual inheritance, part of the book *Pangzi yiquan* ended up in books of distinct genres and readerships across more than two hundred years.

Tizheng bian: Raising the Right Way

Tizheng bian was attributed to Girolamo de Gravina, SJ (1603–1662). The collaborating team involved in composing *Tizheng bian* includes European missionaries and Chinese Christians ranking from high officials at court to lower degree holders residing locally. They are Lodovico Buglio, SJ (1606–1682), Gabriel de Magalhães, SJ (1610–1677), Humbert Augery, SJ (1618–1673), Feliciano Pacheco, SJ (1622–1687), Simão da Cunha, SJ (1589–1660), Zhu Zongyuan 朱宗元 (c.1615–1660), Li Zubai 李祖白 (?–1665), and He Shizhen 何世貞(?–?). These collaborators may have formed the largest team in the history of Chinese Christian books.

Due to multiple editions and reprints, the publication date of this book was registered differently in traditional bibliographies.[22] However, a preface written by a Chinese official, Tong Guoqi 佟國器 (?–?), dated to 1659 suggests that this book was prepared no later than 1659. Among the many copies, I consult two: a facsimiled edition in *CCT ZKW XB* and another print, BnF Chinois 6942, from the National Library of France. Together, they make a complete copy of *Tizheng bian*.

An Abridged Textbook Introducing Systematic Theology

In addition to several paratexts (such as the preface and a table of contents), the extensive composition of *Tizheng bian* takes up six volumes. Its overall theme is major Christian teachings divided into six subjects, namely the virtues of the Lord, the redemption of the Lord, what the Lord rewards, grace and mercy of the Lord, what the Lord values and honors, and what the Lord blesses and protects. While explaining each subject, the book lists a series of key words and then elaborates them. Each key word is explained, and the explanations are developed into subdivisions as theses

---

20. Brunner, *L'euchologe de la mission de Chine*, 36–38.
21. D'Elia, "La passione di Gesù Cristo in un'opera cinese del 1609–1610," 276–307.
22. See CCT Database.

to support its subject matter. All expositions are accompanied by reference materials, such as quotations of church fathers, Bible verses, and other biblical literature. At last, each subject brings about a treatise or persuasive writing structured by an array of key words.

The footwashing text is found in the exposition on the Eucharist, and the Eucharist is one of the key words under the subject about the blessings and protection of God. The full footwashing text in *Tizheng bian* is extracted from the copy in the National Library of France. It reads:

或問　　耶穌定立聖體前。親濯宗徒之足。何意。曰。約有二義。一示吾人領聖體前。身心罪污。洗滌宜盡。一示吾人效法謙遜毋輒自矜。聖經曰。耶穌濯畢宗徒之足云。爾輩非以我爲師爲主者乎。然吾且濯爾足。爾輩亦當互相濯足相下。以徵爲我徒也。

Someone asks, "Before establishing the Eucharist, Jesus in person washed the feet of the apostles. What does this mean?" (One) says, "(There are) about two meanings. One is to show us that before receiving the Eucharist, sins, and filth on the body and in heart should all be cleaned thoroughly. The other is to show us that (we should) imitate the humility but not always praise ourselves." Shengjing once said, "Jesus completed washing the feet of the apostles and said, 'Don't you people consider me as master as lord? Nevertheless, I still wash your feet. You people also should wash feet to each other and lower yourself to each other, in order to certify (you) as my followers.'"[23]

As a narrative piece, this text has been analyzed earlier through the three-layer frame. In terms of composition, it is at first featured with a question and an answer between two rhetorical persons. The first interlocutor mentions the footwashing event and inquires about its meaning; the answer points out two messages while narrating the story. In this case, the footwashing story is out of context but automatically links to the initiation of the Eucharist. As the question asks, "Before establishing the Eucharist, Jesus in person washed the feet of the apostles. What does this mean?"

More important is the implication of such a writing form. That the footwashing scene is mentioned as part of the question suggests that both parties are aware of it. If the one who raises questions can recognize the footwashing account, readers of *Tizheng bian* should be able to do the same in order to follow that passage. The answer reinforces the importance of biblical narrative

---

23. BnF Chinois 6942, vol. 6, f. 30.

with two meanings. If readers have heard of the story, this answer can better their understanding of it as well as of the Eucharist.

It is especially interesting to note that this fragment contains a quote from "shengjing," the very collocation in Chinese. The word in modern Mandarin Chinese exclusively means the Christian Bible; but before the nineteenth century, it was used to promote Christian texts among other religions in China.[24] This quotation corresponds to John 13:13–15. Rather than translating the two verses word by word, it is a simplified paraphrase of the last instruction of Jesus, and it does not resonate with any other Chinese Christian texts at the level of wording. What stands out is that the biblical pericope was freely rendered into Chinese and referred to as part of "shengjing" in the mid-seventeenth century. Apparently, references to Christian "shengjing" had been recognized far earlier, before a Chinese translation of the Bible.

The rest of *Tizheng bian* is composed in a similar pattern. The way in which every subject is outlined and explained in *Tizheng bian* does not differ from non-Christian scholarly writings. For instance, arguments therein are framed as treatises, and some incorporate the form of questions and answers. If judging only from the written form of this book, one can hardly tell its nature in conveying Christian content.

Assisting Missionaries and General Chinese Readers

The book of *Tizheng bian* was produced on the basis of close collaboration between European missionaries and Chinese Christian scholars, as the long list of collaborators shows. At last, it was destined to be used by both missionaries and Chinese readers.

Missionaries used this book as a tool while preaching in Chinese, for which some visible traces can be found on the paper. For instance, in the copy facsimiled in *CCT ZKW XB*, there are handwritten notes jotted down with Romanized pronunciations of certain Chinese characters. It is a print edition, but handwritten notes appear in marginal areas to mark the sound of Chinese characters in alphabets. The marked characters are usually the ones hard to recognize: the character "恙" is noted in "yam" and "甦" is spelled in "sou" (figure 27).

---

24. Chen, "Christian Biblical Tradition in the *Jing* Chinese Culture."

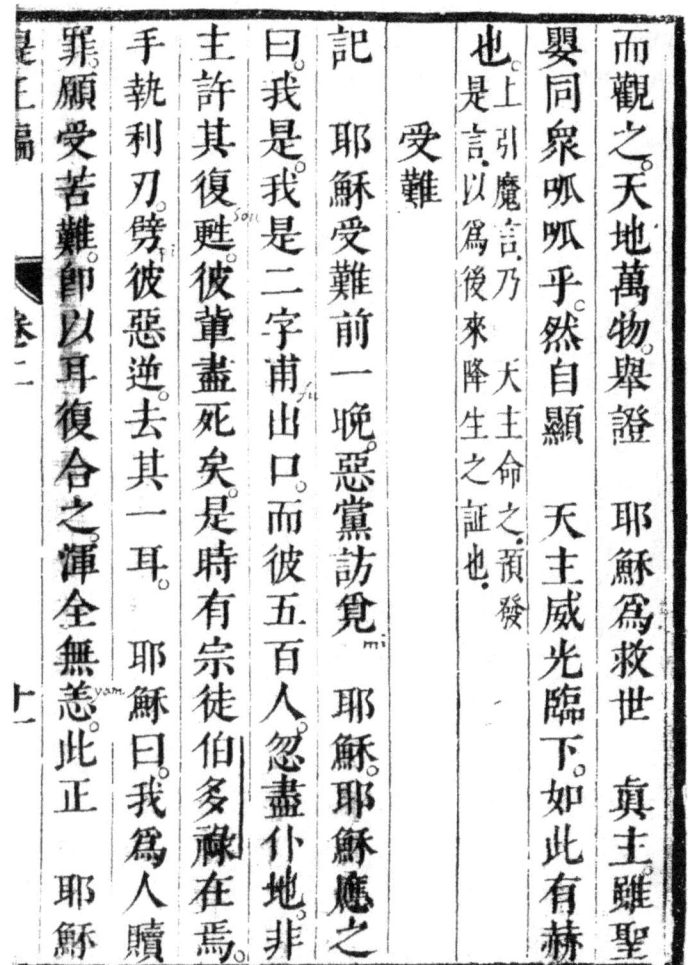

Figure 27

Obviously, these were added after the book had been printed. They are evidence of the use of this book in the hands of missionaries. The book of *Tizheng bian* could prepare missionaries to answer questions from their Chinese converts, catechumens, friends, and acquaintances.

To Chinese readers, *Tizheng bian* was a Christian book open to the outer circle. This book was quoted often and recommended on reading lists, particularly for outsiders. From it, a large number of fragments were included in *Wenda huichao* 問答彙抄 (ca. 1670s), a book compiling numerous passages from other Christian texts.[25] *Budeyi bian* 不得已辨, the aforementioned book responding to anti-Christian attacks, also suggested it as one of the essential books introducing Christianity.[26]

25. *CCT ARSI* vol. 8, 235–604.
26. *WX*, 284–86.

13

Texts to Foster Chinese Christian Religiosity among Insiders

THIS CHAPTER PRESENTS A series of books for Chinese converts and Christians-to-be inside the Christian community. *Wanwu shiyuan* and *Shengjiao yuanliu* are compositions of Christian teachings and doctrine for catechizing purposes. *Yesu shengti daowen* is a prayer book. *Moxiang gongfu* and *Jinshan lu* both are manuals for meditation exercises. These books are less attractive to modern scholars, not as much as sophisticated compositions and philosophical arguments are, but they were essential for practicing Chinese Christians to nurture their religious life.

Wanwu shiyuan: All Beginning with the Origin

Wanwu shiyuan is usually known by another title, *Jingdian jilüe wenda* 經典紀略問答. Its author was Jean Basset, MEP (1662–1707), and its contents were adapted from the historical catechism, *Grand catechism historique* (1683) of Claude Fleury (1640–1723).[1] I consult a copy facsimiled in *CCT BnF*.

This copy of *Wanwu shiyuan* is a handwritten text neatly done. Without paratexts, the body part consists of fifty-two chapters. All the chapters are ordered to form salvation history, starting from the creation in the Old Testament, the genealogy of Jesus, the life circle and ministry of Jesus, the passion, the ascension, and throughout the fall of Rome. Each chapter centers on one biblical subject and consists of two sections: a narration of the subject and a series of questions and answers on the subject.

The footwashing narrative found in this book is part of the thirty-eighth chapter titled "yesu wancan" (耶穌晚餐), meaning "the dinner of Jesus." The text that has been analyzed with the three-layer frame is extracted from the first section of this chapter. Immediately following the narrative

---

1. Dudink, "Jean Basset (1662–1707) and His Catechetical Writings in Chinese," 96–97, 103–6.

text, pairs of questions and answers comprise the other section called "wenda" (問答) in Chinese. It is from the narrative piece that those questions are derived, and the corresponding relations between the two sections are worth exploring. The footwashing text in this book reads:

> 巴斯卦時。耶穌遣使徒脩庭而後親到之。依古禮偕徒食羊羔。此所謂主晚湌也。湌間。耶穌起離席。洗諸徒之足。以設相事之法。而成其潔。

> While the Passover (drew upon), Jesus dispatched the apostles to prepare the (dining) hall and then afterward, he arrived himself. According to the old rite, (he) ate the lamb together with the disciples. This is what is called the dinner of the Lord. During the meal, Jesus rose and stepped away from the feast, washed every apostle's feet, in order to set a rule on how to serve each other, and to help them to achieve their cleanliness.[2]

The narration here is very concise as only several narrative components are included. Even the final speech of Jesus is entirely omitted so that the messages are expressed through the author's interpretation. This piece connects to the following questions and answers. Each question entails an answer that refers to a specific part of the above narration. The other section is:

> （問）吾主未死前行甚麼禮。
> （答）行巴斯卦古禮。湌中食羊羔。
> （問）那時吾主立何謙讓之法。
> （答）親洗使徒之足。立相讓相事之法。
> （問）那時吾主新立何禮。
> （答）新立聖体大禮。...

> Question: What rite did our Lord conduct before his death?

> Answer: (He) did the ancient rite of Passover, eating the lamb during the meal.

> Question: At that time, what kind of rule of modesty did our Lord establish?

> Answer: (He) washed the feet of the apostles in person, establishing the rule to be humble to each other and to treat each other.

> Question: At that time, what kind of new rite did our Lord establish?

2. *CCT BnF* vol. 13, 416–20.

Answer: (He) established the grand rite of the Eucharist. . . .[3]

Three sets of questions and answers respectively punch three significances related to the footwashing story: the ancient rite of Passover, the lesson on humility and service, and the initiation of the Eucharist. The questions, in a way, are set to explore the narrative piece ahead of it by highlighting the matters to which readers should pay attention. In responding to the questions, the answers seem to form a more condensed version of the footwashing story. This section makes the biblical account sharper and easier to understand and to remember.

The footwashing case exemplifies the generic composition of this book. It combines the two sections: a narrative piece provides a storyline, preparing readers to study questions and answers for later; conversely, questions and answers help readers gain an essence of the biblical account that they have read. Such a composition can benefit readers by improving their comprehension, memorization, and appreciation of Christian teachings and doctrines, which makes the book of *Wanwu shiyuan* a useful catechetical text to readers, especially Chinese catechumen.

Shengjiao yuanliu: Origin and Development of the Holy Teaching

Shengjiao yuanliu is a large-volume catechism covering broad subjects of Christianity from theological matters to liturgy practices. It was originally composed during 1635 and 1636, and some corrections were made in 1675.[4] Its author was a Chinese convert, Zhu Yupu 朱毓朴 (?–?), and what he recorded therein might have come from Rui de Figueiredo, SJ (1608–1642).[5] Zhu noted down his conversations with the priest and then compiled them into this book. Therefore, this book is primarily shaped in the form of questions and answers.

Multiple copies of *Shengjiao yuanliu* are available, but most are incomplete. I consult two facsimiles in *CCT ARSI* and *CCT BnF*. The copy in *CCT ARSI* contains handwritten notes and corrections to the print; the copy in *CCT BnF* seems neat, but many characters are not readable because the paper is so thin that prints on both folios overlap. Both copies together provide a complete set of the body part of this book and paratexts that include one piece of preface, a text of editorial norm, table of contents, and a postscript.

3. *CCT BnF* vol. 13, 416–20.
4. See CCT Database.
5. Chan, *Chinese Books and Documents in the Jesuit Archives in Rome*, 186–89.

The body part of this book consists of four sections, namely "jingdian" (經典) on Scriptures, classics, and canons; "zhujie" (主誡) on the Lord's commandments; "huijie" (會誡) about commandments and rules of the Church; and "liyi" (禮儀) containing ritual matters and rites. Each section is developed into several volumes, and each volume entails a specific subject supporting one of the four sections. For instance, the third section of this book is about commandments and rules of the church. The elaboration covers two volumes: one volume on the mass, and the other on fasting. The footwashing piece is found in the volume on the mass that is called "jili zhengyi" (祭禮正義) in Chinese and expounds on meanings of the rite.

The footwashing text is part of the explanatory catechesis regarding stages and processes of the mass. Except for conveying the biblical narrative, its composite features also are interesting to explore. In a conversational form of questions and answers, the whole piece unfolds:

問。神父在臺左用水洗手。是甚麼意思。

曰。解明耶穌將要建定聖體大禮。先脫上衣。親手拿水盆。下跪宗徒面前。一個一個洗他的腳。立個衆人該學法謙遜相幫服事的樣子。另外教我們。凡要領聖體。必須先痛悔解洗諸罪。

(One) questions, "The priest at the left to the altar washes his hands with water. What does that mean?"

(One) says, "(In order to) clearly explain that he was going to establish the grand rite of the Eucharist, (Jesus) at first took off his top garment, with his own hands took a water basin, kneeled in front of the apostle (/s), washed his (/their) feet one by one. This is to set an example that people should learn and model after on how people should be modest to each other, help and treat each other. In addition, (this is) to teach us that everyone to receive the Eucharist must at first do penance and confession to wash and resolve all sins."[6]

Different from other cases, the biblical account is placed in the answer. The footwashing story explains why a priest washed his hand at the left side of the altar during the mass. According to the answer herein, that Jesus washed his disciples' feet for two reasons: one is to establish a moral example on humility and service, and the other is to require "us" to confess and cleanse our souls before receiving the Eucharist. It is indeed the word "us" in Chinese, "wo men" (我們). Since what had been recorded therein are questions and

6. *CCT BnF* vol. 23, 105–6.

answers between two parties, using "us" during conversations is natural. More importantly, it is an instance of a composite feature of *Shengjiao yuanliu*, which is the writing directly speaking to its readers.

As part of the answer, the word "us" includes the priest and the Chinese Christian Zhu, as in this book Zhu is the questioner and, presumably, Rui de Figueiredo provides the answer. After the oral conversations being transformed and modified into a written work, the word "us" remains in writing that would be read by readers. The word "us" then includes the author Zhu and the readers of *Shengjiao yuanliu*. In saying "us," this book indicates a sense of belonging and companionship. It epitomizes the bond between the priest and his questioner Zhu; it also strengthens the bond between the author Zhu and his intended readers.

This manner of encompassing readers in the text is different from "kouduo" text, the composition of sermons on paper, which has been examined in the previous part. Authors who prepared sermons gave away lessons and directly addressed audiences; clergies as immediate users of sermons on paper would use those words in preaching. In *Shengjiao yuanliu*, the author shared with readers the lessons he had studied and the words that he had heard. Readers of *Shengjiao yuanliu* may ask the same question of why the priest washed his hands at the altar, and the answer would be the footwashing story and its messages as provided in this book. It is as if Zhu was a messenger carrying answers from his priest and delivering them to readers who may never meet a priest in person.

Who were readers of *Shengjiao yuanliu*? In his own words, Zhu said:

是書惟為聖教中諸友便看而作。

> This book is just made for friends within the (inner) circle of the holy teaching to read at their convenience.[7]

His readers were "shengjiao zhong zhuyou" (聖教中諸友) who were insiders willing to follow the Christian teaching. He also referred to his Christian fellows as "tonghui zhe" (同會者), meaning "the ones in the same congregation or association."[8] The readership was definitely not restricted to friends within his reach. The author notably advocated his concern for ordinary readers. Zhu was literate, at least literary and scholarly enough to prepare this book, but he gave up sophisticated writing particularly for the sake of people who were not up to a certain literary level. He said:

---

7. *CCT ARSI* vol. 3, 5.
8. *CCT ARSI* vol. 3, 5–6.

非不文也。恐一歸於文。就不便於市民了。

(It is) not because (our conversations are) not literary. (I am just) afraid that as long as (our conversations) are turned into a literary composition, it would not be convenient for people on the street.[9]

Therefore, one can conclude that the intended readers of *Shengjiao yuanliu* were less-learned insiders. What was the recommended reading method and expected effect after reading this book? Zhu also clarified his thought in this regard. He requested:

所以吾輩讀之。只要信得過。信不過便讀之無用。

Therefore, our people read it, just need to believe; if not believing, there is no point in reading it.[10]

Apparently, Zhu planned to impart the contents of this book to readers. He asked readers just to receive what had been written therein if they were not already familiar with them. Moreover, readers were not supposed to discuss this book with an outsider. Zhu did not wish this book to involve debates with other religions or schools, because he knew that for defending Christianity or engaging in dialogues, other Christian books would do.[11]

Among other Christian books, the mission of *Shengjiao yuanliu* was to educate ordinary Chinese catechumen as a catechism by giving detailed explanations of doctrine, prescribing how to observe and carry out the sacraments, and providing examples of Christian attitudes and behavior.[12] It had neither a European nor a Chinese source but was based on oral communications. When the colloquial language was properly polished and edited, this book could be a great help to prepare Chinese catechumens to respond to questions.

Yesu shengti daowen: Eucharistic Litany of Jesus

Yesu shengti daowen is a book of Eucharistic litany adapted from *Fasciculus sacrarum litaniarum ex sanctis scripturis et patribus* (1614).[13] Its author is the Italian Jesuit Giulio Aleni, who also authored the instruction on the

---

9. *CCT ARSI* vol. 3, 5.
10. *CCT ARSI* vol. 3, 5.
11. *CCT ARSI* vol. 3, 5–6.
12. King, "The Gospel for the Ordinary Reader," 182.
13. See CCT Database.

TEXTS TO FOSTER CHINESE CHRISTIAN RELIGIOSITY AMONG INSIDERS 199

Eucharist *Shengti yaoli*, which has been introduced in the previous part. The copy of *Yesu shengti daowen* that I consult is a print made in Fujian Province in 1644 and now facsimiled in *CCT BnF*.

As for the footwashing text from *Yesu shengti daowen*, the narrative analysis has shown that the one-sentence narration underscores the virtue of modesty of Jesus. Tracing it back to its source text in *Fasciculus sacrarum litaniarum* will shed more light on our understanding of this petitionary prayer. The Chinese page extracted from *Yesu shengti daowen* (figure 28) can be traced back to its corresponding page in Latin (figure 29).

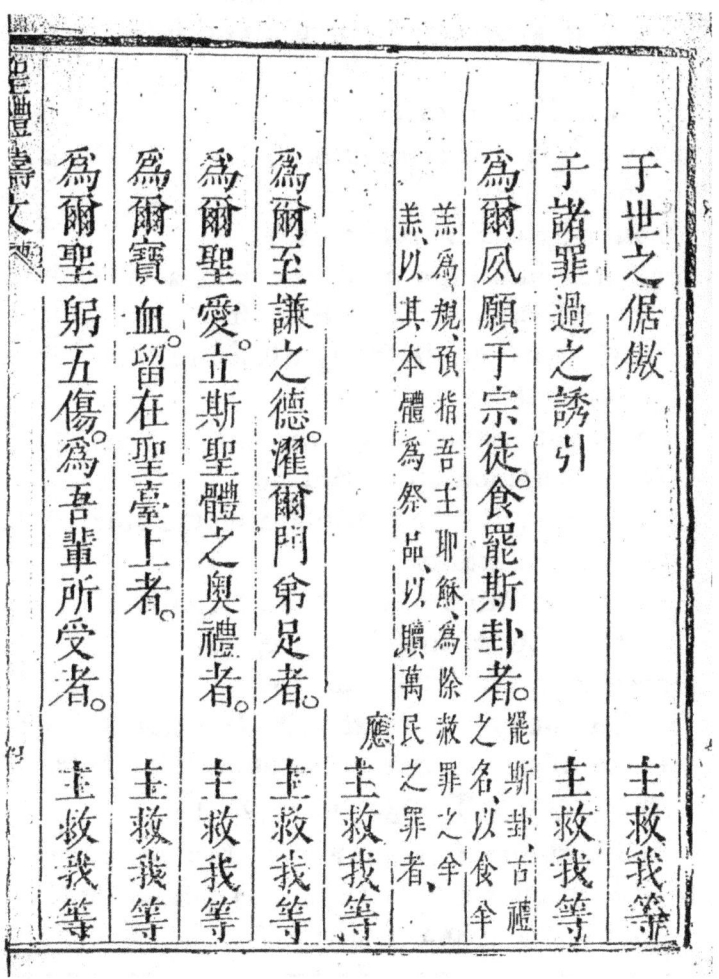

Figure 28

LITANIAE

²95

[V]iaticum in Domino morientium, Miserere nob.
[D]ignus futuræ gloriæ, Miserere nobis.
[P]ropitius esto, Parce nobis Domine.
[P]ropitius esto, Exaudi nos Domine.
[A]b indigna corporis & sanguinis tui susce-
 ptione,
[A] concupiscentia carnis,
[A] concupiscentia oculorum,
[A] superbia vitæ,
[A]b omni peccandi occasione,
[P]er desiderium illud, quo hoc pascha cum
 discipulis manducare desiderasti,
[P]er summam humilitatem, qua discipulorum
 pedes lauisti,
[P]er ardentissimam charitatem qua hoc diui-
 num Sacramentum instituisti,
[P]er sanguinem tuum pretiosum quem nobis
 in Altari reliquisti,
[P]er quinque vulnera huius tui Corporis sa-
 cratissimi, quæ pro nobis suscepisti,

} Libera nos Domine.

[P]eccatores, Te rogamus audi nos.
[V]t nobis fidem, reuerentiam & deuotionem huius admirabilis Sacramenti augere & conser-
 uare digneris, Te rogamus audi nos.
[V]t ad frequentem vsum Eucharistiæ per veram
 peccatorum confessionem nos perducere digneris, Te rogamus audi nos.

Vt

Figure 29

The Latin text "Er summam humilitatem qua discipulorum pedes lavisti" is translated into the Chinese sentence literally. Besides, it is interesting to note that the repetitive response "Libera nos Domine" is printed only once on the Latin page, probably to save typesetting on the same page, but every responding word following every prayer is printed out on the Chinese page. To woodblock carvers, cutting several more characters by hand was not that difficult.

As seen in the footwashing text or other excerpts from the book of *Yesu shengti daowen*, the litany is framed with the same fixed phrase. Practicing Christians learn to say the litany and to memorize those words and structures. A recurring formula helps illiterate minds to memorize and recite prayers; prayers themselves are repetitively and concisely written in colloquial words, giving easy access to everyone.

Texts of this sort were not alien to Chinese folks in the seventeenth century, as Buddhism, Daoism, and folk religions and sects all had prayers in Chinese called "jing" (經), the term referring to Scriptures and classics at the same time. Christian prayers of a great variety also were available, including the Lord's Prayer, the Beatitudes, Ten Commandments, and the Rosary, the Hail Mary, the Apostolic Creed, the Prayer of the Sign of the Cross, etc. So were prayer books. On September 14, 1639 in Fuzhou in Fujian Province, a group was instructed that the Lord's Prayer was needed for examining one's sin, especially when one's mind was disturbed during self-investigation. On another occasion, a distinguished scholar wanted to find out the reason behind [a phenomenon], so "he first made confession and prayed for the Lord's protection."[14]

Just as mantras were used in Buddhist and Daoist practices, prayers were essential for practicing Christians' religiosity. They were needed by ritual experts, catechists, and faithful believers in different contexts. If a faithful recited the prayer incorporating the footwashing scene long enough, the words "the lord was so humble to wash disciples' feet" would become his or her own. Saying Christian prayers would be a sign to differentiate insiders from outsiders. Hence, setting a sort of boundary of the inner circle of the Christian community, prayers and prayer books were useful only for insiders.[15]

---

14. Zürcher, *Kouduo Richao*, 604.
15. For prayer books in Chinese, see Brunner, *L'euchologe de la mission de Chine*.

Moxiang gongfu: Meditation Exercises

Moxiang gongfu was prepared by Gaspar Ferreira, SJ (1571–1649), in the 1630s. It is a guidebook on meditation. It elaborates on ways of spiritual perfection by advancing seven virtues through exercises. In the course of elaboration, references to biblical scenes are included. Most episodes (such as parables and events during the life and ministry of Jesus) are taken from the Gospels.

A copy of this book is facsimiled in *CCT BnF*, which I consult. Two paratexts are included in this book: one piece of editorial norms and a table of contents. The body part of this book consists of seven volumes, respectively focusing on the seven virtues. Each virtue put in Chinese is: "shengwei" (聖畏), meaning "holy awe"; "jianshi" (賤世), meaning "depreciation of the world"; "zijian" (自賤), meaning "self-depreciation"; "shaoyan" (少言), meaning "temperance of words"; "rennai" (忍耐), meaning "patience"; "qianxun" (謙遜), meaning "humility"; and "ren'ai" (仁愛), meaning "charity." Every volume is strictly structured in fifteen chapters, and every chapter is developed on a central theme through both meditation and exercises. Usually, four or five exercises are selected under each theme.

The footwashing text appears in the volume on the virtue of patience, more specifically, in the chapter on how to exercise patience. The headline of this chapter already gives away this theme. It reads:

第十條耶穌甘忍茹荅斯奸徒謀害。尚以友呼之。

> The tenth item, Jesus willingly tolerated the plot of the villainous disciple Judas, still calling him a friend.[16]

The biblical story here is an instance of manifesting the patience and lenience of Jesus toward Judas. As the previous narrative analysis has demonstrated, this version claims that Judas was one of the disciples to meet Jesus, and Jesus did wash the feet of Judas in his hands. This emphasis is a rare case among other Chinese versions, and there is a discrepancy between this and the prototype too. Only reading the context wherein the footwashing text appears can resolve this mystery. In this volume of *Moxiang gongfu*, the footwashing narration is twisted for supporting the central theme of this chapter, which is the tolerance and patience of Jesus on Judas. The more it states that Jesus did for Judas, the more impact this story would have on readers.

It is worth noticing how the author addresses his readers in the book of *Moxiang gongfu*. In the text on doing exercises, almost every instruction

---

16. *CCT BnF* vol. 22, 384.

starts with the word "you," to speak to readers. For instance, the section of exercising on "feeling ashamed" begins with "you should deeply feel sorry and ashamed," and the section of exercising on "giving thanks" starts with "you should at first recognize the greatest grace." In the author's lecturing voice, the nature of this book is further confirmed, which is to guide Chinese Christians to do meditation and exercises.

The actual circulation of *Moxiang gongfu* is not known yet. However, there is a note in the previously introduced *Kouduo richao* that contains information probably about the use of *Moxiang gongfu*. On Sunday, October 1, 1634, Li Jiugong raised questions about spiritual exercises. He said, "I have heard that [our] Doctrine there is the work of meditation. Please tell me about it in outline."[17] The Chinese word that Li used was "moxiang gongfu" (默想工夫), and it may refer to the book of *Moxiang gongfu*. Even if Li just expressed his interests in the general idea of meditation exercises, this piece also suggests the demand of Chinese Christians for instructions on this practice as part of their growing Christian religiosity.

Jinshan lu: On Cultivating the Good

Distinct from other Christian manuals on religious practice, *Jinshan lu* was composed by Chinese scholars rather than by missionary priests. In the facsimiled copy in *CCT BnF*, the names appearing at the beginning of the body text include: one writer, Luis of Yuanling (宛陵本一居士理斯氏); one corrector, Juan of Wulin (武林然真居士若印氏); and three revisers, Miguel of Jinling (金陵士皇居士彌格氏), Julio of Gushe (古歙蕭聞居士儒略氏), and Domingo of Sanshan (三山寄園居士道明氏). Although these are only literary names and Christian names, they line up an impressive team. And, the indicated geolocations are around the areas from Shanghai to Hangzhou, Nanjing, Huangshan, and Suzhou. This range of collaborating Chinese Christians suggests a network centered on the book of *Jinshan lu*, at the least.

Fully in a style of Chinese scholars' work, this book has a series of paratexts that include a table of contents and several appendices. A short preface dated to the feast day of Pentecost in the summer of 1635 articulates the preparation of this book. According to the preface, the writer collected what he learned from the European priests and integrated them into this volume. Initially, this book was compiled only for him to use, for self-cultivation along the journey upwards to heaven. As time went on and his age grew, he

---

17. Zürcher, *Kouduo Richao*, 486.

decided to share this volume with fellows inside the Christian community, by way of carving and printing out this book.[18]

What the author had learned from the priests must have been accumulating gradually in *Jinshan lu*. The miscellaneous contents of this book range from fundamental doctrines to sacraments, from liturgy and meditation to reading books and reciting prayers, from individual reflection to collective activities. Since the author kept track of his own learning process and intended this book for continual study, this book would be a useful tool to encourage the growth of other Chinese Christians.

The footwashing text is found under a section on meditation. Its title is "moxiang shengong" (默想神功), which in Chinese means "marvelous effects of meditation."[19] To be noted, this title is the same as the book of *Moxiang shengong*, the meditation handbook by Pedro de la Piñuela introduced in the previous part, but the two texts are not related. The footwashing narrative in *Jinshan lu* is one particular scene for meditation. It is a simplified version of the biblical story, as has been analyzed earlier. After the narrative piece, the author continues expressing his thoughts while meditating upon this episode. It reads:

> 然先濯宗徒之足。而後賜之領聖體者。必也先潔其心。毫無罪垢。又謙下其志。以卑自處。及大發愛[ ]天主與愛人之真情者。方可領受斯恩。迎[ ]天主降臨吾心。以增諸恩德也。

> As such, (Jesus) firstly washed the feet of the apostles and then granted them to receive the Eucharist. That (sequence of firstly washing and secondly giving the Eucharist indicates that the apostles) must clean their heart at first, making them free from sins and foul matters, and then (they should) make their own wills humble, to place themselves in a lowly position. And (moreover), only the ones greatly express their genuine compassion for loving the Heavenly Lord and caring people can receive and accept this grace, welcome the Heavenly Lord to descend into my heart, in order to increase all of (His) blessings.[20]

The author spells out his understanding of the footwashing narrative. The writing is very personal, especially when the author speaks of welcoming "the Heavenly Lord to descend into my heart" in his words. The expression is about the author himself; it also links to his readers. In his eyes, there are three

18. *CCT BnF* vol. 25, 73.
19. *CCT BnF* vol. 25, 101.
20. *CCT BnF* vol. 25, 101–3.

prerequisite conditions for individuals receiving the grace and blessings: they should be free from sin, they should humble themselves before others, and they should love the Heavenly Lord and people. For one to accept this belief and follow this rule, they should share the views of the author. The readers of *Jinshan lu* were indeed insiders; at least they were the author's fellows within the Christian community, as the preface states.

Perhaps, it is inappropriate to define *Jinshan lu* as a catechism or handbook, and its contents are neither entirely doctrinal nor liturgical. Even so, this book was a Chinese Christian's compilation, and it witnessed his learning journey. As a tool instructing on personal growth in Christianity, it was used for the author's self-cultivation, and his younger Christian fellows could use it for their purposes.

14

Disparate Chinese Compositions

This chapter presents five rather special books. They bear no resemblance to any genre of Christian literature in the European church. As writings in Chinese literary forms, they also seem new due to the Christian contents they convey. *Sizi jingwen* is composed in rhymed doggerel with four characters to a line. So is *Tianxue mengyin*, but in the form of a seven-character line. In addition to verses, it also combines commentary written in prose. Another two books—*Sizheng enyan* and *Chaoxing liyin*—collect poems derived from the prayers provided in a meditation book, *Song wuzhu yesu nianzhu guitiao*. *Qike zhenxun* is another case that is developed from earlier Chinese Christian texts. These texts adopt simple expressions, straightforward narration, and accessible writing forms. Some of them are considered catechesis because they were carved out at first for educational purposes. In this chapter, I call attention to their composite features that could benefit children, young pupils, illiterate or semi-illiterate adults, and beginners in the society of the time.

Rhymed Lines Based on Chinese Primers

There are more than several Christian books written in verse form. In these books, one theme is developed through several rhymed lines, and every line is regulated with four or seven characters. *Sizi jingwen* and *Tianxue mengyin* stand for two examples. Unlike stanza and couplet in the Western literary tradition or strictly regulated classical Chinese poetry, they loosely format narrative poems. Their compositions are close to the primer schoolbooks for educating young pupils. The format could facilitate memorization and improve Christian religious literacy.

Sizi jingwen: Four-Character Classic Text

The book of *Sizi jingwen* was attributed to Giulio Aleni and polished by Chinese Christian scholars. The facsimile that I consult in *CCT ARSI* is a print from Jiangxi Province. A postscript is included to tell a textual history of composing, revising, and publishing this book, which I will discuss later.

This book succinctly documents salvation history. Its entire narration is told from the perspective of Jesus, as he is the protagonist and sole role throughout this book. The footwashing narrative appears as part of the ministry of Jesus. As the narrative analysis has shown earlier, the footwashing text of *Sizi jingwen* is actually very short and contains only a few fabula-layer elements. It reads:

知期巳到　　自願受難
難未到時　　預言來事
受難前夕　　巴斯卦禮
濯足宗徒　　定聖體儀

(He) knew the time had come, willingly (prepared to) receive sufferings.

The suffering had not yet arrived, (he) foretold things in the future.

Before the passion, it was the rite of Passover.

(He) washed the feet of the apostles and established the ritual of the Eucharist.[1]

Although my English translation cannot make the sound of Chinese characters, the signs of rhymes to assist memorization can be explained. These lines mainly rhyme at the close front unrounded vowel [i] (IPA number 301) as the character "shi" (時) rhymes with "shi" (事), "xi" (夕), "li" (禮), "yi" (儀). Stress is always on the last character. The verses are supposed to be recited by readers, and rhymes as such can be handy. The rest of *Sizi jingwen* unfolds similar to this text with loosely rhymed lines.

This book was labeled in traditional bibliographies as a compendium of Christian doctrines for children, or a catechism.[2] The reasoning was that this book was primarily used for children or less educated adults to learn the biblical narration by heart. Still, the composite feature of this

---

1. *CCT ARSI* vol. 2, 340–41.
2. See CCT Database.

book was overlooked. Its particular writing form has caught scholars' eyes in recent years.³

The composition of *Sizi jingwen* is patterned after Chinese primer classics, such as *Three-Character Classic* 三字經. Only in this case, this is a text of "four-character classic." In the traditional Chinese society, primers of this sort (such as *Hundred Surnames* 百家姓 and *Thousand Characters Essay* 千字文) are composed of rhymed sentences in loose parallels, which is effective for quick memorization. They take up the curriculum for imparting moral education to the youngest pupils.⁴ They have laid the foundation of propagating state ideology, and their impact is as profound as it can be because every literate person—erudite scholars and commoners only with basic education—had to learn to read and write from these schoolbooks.⁵

This genre was getting more and more popular along with increasing literacy in society during the Ming Dynasty when European missionaries arrived. Missionaries also took interest in them. The Chinese primers were so useful and easily obtainable that many copies were shipped to Europe.⁶ The Jesuits in China must have been familiar with them; it is no surprise to see that *Sizi jingwen* was composed in this model and welcomed in due course. By way of narrating biblical stories in salvation history and delivering Christian teachings, *Sizi jingwen* played a role in building Christian communities as Confucian educational primers had in society.

In this copy, there is also a postscript telling more stories about the gist, circulation, and editing process of this edition of *Sizi jingwen*. This piece was written by Chinese scholar Li Shihuan 李奭浣 (?–?) in 1663. According to Li, Aleni wrote a fine text, but it was not well organized or widely circulated. Master Tang, who is Johann Adam Schall von Bell, SJ (1592–1666), and Master Nie, who is probably Pietro Canevari, SJ (1596–1675), they both pushed the idea of editing and republishing Aleni's text. Upon this request, Li corrected and revised Aleni's text into this reader-friendly edition.⁷ That is to say that the book of *Sizi jingwen* was at last shaped through communication and collaborations between missionaries and Chinese scholars. Li also talked about the expected readership of this book. Readers of *Sizi jingwen* were ordinary people with basic literacy. Still, Li said that this book

3. Menegon, *Un solo cielo*, 160–62; Criveller, *Preaching Christ in Late Ming China*, 254–59; King, "The Gospel for the Ordinary Reader"; Ku, "*Sizi jingwen*."

4. Schneewind, *Community Schools and the State in Ming China*.

5. Lee, *Education in Traditional China*, 456–78.

6. For a list of books sent from China to Italy made by Carlo Horatii da Castorano (1673–1755), see Civezza, *Saggio di Bibliografia geografica storica etnografica Sanfrancescana*, 92–94.

7. *CCT ARSI* vol. 2, 380.

might be found on anyone's bookshelf because it could be appreciated and cherished as part of one's collection.⁸

At any rate, the book of *Sizi jingwen* was well received, and copies of it ended up everywhere across the country. In the time when Christianity was banned, some were confiscated at a convert's home in Xiangtan District in Huguang Province in Southern China.⁹ An edition was still in production in the twentieth century.¹⁰ It was even revised into a modern text.¹¹ In other words, the life of this book has lasted for four centuries.

Tianxue mengyin: Instructions of the Heavenly Learning

A few copies of *Tianxue mengyin* are known. The one that I consult was originally carved and printed in Jiangxi Province and now preserved in the National Library of France. Without other paratexts, this copy has bibliographic records showing the name of its author Zhou Zhi 周志 (?–?), a Chinese Christian.

Tianxue mengyin adopts seven characters per line. Moreover, its composition contains another feature that *Sizi jingwen* does not have, which is a commentary section to accompany the verses therein. The body part consists of four sections. The first and third sections are composed in the form of heptasyllabic verse with loose rhyming; the second and fourth adopt another genre in the form of prose. In terms of content, the first two sections concern salvation history, the ministry and resurrection of Jesus, and basic doctrines of Christianity; the last two sections focus on the Four Ends. Therefore, the first section outlines Christian teachings in verses, and the second section elaborates on some subjects contained in the first section as a way of commenting. The third and fourth sections operate in the same manner.

The footwashing text that has been analyzed through the three-layer framework is extracted from the first section written in verse form. As it happens, it has a corresponding piece in prose form in the second section. There are even marks linking the two pieces noted on the pages. In the margin of the verse page, a note above the frame highlights the gist of the verses below (figure 30).

---

8. *CCT ARSI* vol. 2, 380. Chan, *Chinese Books and Documents in the Jesuit Archives in Rome*, 239–40.

9. Zhang, "Kanshu chuanjiao," 110.

10. See the official bibliography, *Xuxiu Siku quanshu zongmu tiyao (gaoben)* vol. 2, 635.

11. Ku, "*Sizi jingwen*."

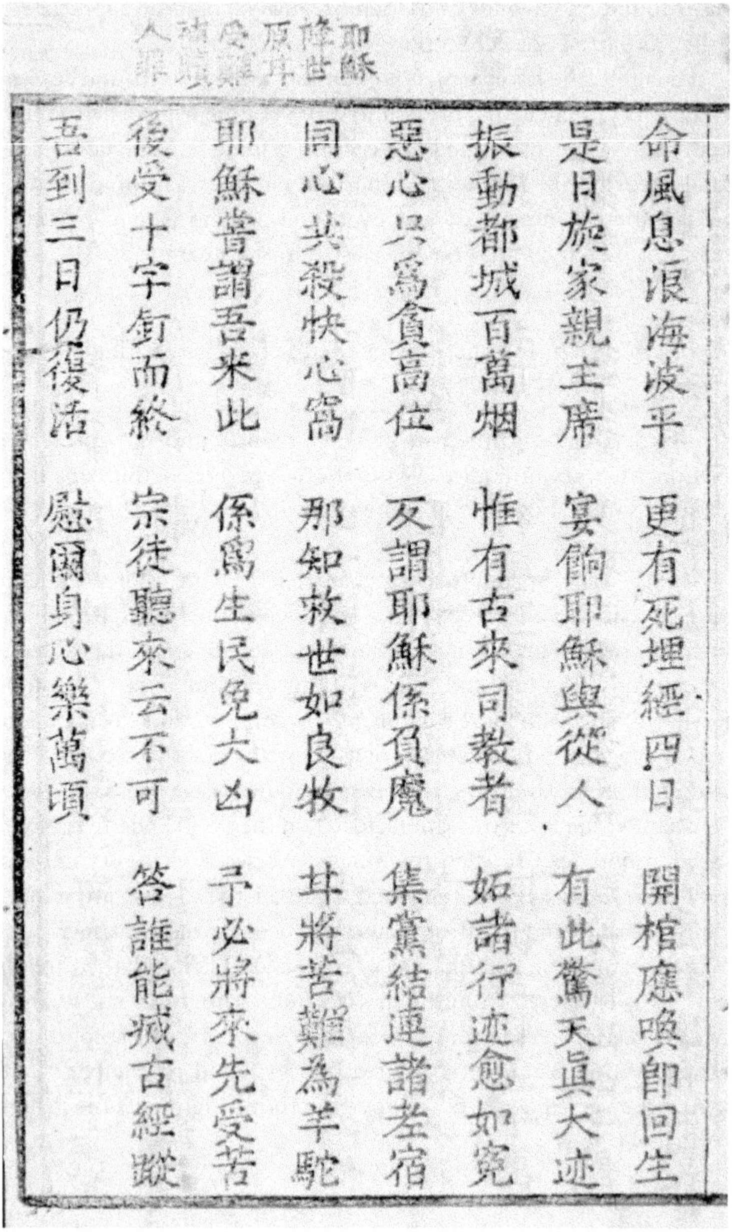
命風息浪海波平　更有死埋經四日　開棺應喚即回生
是日旋家親主席　宴餉耶穌與從人　有此驚天真大迹
振動都城百萬烟　惟有古來司教者　妬諸行迹愈如寃
惡心只爲貪高位　反謂耶穌係負魔　集黨結連諸耆宿
同心共殺快心窩　那知救世如良牧　甘將苦難為羊駝
耶穌嘗謂吾来此　係爲生民免大凶　予必將來先受苦
後受十字釘而終　宗徒聽來云不可　答誰能滅古經蹤
吾到三日仍復活　慰爾身心樂萬頃

Figure 30

The note reads:

耶穌示愛謙表

Jesus shows an example of love and modesty[12]

12. BnF Chinois 7065, f. 8b.

Beneath this note, it is the exact footwashing narrative from *Tianxue mengyin*, in the manifestation of love and modesty. This piece links to the prose section, which is also marked by a note in the page margin (figure 31).

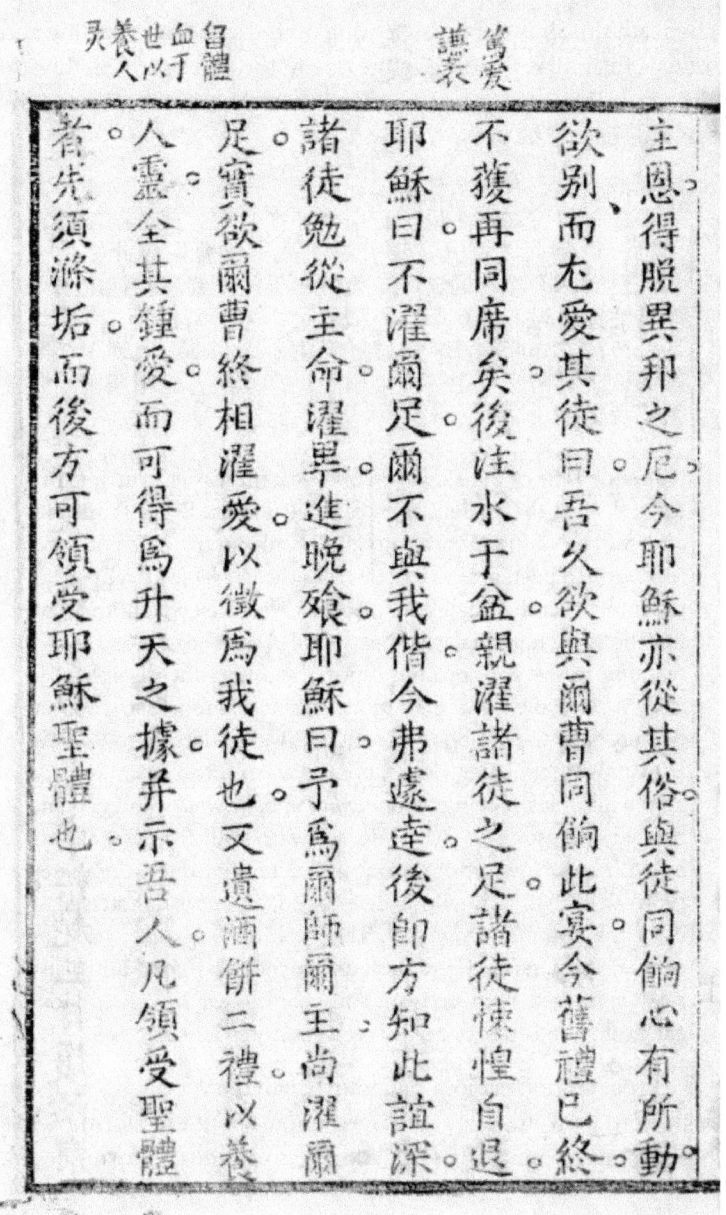

Figure 31

The note to the right side reads:

篤愛謙表

an example of deep love and modesty[13]

Beneath this, it is the prose writing on the same footwashing account. This note is in similar wording as the one in the verse section, thus quickly navigating readers from the footwashing text in the verse section to the passages on this page. The prose text reads:

時如德亞國。有古來佳節曰巴斯卦。家家宴餉一羔羊。為謝主恩。得脫異邦之厄。今耶穌亦從其俗。與徒同餉心有所動。欲別而尤愛其徒曰。吾久欲與爾曹同餉此宴。今舊體已終。不獲再同席矣。後注水于盆。親濯諸徒之足。諸徒悚惶自退。耶穌曰。不濯爾足。爾不與我偕。今弗遽達。後即方知此誼深。諸徒勉從主命。濯畢。進晚飧。耶穌曰。予爲爾師爾主。尚濯爾足。實欲爾曹終相濯愛。以徵爲我徒也。

Upon the time of the Kingdom of Judea, there was an auspicious festival since the ancient time called Passover. Every family ate a feast of the lamb, in order to give thanks to the grace of Lord, for they had been able to escape from the hardships (trapped) in the foreign land. Today Jesus also followed the convention, having the meal together with his disciples. His heart was moved, wanting to say goodbye but especially loving the disciples. He said, "I have always wanted to have this feast together with you people. Now the old body has ended, (we) no longer get to have a feast together." Later, (Jesus) poured water into a basin, washed all the disciples' feet in person. Every apostle was frightened and backed off. Jesus said, "(if) I do not wash your feet, you cannot be with me. Now (you) do not understand at once, then later, (you) will finally know this deep bond." All apostles strived to obey the command of Lord. The washing was done; they ate dinner. Jesus said, "I, being your Teacher and your Lord, still wash your feet. I indeed want you people always wash and love each other, in order to certify (you) as my followers."[14]

The prose section is more elaborative than the verse section. If comparing them word by word, one can observe more about each form's delivery of the footwashing account. The distinction between the two forms lies in their

---

13. BnF Chinois 7065, f. 11b.
14. BnF Chinois 7065, ff. 11a–b.

advantages in engaging readers. The rhymed verse projects a concentrated picture of the footwashing episode. Although some nuances have to be left out as extra expressions are restrained, the regulated format makes memorization and recitation easy for readers. On the contrary, the prose form is in a more liberating manner of writing. It adds narrative components, exegetical points, and references to help readers to understand the biblical account.

The combination of both forms of rhymed verse and prose makes this book appealing to readers at various literacy levels. At last, *Tianxue mengyin* provides a low-access approach for all readers to learn, to recite, and to understand biblical accounts. A handwritten note at the end of the copy that I consult can testify to the reception of this book. It was probably jotted down by a reader or book collector after this print was made. In this note, the person applauded this book by saying:

書中妙義出元根。字字無虛大有憑正。考家傳來戶誦。人人盡得享常生。

The marvelous meaning expressed in this book comes from the original roots; every character is concrete and grounded on proofs. It is circulated and recited among households. Everybody (who reads this book) gets to enjoy the eternity of living.[15]

Poems Derived from Prayers

Rhymed verses prompt popularity and express devotion. The books of *Sizheng enyan* and *Chaoxing liyin* stand for two examples of Chinese Christian books of this type. They can be considered as hymns among other genres of Christian literature in the church. The format of classical Chinese poetry that they adopt is well worth exploring because it is the feature that was appealing to Chinese audiences of the time. Since both *Sizheng enyan* and *Chaoxing liyin* contain poems derived from the same prayer book, I put the three works together.

Song wuzhu yesu nianzhu moxiang guitiao: Rules for Reciting the Rosary and Meditating

Song wuzhu nianzhu moxiang guitiao is a prayer book. It was probably composed by Nicolo Longobardo, SJ (1559–1654), as he wrote the

---

15. BnF Chinois 7065, the last folio.

introduction to this book. The copy that I consult is preserved in the National Library of France.

This book collects thirty-three scenes for contemplation while counting beads, and they are selected from the events during the life and ministry of Jesus. The nineteenth item to ponder over is the footwashing account. It reads:

十九想	吾[ ]主親濯宗徒之足。
The nineteenth thought	Our Lord in person washed the apostles' feet.[16]

The shorter the line is, the more space for imagination. Based on the thirty-three one-sentence prayers, the Chinese faithful expressed their devotion with literary composition. There come the two books of poems: *Sizheng enyan* and *Chaoxing liyin*. Both are independent works that collect poems upon the thirty-three themes but in different verses and different rhymes. In two poems, the footwashing story is expanded beyond a meditation theme or a prayer. Readers could enjoy more fully the imagery and fulfill the sentiment.

Two Poems: *Sizheng enyan* and *Chaoxing liyin*

The copy of *Sizheng enyan* that I consult is a print dated in 1714 and now facsimiled in *CCT BnF*. It contains thirty-three heptasyllabic poems. The footwashing text from *Sizheng enyan* is in a verse form regulated with eight lines of seven characters each. Even lines rhyme, usually, lending the poem to easy oral transmission and memorization. It reads:

謙和有道下爲先
主值離憂更欣然
尊賤不倫分爾我
官骸同類豈天淵
解衣手滌門生足
入座聲明師傅權
千古愛情無限意
長留芳躅望年年

---

16. BnF Chinois 7349, f. 4b.

(There is) a way (to achieve) modesty, lowering (oneself) is the first step.

Lord, when suffering from worries, filled with a sadness deeper and deeper.

The honored and the unworthy are not distinguishable between you and me.

How can the bodies of the same kind be separated, one in the Heaven and the other in gulf?

(Jesus) loosened clothes and washed the feet of his students with his own hands.

(He) returned to the seat and declared his authority as the master.

With forever love, care, and unlimited meanings,

(He) had left a virtuous example and expected others to follow year after year.[17]

Chaoxing liyin is a similar work but written in another verse form, a form of four lines with a loosely rhymed ending. There are multiple copies available nowadays, and the one that I consult is from *CCT ZKW XB*. Its footwashing piece reads:

親行濯足示謙光
提命諄諄黯自傷
幸喜我徒能継述
一宗萬派教無疆

(Jesus) personally performed the footwashing to show the honor of humility.

(He) exhorted (the apostles) earnestly and tirelessly but himself saddened inside.

"Fortunately, my followers could carry on (the lesson of washing feet).

The (Christian) teaching rooted in one origin with numerous branches (spreads) without borders."[18]

The book of *Chaoxing liyin* contains verses narrating the life of Jesus and Mary. It comprises two sections: thirty-three poems on Jesus, written

17. *CCT BnF* vol. 22, 597.
18. *CCT ZKW XB* vol. 17, 48.

in seven-character verses, and sixty-three pieces on Mary, written in five-character verses. In addition, the book includes a series of writings to praise saints and angels. Each piece is a rhymed poem focusing on one theme to contemplate.

The composite style of these poems is close to a poetry school called "Yunjian school," to which their author may relate. The author of *Chaoxing liyin* was Xu Dingjin 許鼎金 (?–?), as stated in the preface dated to 1739. He also recounted that while reading the book of *Song wuzhu nianzhu moxiang guitiao* by Nicolo Longobardo, he was moved and then decided to prepare these poems. The quatrain verses were very easy to chant. He hoped beginners could learn Christian teaching and strengthen their belief by reciting them.[19]

In comparison, *Sizheng enyan* did not leave us much information to trace its authorship and readership. The two works, *Sizheng enyan* and *Chaoxing liyin*, were of the same genre and could bring about a similar literary effect. Practicing Christians could recite them for meditation in private or in demonstration in a group. Their function resonated with hymns, and chants in the church tradition. As Christian poems, they created precedents in the Chinese history of literature and religion.

Qike zhenxun: Developing Earlier Chinese Christian Literature

Qike zhenxun is also a work derived from an existing Christian book. It was composed before 1636, because the title "*Qike zhenxun*" was already put on a list of published books in Fuzhou then.[20] I consult a copy kept in the Hong Kong Baptist University Library. This print is dated in 1857, and a reprint back to 1922. A table of contents and a preface by a Lazarist François-Xavier Danicourt (?–?) are included as well. The front matter tells a textual history of this book, which I will discuss later.

The body text is composed based on *Qike* 七克 (ca. 1610–1615) by Diego de Pantoja, SJ (1571–1618), and the title means "seven victories." Pantoja's *Qike* is an extensive and long-lasting literature on the seven virtues and how to use them to overcome the seven sins. The writing of *Qike zhenxun* is more instructional and straightforward. It skips explanations of the seven sins but only focuses on the seven victories in a didactic manner.

In *Qike zhenxun*, the footwashing account is simple, as the previous three-layer analysis as shown. Even so, the corresponding chapter of *Qike*

19. *CCT ZKW XB* vol. 17, 38.
20. Bernard-Maître, "Les adaptations chinoises d'ouvrages européens," 29.

does not contain the story. The elaboration on humility in *Qike* is very long, literary, and contains many biblical references. It involves pride as an opposition to explain the virtue of modesty. The section on humility in *Qike zhenxun* is short, easy, and focuses on only a few biblical anecdotes. It uses the footwashing account as an instance to illustrate the modesty of both Jesus and the apostle Peter. The articulation effectively highlights the virtue, which is much easier for readers with a low level of education to follow.

The textual relation between *Qike* and *Qike zhenxun* seems to be built in the Chinese literary context. One famous example similar to this case is two emperors' instructions in the Qing time. The Yongzheng Emperor (1678–1735, reign 1723–1735) issued *Shengyu guangxun* 聖諭廣訓 (Amplified Instructions on the Sacred Edict) in 1724. And, this document was based on the *Shengyu* 聖諭 (Sacred Edict, 1670) of the late Kangxi Emperor (1654–1722, reign 1661–1722). The earlier *Shengyu* consisted of sixteen maxims; *Shengyu guangxun* developed the sixteen themes for disciplining people of the country. Both *Shengyu* and *Shengyu guangxun* advocated the state ideology; the latter helped to promote the former in terms of propagation. *Shengyu guangxun* was posted in towns and villages across the country, and it was read aloud two times each month. This educative practice lasted in the Qing Dynasty and continued into the twentieth century.[21] This literary convention seems to be mirrored in the transition from *Qike* to *Qike zhenxun*, at least at a text level.

In reality, *Qike zhenxun* did reach out to broad audiences, especially the ones who did not have a high literary capacity as readers of *Qike* did. According to a preface written in 1857, handwritten copies of *Qike zhenxun* had been in wide circulation before then. François-Xavier Danicourt discovered a copy in Henan Province. He soon realized the great impact of this book upon ordinary audiences. In order to preserve it, Danicourt pushed the course to print it out in book form. That was the edition of 1857, and it was continuously reprinted in 1922. More editions and reprints still continued to appear in different regions during the first half of the twentieth century.[22]

---

21. Mair, "Language and Ideology in the Sacred Edict."
22. Chan, *Chinese Books and Documents in the Jesuit Archives in Rome*, 243.

15

Conclusion: The Footwashing Case and the Bible in China

THIS BOOK HAS ENDEAVORED to seek a new understanding of the history of the Bible in China from the sixteenth century through the eighteenth century. Conventionally, this topic appears as "the history of translating the Bible into Chinese," and existing studies usually address issues related to translation projects (such as persons, logistics, and linguistic debates over terminology). To the previous scholarships that I am indebted, this book pursues an alternative approach in order to understand how the Bible reached out to audiences in China. Instead of fixing Chinese translation works against the Bible in its original language, I shift the heated focus from the absence of a Chinese Bible to a large number of Chinese Christian texts of the time. My research has found that the lack of an official Chinese edition of the Bible did not prevent Chinese reception of the Bible because of numerous Chinese biblical and parabiblical texts, including images.

As seen in the footwashing case, the biblical story was transformed into a range of Chinese versions, and these renditions were featured in the twenty-six Christian books of distinct genres and readerships. The Chinese versions, while differing from the prototype in the Bible, also differ from one another. Each version of the footwashing prototype has been analyzed in this book. So have the twenty-six Christian books.

In three parts, this book has taken multi-dimensional angles to demonstrate the deliveries of the footwashing account at different types of audiences through these Chinese Christian books. Part I presents three versions equivalent to the prototype in the Latin Vulgate, but they are represented in three different books: two scriptural books containing commentaries respectively for erudite readers and unscholarly readers, one liturgical book prescribing the mass that could be read by Chinese clergies. Part II clusters nine varying versions that differ from the prototype in different ways. They are included in the books prepared by European missionaries as well as the ones composed by Chinese Christians. Part III introduces fourteen more disparate versions, and they are shaped in specific forms of Chinese writing. Some were meant for broad audiences to help them learn of Christian teachings; some were produced for educating new believers; some instructed practicing Christians in studying doctrines and doing the exercises.

Integrating the pieces and bits throughout this book into one picture, we can grasp what shapes of the footwashing story that Chinese audiences encountered and how they would connect to the biblical account. Apparently, the prototype was transformed into a wide range of variations and adjusted for target audiences. Sometimes the footwashing story was simplified; but in some versions, narration beyond the biblical pericope was added. Each Chinese version was at variance with the original account in the Gospel of John and distinct from one another. The variety of manners to convey the same biblical story was continuously mixed because of the diverse language styles and literary forms of those Christian books. They were composed for respective readerships, and readers from diverse backgrounds inherently created demands for different books in different contexts. The various genres of those books brought another level of multiplicity to the ways through which Chinese readers connected to the footwashing story.

In light of the fact that the Chinese footwashing texts diverge from the pericope to different degrees and in different dimensions, what is also fascinating is that the varying degrees and aspects can be sorted out. Each Chinese version can be found adjacent to similar versions in a continuous sequence. Besides diversity, my research on the footwashing case has found a continuum during the process of spreading the biblical account. From the texts in Part I to the ones in Part II and Part III, they collectively mark a gradual and widespread diffusion of the story. At last, the footwashing account arrived at all sorts of Chinese audiences, in a manner similar to that a stone causes ripples across a pond when hitting the water. As seen from a reception perspective, the diffusion brought in the assimilation of Christian messages in the Chinese book culture.

These Chinese Christian books mediated the Chinese audiences' encounter and reception of the biblical story as a medium without an official Chinese Bible. As it happens, their production, circulation, and consumption are an understudied phenomenon in book histories. Beyond the scope of primary sources involved in this book, many Chinese Christian texts, if not numberless, consist of various genres, readerships, literary styles, and forms. Their composition range covers Scriptures, handbooks for performing and attending liturgy and rituals, guidebooks for meditation, catechetical texts of different writings, prayers, and images on different materials. Their book forms encompass manuscripts, handwritten copies, reprints, and reproduced editions across more than two hundred years. Except for such a wide range of variation, one can also observe their connections and shared features. Intertextual links between Chinese Christian texts form a textual nexus in many different ways. Through these books, any biblical account can be communicated in a virtual library. This virtual library is an ideal type, an analytical construct, but stands for the China mission's historic achievement as of "apostolate through books."

My outline of the diffusion, the assimilation, and the virtual library may sound conceptual, but the footwashing account being recognized in China was historically real. In 1723, a footwashing ceremony was conducted and documented. Teodorico Pedrini, CM (1671–1746), built a residence in Beijing to organize daily activities and celebrations, where sermons were held usually twice a week. On Holy Thursday, Pedrini reported his pastoral work in the following:

> L'église est à part, et les chrétiens y entrent sans causer le moindre trouble à la maison. J'ai tâché de l'accommoder comme j'ai pu; elle consiste en une assez vaste salle avec une sacristie par derrière et un cour part devant; à cette cour, j'en ai adjoint une autre avec deux chambres, l'une d'un côté et l'autre où les chrétiens se réunissent pour la confrérie. Elle est pauvre et petite, mais assez fréquentée; j'y fais toutes les fonctions que l'on fait dans les autres églises, des sermons deux fois par semaine et même le lavement des pieds du Jeudi-Saint, choses qui ne se font pas dans les autres églises.[1]

In the two small rooms next to the chapel that Pedrini built, the ceremony of washing feet was taking place. Pedrini emphasized that this ritual was special as it may not be done in other churches. Indeed, washing feet was a private activity; to some people, it would not be appropriate to conduct in a public gathering. Nevertheless, Pedrini's note confirms that the ceremony was done in his church, and moreover it suggests from another angle that the same ritual, if had happened elsewhere in China, should have been kept secret or only among small groups of the faithful. Given the limit of sources about any religious practice in China of that time, this piece is already phenomenal, allowing us to take a peek at the environment of washing feet in the Qing Dynasty.

---

1. Planchet, *Histoire de la mission de Pékin*, 337–38.

Building a Chinese Christian Textual Community

This book has demonstrated that without an authorized Chinese Bible in order, the biblical content was verbalized in the Chinese language at the levels of words, verses, and accounts, and the Chinese Christian books communicated biblical messages to Chinese audiences from the late sixteenth century through the eighteenth century. If taking a step further, one can get closer to Chinese audiences, as those books indicate religious and literary backgrounds of their readerships and the contexts to read them.

There are different ways to understand Chinese audiences, and one of them is the distinction between insiders and outsiders. Both are in a correlated set. Insiders had higher clearance in terms of accessing texts confined to a circumscribed circle. They were missionaries, Chinese priests and converts, and catechumen. The rest of the audiences were outsiders, who could only read texts open to all. They consisted of sympathizers, Chinese Christians' social-circle, missionaries' friends and contacts that included several emperors they served, and even opponents. I do not mean to consider Chinese audiences as divided camps; on the contrary, I hope to emphasize their changeable identity and shared experiences based on reading and listening to Chinese Christian texts.

"Insiders" and "outsiders," or "intra-Christianity readers" and "extra-Christianity readers"—it is only a nominal distinction; actually, the dividing line cannot be fixed because of the transition of any identity. Missionaries' friends may become new converts, and some sympathizers may have the intention to do so but have doubts at the same time. When it comes to conversion, the religious identity for Chinese was too complicated. However, their reading experiences can help to scale their engagement with Christian religiosity. Insiders would involve the biblical account more often and deeply as they participated in the liturgy of the Eucharist and the footwashing ceremony. Practicing Christians meditated upon the footwashing moment by memorizing the prayers that recorded it. Clergies prepared sermons developed from the story, and laities would listen to and discuss their reflections upon it. Some outsiders accessed one book, but some may have studied several different versions. Scholars could read literary ones, and commoners may favor pictorial representations. Not only friends but opponents too, they were recommended some books to familiarize themselves with Christian messages. Uninitiated readers without any knowledge of Christianity may have learned of the story as a novel story; no mention that words gradually spread to unintended readers as well. In the long run, the readers' reading experiences could accumulate and eventually bring them to another level of cognition, which may have caused their transition of identity.

The audiences were at first separated because of their ways of connecting to the biblical story, but they all connected to the same biblical story. With quite a few options, the Chinese audiences—both insiders and outsiders—faced a new Christian discourse and shared the same biblical story. After reading or listening to any of the Chinese Christian books, the audiences from different backgrounds converged because of their encounters with the story. At least, they were all able to recognize the footwashing story as a Christian one, the role of Jesus, and some of his messages. Some would continue participating by broadcasting the story.

Those books as a virtual library delivered the biblical story to Chinese audiences. The converse is also true: audiences who came across those books formed a conceptual community by sharing experiences and discourses. It is a community based on texts, or a textual community, a notion coined by scholars. The "textual community" describes religious communities without distinct or strict regulations by bridging the gap between people and texts. It has been used to describe a medieval European phenomenon.[2] A similar situation also is observed in other contexts, cultures, and religions.[3] Nicolas Standaert, in his study of Chinese voices in the Rites Controversy, and Zvi Ben-Dor Benite, in his study of Chinese Muslims' literary identity, also spot a similar observation.[4] If I may draw an apt analogy, this understanding is close to online communities in the digital age. Participants on the same platform or in the same group of interests gather together for the sake of a burst of information or common views, regardless of ones' geolocations—of course, one has to have unrestricted internet access—just as the Chinese audiences, including insiders and outsiders, read or listened to the numerous Christian books regardless of their different backgrounds.

The concept of a Chinese Christian textual community gives us a new understanding of the Chinese who came across Christianity in the late sixteenth century through the eighteenth century. As they encountered Christian teachings, ideas, and words through those Christian books, they were bound as an assembly. Within this textual community, the boundaries of their backgrounds broke down. Men and women ranged from high-ranking officials and low degree holders to commoners and farmers in remote villages. They had different professions, social statuses, and literacy levels.

2. Stock, *After Augustine*; Stock, *The Implications of Literacy*.

3. Stroumsa, "On the Status of Books in Early Christianity"; Stroumsa, "The Scriptural Movement of Late Antiquity and Christian Monasticism"; Bremer, *Formed from This Soil*; Blackburn, *Buddhist Learning and Textual Practice*.

4. Standaert, *Chinese Voices in the Rites Controversy*; Benite, *The Dao of Muhammad*.

Despite that, they shared the experiences of those Christian books, and they could communicate with each other in a new discourse. Missionaries' friends and enemies alike could all recognize that the footwashing story of Jesus was a Christian anecdote, not a Confucian or a Buddhist one. The converted lettered men and women in households who could barely read were saying the same prayers in the same language. Every member of the Chinese Christian textual community commonly shared a Christian discourse communicated through these texts. Thereby, this textual community formed a new sense that can be commonly held among members beyond their identities in other realms.

Afterword

Contextualization is a basic approach to understanding history; through the lens of a specific history, we can return to a big picture as well. Closing this book on the reception history of the Bible in China, what still lingers in my mind are some thoughts. What is the modus operandi in packaging and spreading an idea over the country? What is the resolution of Christianity and China? What does the China chapter bring into the world map of Christianity?

In traditional Chinese society, the central sitting authority is one thing, and the actual power over regions is another, and philosophy of the people belonging to separate divisions is even a different realm. For transmitting messages across these realms, telling stories in target audiences' tongue is persuasive, and a medium of any form operates as an agency. Another prominent example—although a shallow one—to testify for this character is that rumors easily and mysteriously roam quickly in Chinese society. Because of general respect for written words, texts on paper are particularly compelling. An open and liberate environment greatly facilitates producing, reading, and distributing texts, which was precisely the case of China before the mid-eighteenth century, due to the blooming printing industry and book markets.

Creating a Christendom China is not my concern, but I would suggest the significance of context and culture sensitivity in that department. There is a permeable membrane through which any alien idea can be integrated inward but converted as a Chinese version. If China is made part of the universal mission of the church, the baseline of negotiation has to be that Christianity is only part of Chinese religious traditions. The result of Buddhism "conquering" China since the third century BCE has created Chinese Buddhism with various branches and schools that continue shaping cultures and histories in other East Asian countries. What has, is, and will the arrival of Christianity bring about? Cultural imperative does exist, but the religiously pluralistic nature of Chinese culture also needs to be acknowledged.

In world Christianity, the notion of a Chinese Christian textual community stands as a contrapuntal system. Echo once said, "The majority of Christians have read the Gospels in translation (every nation in a different language), but all of them believe that Jesus was crucified and John the Baptist beheaded, and not vice-versa."[5] What Chinese audiences read were various re-composed stories in Chinese, even different styles of the Chinese language, but they believed that "Jesus was crucified and John the Baptist beheaded, and not vice-versa" too. The diffusion, assimilation, and the building of a virtual library also may be observed in other cultures and other times. Christianity is a global phenomenon, in the past as well as in the present. Understanding it requires one to step out from a single Western or Eastern lens. Platforms for new dialogues shall open, for which the China case has its input.

---

5. Eco, *Experiences in Translation*, x.

Bibliography

Auerbach, Erich. *Mimesis: The Representation of Reality in Western Literature*. Translated by Willard R. Trask. 1953. Reprint, Princeton: Princeton University Press, 2013.
Baker, Donald L. "A Note of Jesuit Works in Chinese Which Circulated in Seventeenth- and-Eighteenth Century Korea." *China Mission Studies (1550–1800) Bulletin* 5 (1983) 26–36.
Bal, Mieke. *Narratology: Introduction to the Theory of Narrative*. Toronto: University of Toronto Press, 1997.
Barriquand, François. "First Comprehensive Translation of the New Testament in Chinese: Fr Jean Basset (1662–1707) and the Scholar John Xu." *Verbum SVD* 49 (2008) 91–119.
Benite, Zvi Ben-Dor. *The Dao of Muhammad: A Cultural History of Muslims in Late Imperial China*. Cambridge: Harvard University Asia Center, 2005.
Bernard-Maître, Henri. "Les adaptations chinoises d'ouvrages européens: Bibliographie chronologique. Deuxième partie. Depuis la fondation de la Mission française de Pékin jusqu'à la mort de l'empereur K'ien-long, 1689–1799." *Monumenta Serica* 19 (1960) 349–83.
Blackburn, Anne M. *Buddhist Learning and Textual Practice in Eighteenth-Century Lankan Monastic Culture*. Princeton: Princeton University Press, 2001.
Bontinck, François. *La lutte autour de la liturgie chinoise aux XVIIe et XVIIIe siècles*. Louvain: Nauwelaerts, 1962.
Borko, Harold, and Charles L. Bernier. *Indexing Concepts and Methods*. New York: Academic Press, 1978.
Bremer, Thomas S. *Formed from This Soil: An Introduction to the Diverse History of Religion in America*. Hoboken, NJ: Wiley, 2015.
Brockey, Liam Matthew. *Journey to the East: The Jesuit Mission to China, 1579–1724*. Cambridge: Harvard University Press, 2009.
Brooks, Iveson. *A Discourse Investigating the Doctrine of Washing the Saint's Feet: Delivered at Monticello*. Macon, GA: Rose & Slade, 1830.
Brunner, Paul G. *L'euchologe de la mission de Chine: Editio princeps 1628 et développements jusqu'à nos jours (Contribution à l'histoire des livres des prières)*. Münster: Aschendorff, 1964.
Camps, Arnulf. "Father Gabriele M. Allegra, O. F. M. (1907–1976) and the Studium Biblicum Franciscanum: The First Complete Chinese Catholic Translation of the Bible." In *Bible in Modern China: The Literary and Intellectual Impact*, edited by Irene Eber et al., 55–76. Sankt Augustin: Steyler, 1999.
Chan, Albert. *Chinese Books and Documents in the Jesuit Archives in Rome: A Descriptive Catalogue: Japonica-Sinica I–IV*. London: Sharpe, 2002.

Chauncy, Isaac. *A Discourse Concerning Unction and Washing of Feet, Proving That They Be Not Instituted Sacraments, or Ordinances in the Churches*. London: Hiller, 1697.

Chen, Yanrong. "Christian Biblical Tradition in the *Jing* Chinese Culture." In *The Oxford Handbook of the Bible in China*, edited by K. K. Yeo, 495–510. Oxford: Oxford University Press, 2021.

———. "Jesuit Order (China)." In *Encyclopedia of the Bible and Its Reception*, edited by Hans-Josef Klauck et al., 13:1135–37. Berlin: de Gruyter, 2016.

———. "The *Shengjing zhijie*: A Chinese Text of Commented Gospel Readings in the Encounter between Europe and China in the Seventeenth Century." *Journal of Early Modern Christianity* 1 (2014) 165–93.

Chen, Yuan 陳垣. "Zailun *Zunzhu shengfan* yiben" 再論《遵主聖範》譯本. In *Chen Yuan xueshu lunwen ji* 陳垣學術論文集, 117–23. 北京: 中華書局, 1980.

Civezza, Marcellino de. *Saggio di Bibliografia geografica storica etnografica Sanfrancescana*. Prato: Guasti, 1879.

Coloe, Mary L. "Welcome into the Household of God: The Foot Washing in John 13." *Catholic Biblical Quarterly* 66 (2004) 400–415.

Cox, Steven L., and Kendell H. Easley. *Harmony of the Gospels*. Nashville: Holman Bible, 2006.

Criveller, Gianni. *Preaching Christ in Late Ming China: The Jesuits' Presentation of Christ from Matteo Ricci to Giulio Aleni*. Taipei: Ricci Institute, 1997.

Culpepper, R. Alan. *Anatomy of the Fourth Gospel: A Study in Literary Design*. Fortress, 1983.

Dehergne, Joseph. *Répertoire Des Jésuites de Chine de 1552 à 1800*. Rome: Institutum Historicum S. I., 1973.

———. "Travaux des jésuites sur la Bible en Chine." In *Le siècle des Lumières et la Bible*, edited by Yvon Belaval and Dominique Bourel, 211–28. Paris: Beauchesne, 1986.

———. "Une vie illustrée de Notre-Seigneur au temps des Ming." *Neue Zeitschrift für Missionswissenschaft* 14 (1958) 103–15.

D'Elia, Pasquale M. "La passione di Gesù Cristo in un'opera cinese del 1608–1610." *Archivum Historicum Societatis Iesu* 22 (1953) 276–307.

———. *Le origini dell'arte cristiana cinese (1583–1640)*. Roma: Reale accademia d'Italia, 1939.

Deng, Kent. "China's Population Expansion and Its Causes during the Qing Period, 1644–1911." LSE Economic History Working Papers. London School of Economics and Political Science, 2015.

Dudink, Ad. "Biblical Chronology and the Transmission of the Theory of Six 'World Ages' to China: 'Gezhi Aolüe' 格致奧略 (Outline of the Mystery [Revealed through] Natural Science; before 1723)." *East Asian Science, Technology, and Medicine* 35 (2012) 89–138.

———. "The Japonica-Sinica Collections I–IV in the Roman Archives of the Society of Jesus: An Overview." *Monumenta Serica* 50 (2002) 481–536.

———. "Jean Basset (1662–1707) and His Catechetical Writings in Chinese: A Bibliographical Introduction." In *History of Catechesis in China*, edited by Rachel Lu Yan et al., 87–111. Leuven: Ferdinand Verbiest Institute, 2008.

Dunn, James D. G. "The Washing of the Disciples' Feet in John 13:1–20." *Zeitschrift für die neutestamentliche Wissenschaft und die Kunde der älteren Kirche* 61 (1970) 247–52.

Dunne, George H. "What Happened to the Chinese Liturgy?" *Catholic Historical Review* 47 (1961) 1–14.
Eco, Umberto. *Experiences in Translation*. Translated by Alastair McEwen. Toronto: University of Toronto Press, 2008.
Elman, Benjamin A. "Philosophy (I–Li) versus Philology (K'ao-Cheng): The Jen-Hsin Tao-Hsin Debate." *T'oung Pao* 69 (1983) 175–222.
Forney, Christian Henry. *The Christian Ordinances: Being a Historical Inquiry into the Practice of Trine Immersion, the Washing of the Saints' Feet and the Love-Feast*. Harrisburg, PA: Board of Publication of the General Eldership of the Church of God, 1883.
Golvers, Noël. "D. Papebrochius, S.J., Ph. Couplet en de Vlaamse jezuïeten in China." *De zeventiende eeuw: Cultuur in de Nederlanden in interdisciplinair perspectief* 14 (1998) 39–50.
———. "The Earliest Examples of Chinese Characters Printed in the Southern Low Countries (Leuven, 1672; Antwerp, 1683)." *De Gulden Passer* 94 (2016) 319–33.
———. *Libraries of Western Learning for China: Circulation of Western Books between Europe and China in the Jesuit Mission (ca. 1650–ca. 1750)*. Vol. 2, *Formation of Jesuit Libraries*. Leuven: Ferdinand Verbiest Institute, 2013.
Henderson, John B. *Scripture, Canon and Commentary: A Comparison of Confucian and Western Exegesis*. Princeton: Princeton University Press, 2014.
Huang, Zuo 黃佐. *Liuyi bieliu* 六藝流別. 臺北: 商務印書館, 1973.
King, Gail. "The Gospel for the Ordinary Reader: Aspects of Six Christian Texts in Chinese from the Late Ming Dynasty." *Monumenta Serica* 57 (2009) 167–94.
Ku, Wei-ying 古偉瀛. "*Sizi jingwen*: bendi hua yu Taiwan tianzhujiao" 《四字經文》, 本地化與台灣天主教. In *History of Catechesis in China*, edited by Rachel Lu Yan et al., 319–37. Leuven: Ferdinand Verbiest Institute, 2008.
Lampe, G. W. H. *The Cambridge History of the Bible*. Vol. 2, *The West from the Fathers to the Reformation*. Cambridge: Cambridge University Press, 1975.
Lang, Marijke H. de. "Gospel Synopses from the 16th to the 18th Centuries and the Rise of Literary Criticism of the Gospels." In *The Synoptic Gospels: Source Criticism and the New Literary Criticism*, edited by Camille Focant, 599–607. Leuven: University Press, 1993.
———. "Jean Gerson's Harmony of the Gospels (1420)." *Nederlands archief voor kerkgeschiedenis* 71 (1991) 37–49.
Lapide, Cornelius a. *Commentarius in Evangelium S. Lucae et S. Ioannis*. Antwerp: Meursium, 1670.
Lee, Thomas H. C. *Education in Traditional China: A History*. Leiden: Brill, 2000.
Li, Sher-shiueh 李奭學. "Jindai baihuawen, zongjiao qimeng, yesuhui chuantong: shikui He Qingtai jiqi suoyi *Guxin shengjing* de yuyan wenti" 近代白話文、宗教啟蒙、耶穌會傳統——試窺賀清泰及其所譯《古新聖經》的語言問題. *Zhongguo wenzhe yanjiu jikan* 中國文哲研究集刊 42 (2013) 51–108.
Lohse, Wolfram. "Die Fusswaschung (Joh 13, 1–20): eine Geschichte ihrer Deutung." PhD diss., Friedrich-Alexander-Universität, 1967.
Mair, Victor H. "Language and Ideology in the Sacred Edict." In *Popular Culture in Late Imperial China*, edited by David Johnson et al., 332–59. Berkeley: University of California Press, 1987.
Malek, Roman. "The Bible at the Local Level." *Monumenta Serica* 64 (2016) 137–72.

Marchioron, Luigino. "An Example of Exegesis in the Late Ming Dynasty: The First Annotated Translation of *Sheng Jing Zhi Jie* by the Jesuit Manuel Dias." PhD diss., Fu Jen Faculty of Theology of St. Robert Bellarmine, 2016.

Matson, Mark A. "To Serve as Slave: Footwashing as Paradigmatic Status Reversal." In *One in Christ Jesus: Essays on Early Christianity and "All That Jazz," in Honor of S. Scott Bartchy*, edited by David Lertis Matson and K. C. Richardson, 113–31. Eugene, OR: Pickwick, 2014.

Menegon, Eugenio. *Un solo cielo: Giulio Aleni SJ (1582–1649): geografia, arte, scienza, religione dall'Europa alla Cina*. Brescia: Grafo, 1994.

Missale Romanum. 1570. Reprint, Città del Vaticano: Libreria Editrice Vaticana, 1998.

Mungello, David E. *The Forgotten Christians of Hangzhou*. Honolulu: University of Hawaii Press, 1994.

Murray, Julia K. "Illustrations of the Life of Confucius: Their Evolution, Functions, and Significance in Late Ming China." *Artibus Asiae* 57 (1997) 73–134.

———. *Mirror of Morality: Chinese Narrative Illustration and Confucian Ideology*. Honolulu: University of Hawaii Press, 2007.

Natalis, Hieronymus. *Imagenes de la historia evangelica*. Barcelona: El Albir, 1975.

The New Hollstein Dutch and Flemish Etchings, Engravings and Woodcuts, 1450–1700. Rotterdam: Sound and Vision Interactive, 1993.

Neyrey, Jerome H. "The Footwashing in John 13:6–11: Transformation Ritual or Ceremony." In *The Social World of the First Christians: Essays in Honor of Wayne A. Meeks*, edited by L. Michael White and O. Larry Yarbrough, 198–213. Minneapolis: Fortress, 1995.

Pan, Fengjuan 潘鳳娟. "Shu er bu yi? AI Rulüe *Tianzhu jiangsheng yanxing jilüe* de kuayuyan xushi chutan" 述而不譯？艾儒略《天主降生言行紀略》的跨語言 敘事初探. *Zhongguo wenzhe yanjiu jikan* 中國文哲研究集刊 3 (2009) 111–67.

Pfister, Louis. *Notices biographiques et bibliographiques sur les jésuites de l'ancienne mission de Chine (1552–1773)*. Shanghai: Imprimerie de la mission catholique & Orphelinat de T'ou-sè-wè, 1932.

Planchet, Jean-Marie. *Histoire de la mission de Pékin: Depuis les origines jusqu'à l'arrivée des Lazaristes*. Paris: Louis-Michaud, 1923.

Qing zhongqianqi xiyang tianzhujiao zaihua huodong dang'an shiliao 清中前期西洋天 主教在華活動檔案史料. 北京: 中華書局, 2003.

Ricci, Bartolomeo. *Vita D.N. Iesu Christi, ex uerbis Euangeliorum in ipsismet concinnata, per R.P. Bartholomaeum Riccium, Societatis Iesu è Castrofidardo*. Romæ: Barthol. Zanettum, 1607.

Ricci, Matteo. *Fonti Ricciane: Documenti originali concernenti Matteo Ricci e la storia delle prime relazioni tra l'Europa e la Cina (1579–1615)*. Edited by Pasquale M d'Elia. 3 vols. Roma: La libreria dello stato, 1942.

Richter, Georg. *Die Fusswaschung im Johannesevangelium: Geschichte ihrer Deutung*. Regensburg: Pustet, 1967.

Schneewind, Sarah. *Community Schools and the State in Ming China*. Stanford: Stanford University Press, 2006.

Seah, Audrey. "The 1670 Chinese Missal: A Struggle for Indigenization Amidst the Chinese Rites Controversy." In *China's Christianity: From Missionary to Indigenous Church*, edited by Anthony E. Clark, 86–120. Leiden: Brill, 2017.

Shioyama, Masazumi 塩山正純. "カソリックによる聖書抄訳 ディアスの『聖経 直解』." *Civilization* 文明 21 (2008) 57–77.

Shore, Paul. *The Vita Christi of Ludolph of Saxony and Its Influence on the Spiritual Exercises of Ignatius of Loyola*. St. Louis: Seminar on Jesuit Spirituality, 1998.
Song, Gang 宋剛. "'Benyi' yu 'tuyu' zhijian: Qingdai yesuhuishi He Qingtai de *Shengjing* hanyi ji quanshi" '本意'与'土语'之间：清代耶稣会士贺清泰的《圣经》汉译及诠释. *Guoji hanxue* 国际汉学 5 (2015) 23–49.
———. "Cong jingdian dao tongsu: *Tianzhu jiangsheng yanxing jilüe* jiqi Qingdai gaibianben de liubian" 從經典到通俗：《天主降生言行紀略》及其清代改編本的流變. *Tianzhujiao yanjiu xuebao* 天主教研究學報 2 (2011) 208–60.
Standaert, Nicolas. "The Bible in Early Seventeenth-Century China." In *Bible in Modern China: The Literary and Intellectual Impact*, edited by Irene Eber et al., 31–54. Sankt Augustin: Steyler, 1999.
———. *Chinese Voices in the Rites Controversy: Travelling Books, Community Networks, Intercultural Arguments*. Rome: Institutum historicum Societatis Iesu, 2012.
———. "The Composition of Place." *Way* 46 (2007) 7–20.
———, ed. *Handbook of Christianity in China*. Vol. 1, *635–1800*. Leiden: Brill, 2001.
———. *An Illustrated Life of Christ Presented to the Chinese Emperor: The History of Jincheng Shuxiang (1640)*. Sankt Augustin: Institut Monumenta Serica, 2007.
———. "The Spiritual Exercises of Ignatius of Loyola in the China Mission of the 17th and 18th Centuries." *Archivum Historicum Societatis Iesu* 161 (2012) 73–124.
Starr, Chloë. *Chinese Theology: Text and Context*. New Haven: Yale University Press, 2016.
———. "Reading Scripture in Nineteenth-Century China." In *Reading Christian Scriptures in China*, 32–48. New York: T&T Clark, 2008.
Stock, Brian. *After Augustine: The Meditative Reader and the Text*. Philadelphia: University of Pennsylvania Press, 2001.
———. *The Implications of Literacy: Written Language and Models of Interpretation in the Eleventh and Twelfth Centuries*. Princeton: Princeton University Press, 1983.
Stroumsa, Guy G. "On the Status of Books in Early Christianity." In *Being Christian in Late Antiquity: A Festschrift for Gillian Clark*, edited by Carol Harrison et al., 57–73. Oxford: Oxford University Press, 2014.
———. "The Scriptural Movement of Late Antiquity and Christian Monasticism." *Journal of Early Christian Studies* 16 (2008) 61–77.
Sun, Yuming. "Cultural Translatability and the Presentation of Christ as Portrayed in Visual Images from Ricci to Aleni." In *The Chinese Face of Jesus Christ*, edited by Roman Malek, 2:461–98. Nettetal: Steyler, 2003.
Tenney, Merrill C. "The Footnotes of John's Gospel." *Bibliotheca Sacra* 117 (1960) 350–64.
Thomas, John Christopher. *Footwashing in John 13 and the Johannine Community*. Cleveland, TN: CPT, 2014.
Verhaeren, Hubert Germain. *Beitang tushuguan cang xiwen shanben mulu* 北堂图书馆藏西文善本目录. 北京：国家图书馆出版社，2009.
Vulgata Clementina, 1592. "Clementine Vulgate Project." Bishops' Conference of England and Wales. http://vulsearch.sourceforge.net/html/index.html.
Weiss, Herold. "Foot Washing in the Johannine Community." *Novum Testamentum* 21 (1979) 298–325.
Wheatley, Henry Benjamin. *What Is an Index? A Few Notes on Indexes and Indexers*. New York: Cambridge University Press, 2010.

Wylie, Alexander. *Notes on Chinese Literature: With Introductory Remarks on the Progressive Advancement of the Art; and a List of Translations from the Chinese into Various European Languages.* Shanghai: American Presbyterian Mission Press, 1901.

Xiao, Qinghe 肖清和. "'Qiutong' yu 'bianyi': MingQing disandai jidutu Zhang Xingyao de sixiang yu xinyang chutan" "求同" 与 "辨异": 明清第三代基督教徒张星曜的思想与信仰初探. *Bijiao jingxue* 比较经学 1 (2013) 38–83.

Xuxiu Siku quanshu zongmu tiyao (gaoben) 續修四庫全書總目提要(稿本). 濟南: 齊魯書社, 1996.

Xu, Zongze 徐宗澤. *MingQingjian yesuhuishi yizhu tiyao* 明清間耶穌會士譯著提要. 上海: 中華書局, 1949.

Yang, Shaofang 杨少芳. "Tianxue zai Qingchu de chuanbo: *Tianjiao mingbian* chutan" 天学在清初的传播:《天教明辨》初探. In *Dongya yu ouzhou wenhua de zaoqi xiangyu: Dongxi wenhua jiaoliu shilun* 东亚与欧洲文化的早期相遇：东西文化交流史论, edited by Zhang Xiping 张西平 and Luo Ying 罗莹, translated by Federico Masini, 109–207. 上海: 华东师范大学出版社, 2011.

Yu, Yating 余雅婷. "聖書福音書の漢訳をめぐって－『天主降生言行紀畧』から『古新聖経』へ." *Journal of East Asian Cultural Interaction Studies* 東アジア文化交渉研究 10 (2017) 153–62.

Zetzsche, Jost Oliver. *The Bible in China: The History of the Union Version or the Culmination of Protestant Missionary Bible Translation in China.* Nettetal: Steyler, 1999.

Zhang, Xianqing 张先清. "Kanshu chuanjiao: Qingdai jinjiaoqi tianzhujiao jingjuan zai minjian shehui de liuchuan" 刊书传教: 清代禁教期天主教经卷在民间社会的流传. In *Shiliao yu shijie: Zhongwen wenxian yu Zhongguo jidujiaoshi yanjiu* 史料与视界: 中文文献与中国基督教史研究, 83–141. 上海: 上海人民出版社, 2007.

Zheng, Haijuan 郑海娟. "He Qingtai *Guxin shengjing* yanjiu" 贺清泰《古新圣经》研究. PhD diss., 北京大学, 2012.

———. "Xinchuan yu xinquan: *Guxin shengjing* de jiejing zhidao" 薪传与新诠:《古新圣经》的解经之道. *Wenbei: Bijiao jingxue yu bijiao wenhua* 文贝:比较文学与比较文化 1 (2014) 55–84.

Zürcher, Erik. *Kouduo Richao: Li Jiubiao's Diary of Oral Admonitions: A Late Ming Christian Journal.* Sankt Augustin: Institut Monumenta Serica, 2007.

Index of Authors

Aleni, Giulio 艾儒略, 45n14, 98–100, 104–5, 109, 114, 116, 118, 120, 129, 136, 183, 198, 207–8
Allegra, Gabriele 雷永明, xxii, 73
Augery, Humbert 洪度貞, 188

Basset, Jean 白日昇, 2, 63, 193
Buglio, Lodovico 利類思, 46–47, 51, 53, 60, 62, 185, 188

Canevari, Pietro 聶伯多, 208
Cattaneo, Lazzaro 郭居靜, 120
Chan, Albert, 186
Chen, Yuan 陳垣, 45
Couplet, Philippe 柏應理, 62–63

da Cunha, Simão 瞿西滿, 136, 188
Danicourt, François-Xavier, 216–17
de Gravina, Girolamo 賈宜睦, 188
Dejean, Joseph, 2
de la Piñuela, Pedro 石鐸琭, 120, 124, 204
de Mailla, Joseph M. A. de Moyriac 馮秉正, 46–47
de Matos, Bento 林本篤, 136
d'Entrecolles, François 殷弘緒, 1
de Seixas, João 林德瑤, 124, 126–28
Dias, Manuel 陽瑪諾, 3, 36–37, 44–45, 64

Fei, Jinbiao 費金標, 73
Ferreira, Gaspar 費奇規, 45n14, 202
Francisco, Inácio 張舒, 127

Gerson, Jean, 100

He, Shizhen 何世貞, 188

Jovino, Francesco, 1

Laghi, Antonio, 1
Li, Di 李杕, 2
Li, Jiubiao 李九標, 136–38
Li, Jiugong 李九功, 47, 103, 203
Li, Shihuan 李奭浣, 208
Li, Zubai 李祖白, 188
Longobardo, Nicolo 龍華民, 45n14, 213, 216
Lu, Xiyan 陸希言, 33

Ma, Xiangbo 馬相伯, 2
Magalhães, Gabriel de 安文思, 188
Marshman, Joshua 馬士曼, 2
Michele, Ruggieri 羅明堅, xxi, 3
Morrison, Robert 馬禮遜, 2

Nadal, Jerónimo, 105, 109–10

Pacheco, Feliciano 成際理, 188
Pantoja, Diego de 龐迪我, 186, 216
Poirot, Louis 賀清泰, 2, 64–67, 69, 71–73

Ricci, Bartolomeo, 104
Ricci, Matteo 利瑪竇, xxi, 3, 78n2, 115
Rudamina, Andrius 盧安德, 129, 136

Schall von Bell, Johann Adam 湯若望, 179, 181, 183–84, 208

Tong, Guoqi 佟國器, 188

Verbiest, Ferdinand 南懷仁, 116

Wu, Dani 吳達尼, 124, 128
Wu, Jingxiong 吳經熊, 2
Wu, Li 吳歷, 138

Xiao, Jingshan 蕭靜山, 2
Xu, Dingjin 許鼎金, 216
Xu, Zongze 徐宗澤, 115, 136, 145, 186

Yang, Guangxian 楊光先, 47, 185
Yang, Tingyun 楊廷筠, 104

Zhang, Xingyao 張星曜, 103, 120, 138–39, 142–45
Zhou, Zhi 周志, 103, 209
Zhu, Yupu 朱毓朴, 195
Zhu, Zongyuan 朱宗元, 188

Index of Subjects

Abraham, 142, 183
Antwerp, 1, 69
Augustinians, xxi

Beijing, xxi, 1, 36, 46n19, 49, 69, 127, 186, 220
Bible translation/translation of the Bible, xxii–iv, 2, 64, 73, 190
biblical and parabiblical texts, xxiii–v, 2, 7, 76, 218
biblical stories/story, 3, 5–7, 10, 17, 32, 73, 90, 93, 126, 151, 176–77, 184, 202, 204, 208, 218–19, 222
Buddha, 5, 101, 104, 114
Buddhism/Buddhist, 3, 45–46, 104, 120, 144–45, 201, 223
Budeyi bian 不得已辨, 185, 187, 192

catechesis, 115, 118, 196, 206
catechetical books/texts/text, xxvi, 149, 195, 219
catechisms/catechism, xxvi, 115–16, 115n1, 193, 195, 198, 205, 207
catechumen, 40, 115, 138, 142, 187, 191, 195, 198, 221
Chinese Bible, xxii–xxiv, 1–2, 6, 32, 36, 98, 218–19, 221
Chinese Christian books/texts/writings, xvi, xxiii–vii, 2–3, 6, 7, 9, 10, 12, 16, 19, 28, 31, 36, 47, 63, 65, 75, 98, 101, 103, 129, 138–39, 142–43, 147, 183–85, 187–88, 190, 206, 213, 218–22

Chinese Christian scholar, 47, 103, 137–38, 143
Chinese Christians, xxii, xxvi, xxiii, 2–3, 46–47, 75, 77, 103, 115, 124, 129–30, 134, 187–88, 193, 203–4, 218
Chinese readers, xxii–xxiv, 3, 44, 47, 71–72, 80, 81, 100, 110, 117–118, 124–125, 181, 183, 190–191, 219
Chinese translation/translations, 1, 64, 186, 190, 218
Christianity, xxi–ii, xxiv, xxvi, 38–39, 45–48, 63, 98, 103–4, 108–9, 114–15, 128, 137, 144–45, 179, 181, 192, 195, 198, 205, 209, 221–24
Classic of Documents 尚書, 45
commentary/commentaries, xxiii, xxvi, 19, 40–41, 43–44, 64, 67–72, 95, 102, 206, 209, 218
community/communities
    Christian community/communities, xxi, xxvi, 3, 72, 98, 113, 129, 137, 142–43, 193, 201, 204, 205, 208
    textual community, 221–23
Confucianism/Confucian/Confucians, 45, 138, 144, 208, 223
Confucius Sinarum Philosophus, 63
Confucius, 5, 45, 101, 114, 144
Council of Trent, xxii, 49

Daoism/Daoist, 114, 144–45, 201
Dominicans, xxi

Eucharist, 16, 33–34, 40, 53, 78–79, 88–89, 95–97, 99, 102, 115–18, 121, 125, 130, 132, 134, 137, 142, 147–48, 150–53, 161, 166, 168, 172, 174–78, 189–90, 195–96, 198–99, 204, 207, 221
Evangelicae Historiae Imagines, 107–10, 113

Five Classics, 45
Four Books, 45
Franciscans, xxi

genre/genres, 15, 19, 45, 92, 100–101, 103, 114, 129, 147, 178, 188, 206, 208, 209, 213, 216, 218–19
Gospels, 2, 4, 56, 60, 63, 78, 89, 95, 98–100, 104, 108–109, 113, 154, 162, 186, 202, 224
Gospel verses, 1, 19, 38, 43–46, 53, 71

Hundred Surnames 百家姓, 208

Islam
    Islamic, 3
    Muslim/Muslims, 47, 185, 222

Jesuit/Jesuits, xxi, 1, 45, 47, 63, 99, 124, 133, 136, 185, 187, 198, 208
Judas, 11, 13–14, 21–23, 29–30, 77–78, 80, 90–91, 149, 153–55, 162, 166–67, 174, 202

Kangxi Emperor, 134, 217

Lapide, Cornelius, 69–71
Lazarist/Lazarists, xxi, 216
Ludolph/Ludolphus de Saxonia, 99–100

Mei, Wending 梅文鼎, 47
Mgr Domencio Coppola, 73
Missal
    Roman Missal, 1, 38, 44, 49, 51–53, 55, 57, 60–61, 117
    Chinese Missal, 49, 51, 52, 57
Missions Étrangères, xxi
Mohists, 144

New Testament, xxiii, 2, 64–65

Old Testament, xxiii, 1, 3, 64, 116, 142, 183, 193

Papebrochius, Daniël, 62
Pedrini, Teodorico, 220
Peter, 8, 11, 13–14, 21, 24–27, 29, 30–33, 53, 77–78, 83–92, 94, 125–26, 131, 149, 156–59, 163, 165–167, 172–173, 217
Pope
    Pope Clement VIII, 49
    Pope Paul V, 1, 51, 63
    Pope Pius V, 49, 52, 55
    Pope Urban VIII, 49
Propaganda Fide, xxi
Province
    Fujian, 98, 105, 116, 136, 187, 199, 201
    Hebei, 127
    Henan, 217
    Huguang, 209
    Jiangxi, 207, 209
    Zhejiang, 187

readership/readerships, 7, 15, 19, 21, 32, 35, 36, 47, 75, 93, 110, 126–28, 137, 139, 142, 147–48, 172, 178, 188, 197, 208, 216, 218–19, 221
religiosity, 73, 115, 147, 149, 193, 201, 203, 221

shengjing 聖經 (not in book titles), xxii–iii, 189–90
Shengyu 聖諭, 217
Shengyu guangxun 聖諭廣訓, 217
Siberian Orthodox missionaries, xxi
Sigao shengjing 思高聖經, xxii, 73

the Bible in China, xxi–iv, 218, 223
Thousand Characters Essay 千字文, 208
Three-Character Classic 三字經, 208
three layers
    three-layer analysis, 21, 139, 172, 186, 216

three-layer framework/frame, xxv, 8–10, 19, 21, 34, 40, 53, 67, 75, 93, 189, 193, 209

fabula/fabula-layer/fabula layer, 9–13, 15, 21–22, 24–30, 32, 35, 77–78, 80, 82–89, 92, 94–96, 121, 125, 131, 139, 149–51, 153–54, 160–61, 163, 172–73, 207

story/story-layer/story layer, 9–10, 12–15, 28–32, 35, 87–90, 93, 131, 139, 160, 165, 172

text/text-layer/text layer, 9–10, 15–16, 23, 25, 31–32, 35, 84, 90–91, 93, 96–97, 131, 139, 172, 174

Trigault, Nicolas 金尼閣, 63

Vita Christi, 99–100, 104

Vulgate, xxv, 1, 3–4, 6, 10, 21, 53, 93, 218

Yongzheng Emperor, xxi, 217

Scripture Index

Genesis

18:4	183
18:1–8	142

Job

1:12	3

Matthew

26:17–25	154
26:21–25	154
26:25	80

Mark

14:12–21	154

Luke

22:7–17	154
22:14	154
22:15–16	80, 135
22:15	80
22:16	80

John

13:1–15	4–5, 8, 10, 15, 21, 28, 35, 43, 53, 65, 68, 69, 78, 149, 172
13:1–3	22, 78
13:1	44, 78, 151
13:2	30, 91
13:3	78, 151
13:4–5	184
13:5	81
13:6–11	30, 91
13:6–10	24, 83, 157
13:8	84
13:9	131
13:10	84
13:12–15	27, 85
13:12	85
13:13–15	159, 190
13:13	164
13:14–15	85, 160
13:15	31, 85

1 Corinthians

11:20–32	53

www.ingramcontent.com/pod-product-compliance
Lightning Source LLC
Chambersburg PA
CBHW050347230426
43663CB00010B/2020